METROPOLITAN COLLEGE
OF NEW YORK LIBRARY
75 Varick Street 12th Fl.
New York, NY 10013

# Citizenship and Cultural Policy

# Citizenship and Cultural Policy

edited by

Denise Meredyth and Jeffrey Minson

SAGE Publications
London • Thousand Oaks • New Delhi

© Sage Publications 2000, 2001

Originally published as a special issue of the *American Behavioral Scientist* (Volume 43, Number 9, June/July 2000)

Revised edition published as *Citizenship and Cultural Policy* 2001

All rights reserved. No part of this publication may be reproduced, stored in a retrieval system, transmitted or utilized in any form or by any means, electronic, mechanical, photocopying, recording or otherwise, without permission in writing from the Publishers.

SAGE Publications Ltd
6 Bonhill Street
London EC2A 4PU

SAGE Publications Inc
2455 Teller Road
Thousand Oaks, California 91320

SAGE Publications India Pvt Ltd
32, M-Block Market
Greater Kailash - I
New Delhi 110 048

**British Library Cataloguing in Publication data**

A catalogue record for this book is available from the British Library.

ISBN 0 7619 6293 X

**Library of Congress catalog card number available from the publisher**

Printed in Great Britain by Athenaeum Press, Gateshead

# Contents

|  | The Authors | vii |
|---|---|---|
|  | Introduction: Resourcing Citizenries<br>*Denise Meredyth and Jeffrey Minson* | x |
| 1 | Community, Citizenship and the Third Way<br>*Nikolas Rose* | 1 |
| 2 | Acting on the Social: Art, Culture, and Government<br>*Tony Bennett* | 18 |
| 3 | The National Endowment for the Arts in the 1990s: A Black Eye on the Arts?<br>*Toby Miller* | 35 |
| 4 | Participatory Policy Making, Ethics, and the Arts<br>*Janice Besch and Jeffrey Minson* | 52 |
| 5 | Popular Sovereignty and Civic Education<br>*Ian Hunter and Denise Meredyth* | 68 |
| 6 | Citizenship in the International Management of Populations<br>*Barry Hindess* | 92 |
| 7 | Who Is the Subject of Human Rights?<br>*Anna Yeatman* | 104 |
| 8 | Culturally Appropriate Indigenous Accountability<br>*Tim Rowse* | 120 |
| 9 | Multicultural Broadcasting and Diasporic Video as Public Sphericules<br>*Stuart Cunningham, Gay Hawkins, Audrey Yue, Tina Nguyen, and John Sinclair* | 139 |
| 10 | Liberal Machines<br>*Julian Thomas* | 154 |

# The Authors

**TONY BENNETT** is a professor of sociology and the director of the Pavis Centre for Social and Cultural Research at the Open University. He was previously a professor of cultural studies at Griffith University and the director of the Australian Key Centre for Cultural and Media Policy. His recent publications include *The Birth of the Museum* (1995), *Culture: A Reformer's Science*, and (with Michael Emmison and John Frow) *Accounting for Tastes: Australian Everyday Cultures* (1999).

**JANICE BESCH** is a cultural policy researcher and analyst currently employed by the Australia Council, the Australian Government's arts funding and advisory body. She has previous experience in state and local government contexts and is currently engaged in doctoral research exploring policy and accountability frameworks for the arts.

**STUART CUNNINGHAM** is a professor and head of the School of Media and Journalism, Queensland University of Technology, Brisbane, Australia. He is an author or editor of several books on Australian media, cultural policy, and global television, the most recent of which are *The Media in Australia: Industries, Texts, Audiences* (with Graeme Turner, 1997), *New Patterns in Global Television* (with John Sinclair and Elizabeth Jacka, 1996), and *Floating Lives: The Media of Asian Diasporas* (with John Sinclair, 2000).

**GAY HAWKINS** is a senior lecturer in sociology at the University of New South Wales, Sydney, Australia. She has published a book on the invocation of community in arts policy: *From Nimbin to Mardi Gras: Constructing Community Arts* (1993) as well as numerous articles on transformations in public service broadcasting and television value and difference.

**BARRY HINDESS** is a professor of political science in the Research School of Social Sciences at the Australian National University. His most recent books are *Discourses of Power: From Hobbes to Foucault* (1996) and (edited with Mitchell Dean) *Governing Australia: Studies in Contemporary Rationalities of Government* (1998). He is currently preparing a book on democracy to be published by Routledge.

**IAN HUNTER** is the director of the Centre for Advanced Studies in the Humanities at Griffith University, Brisbane. He is the author of a number of books and articles dealing with the history of ethical disciplines and deportments. These include *Culture and Government: The Emergence of Literary Education* (1988) and *Rethinking the School* (1994). He has recently completed a book on the relation between civil and metaphysical philosophy in early modern Germany.

**DENISE MEREDYTH** is a research fellow at the Institute for Social Research, Swinburne University of Technology, Melbourne, Australia. She has published on issues related to the historical and contemporary study of education, citizenship, and governance and is currently completing work on civics, ethics, and pluralism, as well as a policy report on information technology and Australian education. Publications include *Child and Citizen: Genealogies of Schooling and Subjectivity* (1993, coedited with Deborah Tyler).

**TOBY MILLER** is a professor of cultural studies and cultural policy at New York University. He is the author of *The Well-Tempered Self: Citizenship, Culture, and the Postmodern Subject* (1993), *Contemporary Australian Television* (with S. Cunningham, 1994), *The Avengers* (1997), *Technologies of Truth: Cultural Citizenship and the Popular Media* (1998), and *Popular Culture and Everyday Life* (with A. McHoul, 1998). He is the editor of *Television and New Media*, is coeditor of *Social Text*, and has also edited the following three books: *SportCult* (with R. Martin, 1999), *Film and Theory: An Anthology* (with R. Stam, 2000), and *A Companion to Film Theory* (with R. Stam, 2000).

**JEFFREY MINSON** is currently a research fellow at the University of Technology, Sydney, Australia. He is the author of *Questions of Conduct: Sexual Harassment, Citizenship, Government* (1993) and of *Genealogies of Morals: Nietzsche, Foucault, Donzelot and the Eccentricity of Ethics* (1985). He has written on ethics, public policy, legal studies, and cultural history. He is preparing a book on the significance of the history of civility for current debates about the alleged deficiencies of democratic politics and government.

**TINA NGUYEN** is a postgraduate student in the Australian Key Centre for Cultural and Media Policy, Queensland University of Technology, Brisbane, Australia.

**NIKOLAS ROSE** is a professor of sociology at Goldsmiths College, University of London. His recent books include *Inventing Ourselves* (1996), *Governing the Soul* (2nd ed., 1999), and *Powers of Freedom* (1999).

**TIM ROWSE** is a research fellow in the Department of Government and Public Administration, University of Sydney, Sydney, Australia. His studies of the application of ethnographic knowledge to public policy have found expression in his books *Remote Possibilities: The Aboriginal Domain and the Administrative Imagination* (1992) and *Traditions for Health: Studies in Aboriginal Reconstruction* (1996).

**JOHN SINCLAIR** is a professor in the Department of Communication, Language and Cultural Studies, Victoria University of Technology, Melbourne, Australia. He has published widely on the globalization of the television and advertising industries, with special attention to Asia and Latin America.

**JULIAN THOMAS** is senior research fellow with the Australian Key Centre for Cultural and Media Policy, Griffith University. He has written widely on information policy, cultural history, and intellectual property.

**ANNA YEATMAN** is a professor of sociology at Macquarie University in Sydney, Australia. She is the author of *Bureaucrats, Technocrats, Femocrats* (1990) and *Postmodern Revisionings of the Political* (1994); and of a forthcoming book, *The Politics of Individuality*. She is also the editor or coeditor of a number of collections, the three most recent of which are *Activism and the Policy Process* (1998), *The New Contractualism* (1997), and *Justice and Identity* (1995).

**AUDREY YUE** is a lecturer in cultural studies, Melbourne University, Melbourne, Australia.

# Introduction

**Resourcing Citizenries**

DENISE MEREDYTH
*Swinburne University of Technology*
JEFFREY MINSON
*University of Technology, Sydney*

**This collection of articles is designed** to explore the overlap between the social and political analysis of citizenship and applied work in cultural and media policy. The articles in this volume tackle a variety of topics from different theoretical and disciplinary perspectives, but each bears on some central questions: To what extent are national governments responsible for providing common cultural resources to rights-bearing citizens? What is the range of rationales available for states to use in allocating such resources? And how are such rationales likely to be affected by economic internationalization, supranational agreements, diasporic migration, multiethnicity, and grassroots community politics?

These issues bear on debates in two territories, across a borderline that is often crossed, but rarely marked (see Bridges, 1994; Corrigan & Sayer, 1985; Dahlgren & Sparks, 1991; Kaplan, 1993; Rabinow, 1989).

The first of these is the burgeoning field of citizenship studies, which sprawls across sociology, political science, philosophy, intellectual history, and ethics (see, e.g., Beiner, 1995; Commen, 1997; Klusmeyer, 1996; Mouffe, 1992; Turner, 1993, Turner & Hamilton, 1994; Van Steenbergen, 1994; Walzer, 1997). The second is the emergent area of cultural and media policy studies.[1] Working across these fields, we aim to avoid the disciplinary segmentation and hermeticism that often prevails within citizenship studies and, more generally, within normative political theory (see Hindess, 1998). Accordingly, the collection is deliberately eclectic. Some contributions engage with issues in arts, media, and cultural policy, from arts and information policy to museums and diasporic media. We have also solicited work from political and social theorists influenced, variously, by post-Foucauldian work on governmentality, feminist

---

**Editors' Note:** *The editors would like to thank Louise Goebel for her careful subediting work on this volume. For discussion of the ideas and directions contained in this introduction and in the shaping of the volume as a whole, we would also like to thank Julian Thomas, Janice Besch, Louise Goebel, and our contributors. We are also grateful to the Australian Research Council for the Large Grant and Postdoctoral Fellowship Grant that have made this work possible. Thanks also to Tony Bennett for his support for this project.*

and psychoanalytic theory, public policy–based ethics, and recent historical research on traditions of civil science and philosophy.

In commissioning work that can be placed on the borderline between political theory, history, applied ethics, and cultural policy, we are filling a well-marked gap in studies of citizenship. In a widely cited survey of the field, Kymlicka and Norman (1995) comment that, for all the sophistication of current ethical-political analyses of the civic deficit, "a striking feature . . . is the timidity with which authors apply their theories of citizenship to questions of public policy" (p. 300). It is not that confidence is wanting: Theorists are quite ready to diagnose social ills, usually through the ritual application of "assymetric [sic] counter-concepts" (Koselleck, 1985). The result, on one hand, is a perpetual rediscovery of unhealthy imbalances in our democracies: between active and passive citizenship, between the public-spirited citizen and the self-interested consumer and claimer of duty-free rights, and between bureaucratic guardianship and the promise of popular sovereignty (Barber, 1982; Clarke, 1996; Cleveland, 1996; Dagger, 1997). On the other hand, where theorists are bold enough to go beyond schematic diagnoses of the civic deficit, the results are often summary and heavy-handed policy prescriptions, such as compulsory community service. Either political theory issues in mandatory prescriptions or prohibitions, or it appears impotent—"gentle and relatively unobtrusive" methods of engendering civic dispositions being dismissed as inconsequential (Kymlicka & Norman, 1995, p. 301): "If civility is important," comment Kymlicka and Norman (1995), "why not pass Good Samaritan laws?" (p. 300).

Such suggestions typify citizenship theorists' limited engagement (despite emphasis on the *idea* of forming character in applications of virtue ethics to citizenship) with the repertoire of actual techniques for the indirect "conduct of conduct." Perhaps this is in part an effect of the longstanding influence over normative social and political theory of juristic or "juridico-discursive" paradigms of power, politics, and government (Pocock, 1993, pp. 394-395; see also Foucault, 1978; Minson, 1985). To be legitimate, citizenship theorists assume, government must be reducible to the ideal of the polity as a democratic comity, a product of conversations, covenants, or bargains between presumably rational citizens about the obligatory rules of their collective coexistence.[2]

For all its nobility, this postulate has trouble in dealing with the myriad and generally unexceptionable aspects of the private and public governance of citizens (including legal regulation itself) that do not conform to this ideal form (Burchell, Gordon, & Miller, 1991; Dean & Hindess, 1998; Donzelot, 1979, 1988; Rose, 1990, 1996a, 1996b). To engage with the practical and political challenges of putting liberal pluralist conceptions of civic formation to work requires taking seriously the empirical means of forming civic and civil attributes. Cultural policy is one of the zones of social governance in which this work of making up citizens takes place. Studies of cultural policy are centrally concerned with such modes of neoliberal governance, which work between public institutions and private lives and at both national and international levels, shaping civic or civil habits, tastes, and dispositions in ways that are all the more effective for not being experienced as obtrusive (Bennett, 1995; Hunter, 1988, 1994; Mercer, 1997; Miller, 1998).

From this corner of public policy, we can plot the angle at which critique, advocacy, and community politics intersect with expertise and varieties of political, legal, and governmental reasoning. At the same time, we can monitor the effects of the international trends in governance that are supposed to be shaking public policy to its historical foundations. These include the impact on public policy of neoliberal economic doctrines, the tension between market rationality and community values, and the prospects for a regeneration of civil society through the mobilization of participatory communities.

In the search for supplementary funds, cultural institutions are becoming increasingly market driven, seeking ways of attracting new audiences.[3] The pattern is one of devolution of cultural funding and planning to local governments and independent agencies and local initiatives. In place of the centralized civil service authorities, semiautonomous agencies and brokers now provide cultural services to client groups within cultural and media industries, generating new consumer relations (see, e.g., Bennett, 1997; Craik, James Bailey, & Moran, 1995; Cunningham & Jacka, 1996; Mercer & Stephens, 1997; Mulcahy, 1998; Wyszomirski, 1998). Communities have been incited to tap into a tradition of volunteerism, identifying their own cultural needs and planning for themselves and generating funding for cultural initiatives (McNulty, 1994). Support for these community participation programs has come from across the political spectrum—from market liberals concerned with minimizing state interference, from conservatives concerned about declining community values and civility, and from leftist champions of popular sovereignty and community participation.

Surveying these developments, this collection of articles hinges applied policy on culture and citizenship with studies of governance. On one hand, case studies from cultural and media policy test the limits of political-theoretical diagnosis and prescription. On the other hand, they suggest ways of translating theoretical-political concerns into more effective advocacy and practicable cultural reforms to civic life. But before introducing our contributors, we need a clearer angle on cultural policy and its bearing on citizenship.

## CULTURAL POLICY: DEBATES AND DIALECTS

As a field, cultural policy studies is still inchoate, with no single institutional home. The umbrella term *cultural policy* can place cultural studies gurus and identity politics activists next to experts on the cultural industries (e.g., Crawley, 1997; DiMaggio, 1987). It can cover those who champion the traditional arts and government support for heritage, public libraries, and cultural community development, those concerned with language policies for ethnic minorities, and those engaged in ground-level research and consultation on the cultural resources of communities, audiences, consumers, and subcultures.

In the academy, cultural policy studies appears on the cusp of cultural studies, urban planning, cultural history, sociology, and political theory. American cultural planners such as DiMaggio are cited as progenitors (see DiMaggio, 1987; Miller, 1996), along with British intellectuals who in the 1980s combined Birmingham-school cultural studies with the local government traditions of the United Kingdom (Bennett, 1998; Jones, 1994). Cultural policy thinking in that decade also owed something to social-democratic intellectuals seeking a rapprochement between leftist politics and commerce via industry policy.

During the 1980s in Britain, for instance, cultural policy gradually shifted from a focus on high culture and heritage to include what became known as the *cultural industries* of broadcasting, film, popular music, video, fashion, and so on. Setting aside established moral-political contrasts between self-sacrificing citizens and pleasure-driven consumers, these social-democratic arguments combined concerns about the conditions for employment growth with attention to the liberating potential of popular consumption patterns (Mulgan & Worpole, 1986).

As a strain of public policy debate, cultural policy discussion is made up of polyglot dialects. Debates on the politics of difference and the politics of entitlement, for example, tend to be articulated mostly in the idiom of cultural rights (Balibar, 1991; Kymlicka, 1995; Taylor, 1989). One influential formulation holds, for instance, that the principal rationale for government-instigated cultural policies in a liberal polity committed to fostering individual self-fulfillment is citizens' entitlement to one of its preconditions, namely, the cultural resources that for many citizens are a vital source of the self (Taylor, 1989, 1992). Citizens have a suprapolitical human right to culture, it is said, because culture defines humanity. As humans, citizens have a right in particular to the full experiential range of intellectual and artistic experience provided by their unique culture: "the reflective self-consciousness operating at the highest level of intensity," beyond "the common experience of day to day living," as the 1948 Declaration on Human Rights puts it (General Assembly of the United Nations, 1948, cited in Schensul, 1990, p. 337). Accordingly, cultural rights cannot be the privilege of a national or universal elite—there must be full recognition of all the culturally diverse forms of humanity and their artistic expression.

Some have qualified these formulations with the argument that there is no clear distinction between elite intellectual and artistic expression and the common experience of day-to-day living. The point is not to democratize culture (by creating greater access to the mainstream arts). Rather, moving beyond the instrumentalist, market-dominated obsessions of most current cultural policy, we need an alternative form of cultural policy that could be a vehicle for building a citizen-oriented cultural democracy (Dunn, 1997; Evrard, 1997; Lewis, 1994).

Where the debate turns to the cultural resources needed by multiethnic communities, this discourse on democracy and culture meets the politics of entitlement

(Castles, 1997). Debates on multiculturalism have explored ways in which language policy and other cultural policy frameworks might provide the resources that would enable ethnically divided populations to learn to accommodate cultural differences, rather than subordinating them within common cultural institutions (Kymlicka, 1989, 1995; Parekh, 1997). Moving beyond theoretical oppositions between communitarianism and liberalism, it is argued, cultural policy frameworks should be able to recognize the rights of *cultures*, negotiating with collective political identities while anticipating the potentially coercive or exclusive impact of group identification. Given both external protections and internal cultural restraints against such communities, it is hoped, collective cultural groups may find ways to negotiate defensible moral rules for pluralistic civic conduct.

> A community of orthodox Jews sharing public space on the Sabbath without commercial life polluting that space; a neighborhood of West Indians playing cricket on the streets of Brooklyn during carnival; a Quebecoise going into a supermarket and getting asked what she wants in French; a community of Moslems within the U.S. Army sharing Friday prayer in a public space reserved for them: these examples in cosmopolitan society will surely encroach upon the rights of others, in that public space is appropriated for group activity, and sometimes the activities will create (for others) a public nuisance . . . [nevertheless] these activities provide meaning for many people's lives in a cosmopolitan society. (Laitin, 1998, p. 226)

Such aspirations have not gone unchallenged, given the problems entailed in tying individual citizens and their claims on public culture to ethnically specific cultural identities (Carens, 1997; Kukathas, 1992; Margalit & Halbertal, 1994; Rorty, 1994, 1995; Young, 1997). Nevertheless, critics and defenders of cultural rights engage in a common mode of citizenship talk about cultural policy, one that is intellectually oriented around contending suprainstitutional principles or ideals. This idealistic language is at home in the academy, but it also functions as a rhetorical and ethical resource for those seeking to inject *gravitas* and vision into political, diplomatic, and legal deliberations (e.g., Clinton, 1994).

True, in the archipelagos of government decision making, commentary, advocacy, and intervention that make up public policy debate, such invocations of the higher principles of culture—elite or democratic—tend to sound like motherhood statements. They can seem particularly unworldly when juxtaposed to political realities such as budgetary exigencies and financial risk, electoral pressures, rivalrous class, ethnic, or gender politics, or clashes of interests between artforms, advocacy bodies, and agencies. It would be mistaken to portray cultural policy discussion as a clash between political idealism and capitalist calculation. Instead, we could talk about distinct but by no means polarized idioms of cultural policy discourse, some of which are certainly oriented to economic and political advantage.

Talk about synergies between art and national economic vitality has become the argot of the advisers, bureaucrats, lobbyists, and advocates attached to cultural industries, heritage, entertainment, broadcasting, information policy, and communications (e.g., Casey, Dunlop, & Selwood, 1996). In these environments in which centralized cultural planning and funding is now construed as intrusive, expensive, and inefficient, many of these policy intellectuals endeavor to balance public-good considerations against the imperative to foster markets, build client relations, and promote consumer choice (Colbert, 1997; Jacka, 1997; Zolberg, 1994). Many are remaking themselves as generic managers while finding places for administrative expertise and specialist judgment (cf. Du Gay, 1995). At the same time, many see themselves as advocates, exemplary citizens, and activists linked by reciprocal commitments to arts workers, communities, or cultural institutions (Christie, 1999). At such points, where experts engage with the demands of effective advocacy and advice in the face of fiscal restrictions, electoral pressure, and political trade-offs, we find practical instances of the connection (and disconnection) between democratic discourse and the imperatives of actionable policy and social governance (Daniels, 1997; Radbourne, 1997; Throsby, 1997).

We see just these sorts of (dis-) connections, for instance, in the 1994 Australian cultural policy statement, *Creative Nation* (Commonwealth of Australia, 1994), now a model for the cultural planning exercises of Britain's New Labour. The statement combined arts, film, media, and information policy within a "whole-of-government" cultural policy framework intended "to bring cultural issues into the mainstream of our national life" (Commonwealth of Australia, 1994, p. 12). The preamble affirmed a commitment to fostering artistic excellence and cultural democracy, ending with a charter of cultural rights. Thereafter, *Creative Nation* gets down to business.

> This cultural policy is also an economic policy. Culture creates wealth. Broadly speaking our cultural industries generate thirteen billion dollars a year. Culture employs ... adds value ... it makes an essential contribution to innovation, marketing and design. ... It is a badge of our industry. The level of our creativity substantially determines our ability to respond to new economic imperatives. ... It is a valuable export in itself and a valuable accompaniment to the export of other commodities. (Commonwealth of Australia, 1994, p. 7)

These images of the arts as the ornament and accompanist of commerce reappear in a subsequent discussion of national art and culture as an instrument of foreign policy, providing "a blend of culture and commerce to project a contemporary image of Australia overseas" (Commonwealth of Australia, 1994, p. 93). So even in this most instrumentalist of arguments, markets are not everything. Art also helps to enhance the international profile of the state: For all its limitations, the document is an argument for significant state support for the arts and cultural industries. We need to pause before assuming too quickly that this state interest in culture is unmindful of the welfare of citizens.

Debates about state interest in the health of culture and the arts and tensions between higher public good considerations and instrumentalism are far from new, at either a national or an international level. It may be useful to think of these tensions as part of the historical "steady diet of conflicts" (Hirschmann, 1994, p. 212) through which we have arrived at the present-day uneasy fit, within liberal democratic discourse, between different domains of reasoning: state interest, social governance, and democratic politics.

Since at least the 18th century (in France and Germany), Western states have pursued the end of social settlement and pastoral governance through the bureaucratic coordination of local and municipal cultural activities and civic life (Bennett, 1995, 1998; Hunter, 1988, 1994; Mercer, 1997; Miller, 1993, 1998; Mulcahy, 1998). Public arts, media, and cultural institutions have had a nation-building role not only in consolidating nations of immigrants and displaying national prestige but also in forming the habits and ethical attributes of urban populations. Alongside schools and prisons, museums and art galleries were purpose-built instruments of moral reformation. However, their rationales also had to be adapted to the expansion of social and political rights early this century. National debates occurred on citizens' social rights to equal access to common cultural resources and their promises of self-improvement—debates that are broadly comparable with contemporary controversies.

A measure of conflict was and is inevitable. As tutelary institutions, schools, public broadcasters, museums, art galleries, and so on have been charged with the responsibility to assist in forming public cultures, collective cultural identities, and self-governing citizens, extending the latter's repertoire of interests and abilities. It also falls to these institutions of social governance to save the people from themselves, maintaining a neutral and expert judgment that arbitrates in battles over common resources, combats popular ignorance, and in some instances defuses destructive conducts. At the same time, as democratic institutions, cultural and social institutions are supposed to be conduits for the expression of popular aspirations and critical reason, for instance, as articulated in equity and access programs.

Equivalent points can be made about the conflicting dimensions of international cultural policy, the terrain of rivalry and cooperation between states, and of negotiation between commercial and governmental interest. Cultural affairs has a long-standing role as a national foreign policy instrument conducted as part of the business of government between and within nations and between sovereign states and corporations (Chartrand, 1992). The United States, for instance, has a long history of pursuing cultural exchange as an instrument of diplomacy, combining neutral philanthropic ends of mutuality with the securing of national trade and security interests and using scholarly exchange and fellowships to keep a competitive edge in ideas, while preselecting future elites and introducing conceptions of human rights and intellectual freedom into nondemocratic regimes. As the Librarian of Congress, James Billington (1992) remarks, while putting the case for government cultural patronage in intellectual exchange schemes such as Fulbright Fellowships, "stronger cultural and educational programs enable us to sustain and support longer-term forces working towards democratization, even when we feel compelled, from understandable short-term reasons of state, to work tactically with non-democratic or even repressive leaders" (p. 103). Mediating between cultures through the arts and cultural exchange, he argues, America can present itself as a "uniquely experimental frontier civilization" (p. 109), tolerant of the right to affirm and express unique cultures while meeting "the desire of everyone . . . to participate in the common world of television communications and secular knowledge" (p. 110). This is properly portrayed, he suggests, not as an "imperialist policy," but as an exercise in "symphonic" international cultural policy (p.109).

Needless to say, these are hardly the kinds of overlap between theory and cultural policy portended in political theorists' appeals to supranational recognition of cultural rights (Archibugi & Held, 1995). Once cosmopolitan principles are tagged to cultural rights through agencies of supranational bodies such as the United Nations and United Nations Educational, Scientific, and Cultural Organization (UNESCO), civic idealists speculate, national citizenship will be erased, and community will be reinvented in a global mode (Featherstone, 1990; Heater, 1996; Linklater, 1998; Mayor, 1993). *Culture* will become the new language of international statecraft as supranational forms of governance seek a universal moral counterweight to the chaos created by international capitalist expansion and panicking nation states (Jacques, 1996, p. 25). A cosmopolitan conception of citizenship will be realized at local levels within a complex configuration of "community institutions, state, nations and transnational voluntary associations, regions and alliances of regions" (Meehan, 1993, p. 1, cited in Lemke, 1998, p. 213). Human rights abuses and the dispossession of indigenous peoples will be able to be addressed by appeal to a higher international court and by reference to liberal cosmopolitan principles enforced through international law (Caney, George, & Jones, 1996).

The gap between civic idealism and political application is likely to remain marked in cultural policy discussions. For some cultural policy experts, current liberal pluralist conceptions of the "mutual bliss points" to be found through good will and negotiation seem "wildly intellectual in a realm of politics that arouses deep emotions" (Laitin, 1998, p. 236). The problem with treating culture as our sole source of moral guidance in debates on cultural policy is that "in the very nature of minority organization, there is the potential for ugliness that goes far beyond a liberal vision of politics" (Laitin, 1998, p. 236). Theorists of cosmopolitan accord too easily assume that collective cultural identities are willing to negotiate using rational democratic forms of discussion, putting aside the commitment to inalienable articles of faith and managing internal differences, including those between leaders and constituencies, extremists and moderates. As Everitt (1996) argues, commenting on UNESCO's *Our Creative Diversity* (World Commission on Culture and Development, 1995), which calls for a new global ethic to address cultural fragmentation, the appeal to universal values and collective reason misses the point about the need for street-level cultural resourcing and for a more pragmatic understanding of the endemic problems that plague the governance of cultural life.

> While it is true that all cultures object to murder, they disagree fundamentally on many other matters—and, in particular some of those dear to the commission's heart. A theocrat will have a very different view of democracy and human rights—a view that can be honestly held and culturally authentic. To take a practical example, what should teachers in front of a multiracial class in this country do when discussing such issues with their students? Should they let themselves be guided by a certain sense of relativity and not insist, say, on the equality of the sexes? Or should they assert the primacy of European values come what may? The recent rebellion among Muslim parents in Bradford about religious education in schools suggests that this is not an abstract question; for them tolerance is no virtue and it is not merciful to countenance heresy. The point is that today's culture is taking place messily on the streets, in under-funded schools, in video arcades and in bleak suburbs and favelas from Cairo to the Caucasus. It is a million miles away from the committee rooms of the great and is not readily susceptible to the application of reason, of sweetness and light. (Everitt, 1996, p. 32)[4]

The comment brings us back to our core question of the responsibilities of states (or of communities themselves) for resourcing citizenries. We doubt whether it suffices to defer such problems to the collective conscience of ethnic communities or to the global community as a moral arbiter (cf. Stevenson, 1997). We also doubt whether advanced liberal societies have (morally speaking) outgrown the need for all forms of governance that fail to comply with the ethos of moral self-governance. This ethos may permit some political theorists to wash their hands of the dirty work of politics and government, but this is a luxury not afforded to those who make everyday decisions about the allocation of cultural resources, the arbitration of rights claims, and the trade-off between the common entitlements of citizens and the claims made in the name of collective political identities.

To conclude, one reason why citizenship theorists may find applied cultural policy thinking good to think with is because it exemplifies the sheer variety of the political vocabularies, rationalities, and ethical, person-forming regimens at work in public policy. If political theory of citizenship and governance is to become less heavy handed in its applied approach to cultural policy, it will need to be able to recognize the difference between these cultural policy idioms, if not to speak them. To this end, let us now turn to the individual contributions to this volume, which offer fresh angles on these themes.

## THE SCOPE AND FOCUS OF THE COLLECTION

We turn first to a study of the politics of community in contemporary Britain. Nikolas Rose's chapter is the first of some broad-ranging discussions that undercut the theoretical counterconcepts through which the citizenship ethos is commonly defined: community being pitted against liberal-commercial values, the citizen against the consumer, and so on.

Rose attempts to tease out what is distinctive about the expectations and practices attached to the current Blair government's much vaunted "Third Way" between the axial organizational principles of the market and the social-democratic/collectivist welfare state. Blair's program appears as a curious mixture of dog-eared agendas and warm words drawn from the lexicons of social democracy and Victorian philanthropy (virtue, character, personal responsibility, etc.). The potent new ingredient slipped into this cocktail is a communitarian etho-politics inserted into British electoral political discourse and into ways of defining and addressing social policy problems.

New Labour's philosophical template for an ethical overlay to supplement its neoliberal economic reform programs leans toward a fixed set of often traditional moral obligations, even if it is perhaps more open than its Conservative party predecessors were to the proliferation of new kinds of community and their distinctive ethical styles. Rose suggests that the current turn to governing through community is in part linked to the acculturating effects of attachments to commercially based lifestyle communities, some of which invent new ethical possibilities and contribute to societies' funds of civility. Nevertheless, the predominant thrust of Blairite etho-politics, argues Rose, is to drive government to abdicate its responsibilities in some areas, while either cruelly or absurdly overreaching itself in its zeal to make social policies across the board—from parental responsibility to social security—conform to a single moralizing vision.

Whereas Rose was interested in recent developments, by which communal cultures have become targets and effects of government, Tony Bennett uses a Foucauldian frame of reference to explore historical continuities and shifts in the ways in which a staple object of cultural policy, the art museum, has been connected with social governance, including forms of community outreach. Bennett's genealogy points to the mundane origins of current museum practices, in 19th-century programs that pressed museums and other public utilities into campaigns against working-class drunkenness. In this way, he ironizes the language of citizen empowerment in current community-friendly deployments of art while casting a wry eye on critiques of the art world as socially exclusive.

There is a further, theoretical twist to Bennett's argument. Historical comparison between governmental uses of art as a "means of acting on the social" offers a counterargument to social theory's tendency to make the cultural and the social coeval. Versions of this theoretical impulse in the cultural policy field can be found in arguments on cultural democracy, which tend to conceive every social practice or artefact as a bearer of cultural significance and as potentially formative of identity (e.g., Evrard, 1997; Stratton & Ang, 1994). Equity and diversity are invoked to criticize types of arts and cultural policy that, in the name of excellence, are said to privilege the mainstream Euro-American fine arts.

This is the terrain investigated by Toby Miller in a study of a prominent flashpoint in the U.S. culture wars of the 1980s and 1990s, when the very idea of federal government subsidy for high art was brought into question. Miller's starting point is the moment when the U.S.'s peak arts funding body, the National Endowment for the Arts (NEA), came close to extinction in the mid-1990s at the hands of a resurgent Republican party captured by moral/religious die hards and a more diffuse anti-Federalist populism. Miller sketches a history of the NEA and tracks the evolution of the conservative-populist campaign to defund a perceived bastion of left-liberal or elite arts, paying careful attention to the range of ideologies mobilized by the NEA's defenders and critics. Future arguments on the ethical basis for public cultural support of the arts, Miller concludes, in a prostatist version of the cultural democracy argument, will need to find new rationales with deeper roots in an ethic of democratic political decision making.

Certainly, arts policy in liberal democracies cannot afford to turn its back on demands for a more equitable distribution of cultural resources and for more civic participation regarding such matters. As we have seen, democratic citizenship can only be one consideration among others. Cultural equity is limited *inter alia* by "reasons of good government," which derive from the specific characteristics, or convenience, of the activities to be governed (Foucault, 1991, p. 95). There can only be a limited number of intrinsically expensive and relatively unpopular cultural institutions such as opera to spread around. It has been observed that in the United States, during the 1980s culture war around arts subsidies,

> states and cities in which artists and art organisations are concentrated get more funding than one would expect on the basis of their population, but less than one would anticipate on the basis of their proportion of artists and artistic activities. (DiMaggio, 1991, p. 229)

Principles of justice, democracy, or citizenship are too multifarious and contentious for there to be a single right answer to allocative questions. Yet, in the compromises, expert advice, and coalition building between government arts agencies and the cultural sector, upon which the survival, as well as the balance, of allocations depends (DiMaggio, 1991, p. 229), ethical considerations are still a factor. The ethical questions that are most likely to spring to mind are about the relative access and influence of prestigious arts institutions and less-established cultural traditions. But as the next chapter shows, there is more to the ethics of civic participation than the right to have one's say.

Janice Besch and Jeffrey Minson attempt to cast the concept of citizen participation in policy making in a fresh light, as a prelude to formulating some ideas about the conflicting place of democratic opinion and the participation of cultural sector professionals in arts policy development. Drawing on an array of intellectual sources and firsthand experience in the arts policy field, their chapter sketches an alternative to the idealized image of the moral community of self-governing citizens that overarches most political advocacy and theoretical discussion of democratic participation. The authors draw attention to the multiple roles into which "actually existing" participation dissolves and to the more worldly ethical dispositions (and conflicting obligations) that are inseparable from responsible participation in those different capacities. The assumption that citizen participation is the highest form of democracy is further questioned by reference to the place of polling techniques in the policy process. The chapter then turns to some problems facing the cultural sector as a consequence of neoliberal microeconomic reform agendas and Australia's own version of the anti-elitist political challenges. These problems, it is suggested, require imaginative and supple responses: There does need to be more participation. Yet, even taking into account considerations such as cultural access and equity, identifying the kinds of participation required (and the kinds of participant) entails departing from the scripts provided by citizenship theory and civics manuals.

Ian Hunter and Denise Meredyth mount a more direct and disquieting challenge to the grip on political theory of the image of the self-governing community. They put the case that a limited type of nondemocratic political sovereignty and its correlate, the political subjection of citizens to that authority, is not just a regrettable political fact but a historical prerequisite of liberal-democratic government itself. To separate state authority from democratic government is to situate one's thought in the vicinity of the notorious and largely forgotten early modern reason-of-state tradition. This chapter justifies a cautious renewal of interest in this tradition, or, more accurately, in the antimetaphysical tradition of civil political thought in which certain versions of reason-of-state doctrine were imbricated.

The interest of this tradition is initially foreshadowed in a discussion of certain persistent aporia in contemporary international civic education programs and political theory. These problems can be sheeted home to a conception of legitimate state authority as founded in the reflectively based consensus of a self-governing citizenry. Intercultural antagonism of the sort displayed in *l'affaire du foulard*—the bitter controversy that broke out in France in 1989 over Muslim girls wearing the veil at school—is one such stumbling block for this variety of enlightened thinking. The inadequacy of all the main normative theoretical contenders in dealing with intercultural conflicts is a subject of repeated commentary in the academic literature (e.g., Bammer, 1994; Benhabib, 1992; Gergen, 1991; Hall & Du Gay, 1996), but the critics are seldom prepared to grasp the nettle of the necessary coexistence of democratic government and limited forms of subjection to a political sovereign as a condition for setting limits to destructive forms of communitarian conflict. Turning to history, the chapter suggests that these problems in contemporary political theory and civics are present *in nuce* both in Kant's philosophy and in the early modern German Protestant metaphysics of which that philosophy is a variant. In turn, these imperializing forms of thought and the incendiary forms of cultural politics to which they gave rise were the prime targets of a rival form of enlightenment, that of civil philosophy. An outline of this philosophy shows that not all reason-of-state doctrines are inimical to liberal-democratic government. Moreover, elements of this civil philosophy provide a way of clarifying modern problems of cultural and educational policy.

The civic renewal and democratic education programs described by Hunter and Meredyth provide a vivid example of the global face of governmentality, which Barry Hindess discusses, reflecting on the consequences of relating national citizenship to its international conditions of existence. Hindess's argument partly parallels Hunter and Meredyth's, with its contrast between the reason-of-state thinking that undergirds the location of citizenship in nation states and the Kantian political metaphysics behind the whiggish view that the international spread of democratic citizenship represents a self-evident advance in human well-being. Optimism about democratic citizenship conventionally goes hand in hand with ideals of a cosmopolitan global citizenship (paradigmatically, human rights and environmental obligations) as a remedy for the contingent moral limits of national citizenship. But can this sanguine view be sustained if the spread of national citizenship and an international moral order in fact have little to do with human beings progressively acquiring the capacity to govern their own affairs? Citizenship appears in a harsher light when it is seen as the historical artefact of a supranational regime for the government of populations that works by partitioning everyone into discrete, territorially based competing national units under nominally sovereign governments. Citizenship in this perspective is unavoidably exclusivist and divisive, "a conspiracy against the rest of the world" (Hindess, this volume, p. 94). The political implications of this picture of international governance are unclear, but we are reminded that reason-of-state thinking is not something we should learn to love. It can still be chilling even if we learn to stop identifying it with its abuses and understand its more benign rationale.

The expansion of international human rights conventions discussed by Anna Yeatman, in the subsequent chapter, could also be redescribed in terms of a regime of international governance. Yeatman herself is alert to the dangers of both underplaying the realpolitik dimension of human rights discourse and of envisioning a time when the tensions between human rights and national citizenship will be resolved: "They implicate phenomenologically different territories of right and being" (Yeatman, this volume, p. 105). Her main interest is in arriving at a better understanding of the ethical core of human rights claims. She asks what it is about human individuality in virtue of which it can be the source of the dignity that, according to United Nations conventions, is lost in human rights violations. How can the concept of the human as such bear this ethical weight, not in spite of but by virtue of its being so empty and abstract, in respect to sexual difference, class, culture, and so on? These considerations of what humanness consists form the basis of Yeatman's argument that human rights and liberal individualist citizen rights are distinct, overlaps notwithstanding.[5]

One implication of Yeatman's discussion is that if cultural rights are to count as human rights, cultures have to be construed as communities of individual choice, not of fate. Then, at least in one respect, Yeatman argues, human rights entail placing some limits on cultures' rights of self-determination. She also contends that, in light of the exclusionary and subordinative implications of citizenship, "it is problematic for national state governments to be the only agents responsible for ... the implementation and monitoring of human rights" (p. 115).

These points return us to the tensions, but also interdependencies, between national and international governance. Limited acquiescence in United Nations conventions on economic, social, and political rights, especially by the United States, induces a certain pessimism about the range of conditions under which the international order can be expected to supply the human rights supplement that liberal national political orders cannot meet. Perhaps we should also resist the temptation to assume that the limits imposed on citizenship rights by their foundation in the legal and political decisions of sovereign states always have to be treated, morally speaking, as limitations to be overcome by reference to cosmopolitan citizenship. Attempting to institutionalize human rights claims within a democratic polity is likely to strike political, moral, and technical problems that cannot be solved at a higher global level.

This is one of the lessons of the next chapter. Tim Rowse's study is about how social limits to aboriginal Australians' cultural autonomy might be negotiated. Moving between developments in Australian anthropology, politics, and public policy and international debates in political theory, Rowse suggests ways of rethinking some problems that have arisen in attempting to operate the principle of self-determination in aboriginal governance—for instance, around the so-called cultural appropriateness of applying standard accountability procedures regarding public resources within partly community-based apparatuses of government. Rowse constructs an argument that brings together Kukathas's (1992) attempt to steer a middle path based on the notion of associations between liberal individualist and communitarian/culturalist approaches to cultural rights and the instructive ways in which some Australian bureaucrats, consultants, and anthropologists—in submissions to a government review of aboriginal representative councils—picked their way through competing notions of accountability.

The suggestion is that there are advantages in reworking public definitions of aboriginal collectivities around the associational idea. It allows space for distinctions to be made between private and public; associations are entitled to certain kinds of autonomy from big government, both public and private, in the way their group life evolves. One advantage of the long-neglected associationalist tradition in political theory (see Hirst, 1993; Nichols, 1975) is that although it is not exclusively obsessed with individual rights, it is not normative on the question of whether associations are based on mutual convenience or common affective bonds. An associationalist framework does not pressure citizens to bind themselves into fixed communal arrangements and customs. It is not antistatist and can contemplate the need for nation states to develop the capacities that some indigenous people need to acquire if they are to successfully practice a policy of self-determination.

Rowse illustrates the flexibility afforded by this framework. Liberal arguments for limiting cultural rights usually turn on the need to protect individual liberties, including individual exit rights, from oppressive "internal restrictions" (Kymlicka, 1995, pp. 33-48), but a widespread problem that the governance and self-governance of aboriginal communities has to confront, inter alia exacerbating the problems of public support and accountability, is the frequent inclination of whole families and groups in a community to split off and form a new collectivity when conflicts arise. In these circumstances, public definitions of aboriginal collectivities as set cultural wholes are an obstacle, Rowse argues, to negotiating a settlement between concerns about aboriginal people misusing public monies (often but not entirely driven by right-wing complaints about special treatment), and aboriginal aspirations to make self-determination work for their own people and for the public good.

Rowse's chapter, with its synthesis of theoretical, anthropological, and administrative thinking, further suggests that, as Rose points out, we should not underestimate the intellectual and political inventiveness exhibited in emerging tactics for governing through the relay of community—forms of inventiveness little dreamt of in communitarian philosophies and avant-garde experiments in living.

In their chapter, Cunningham, Hawkins, Nguyen, Sinclair, and Yue also upset conventional expectations about the fit between citizenship and the public-private distinction. As well, they show how work in cultural policy provides alternatives to the tired theoretical trope that sets the figures of the citizen and the consumer in antithesis. The object of this essay is the media of multiculturalism. The chapter examines the ways in which diasporic communities in Australia (especially Vietnamese and Chinese Australians) organize to consume and produce media to dwell both within and outside the spaces of Asia, Australia, and the West. These practices occur beside and around the regulatory provisions of national media and cultural policy. Nevertheless, argue the authors, they cannot be taken as instances of either the decline of national state planning or the advance of globalization at the expense of the public sphere. Instead, a new take has to be developed on globalization, with the focus being on diasporic media serving global "narrowcast" audiences.

The two diasporic communities at the center of the case studies defy categorization in terms of the familiar contrasts of citizenship theory. For example, Vietnamese Australians' use of VCRs illustrates a sociable face of commerce—supplying a demand for internationally distributed video entertainment shows, made in California, which afford one of the ways in which Vietnamese boat people and subsequent migrants have made themselves at home in a foreign land, while reaffirming and redefining their attachments to their nation if not their state of origin. These are, in significant respects, commercially organized communities. Citizenship literature, worried about passive citizenship, normally pays little attention and still less respect to peaceful consumption practices. Champions of democratic citizenship would like to see citizens with different identities and interests publicly engaged in a more obviously public "agonistic reciprocity" with one another (Ivison, 1997, p. 165, citing William Connelly), not sitting down to watch videos in their lounge rooms. Cunningham and his collaborators put a case for seeing the living rooms of Vietnamese Australians and their compatriots in related countries as "vibrant spaces of self- and community-making," internationally embedded components of a public sphere or "sphericule" formed along diasporic trade routes. It is a further instantiation of the consumer- and lifestyle-based civility-community game that Rose has suggested is so central nowadays to the ways in which identity is being formed. Here is a small, unprogrammed way in which problems of peaceful coexistence in diversity and cultural maintenance come to be settled without reference to theoretical questions of how to reconcile ideals of the common good with respect for cultural difference.

Finally, as an antidote to both pessimistic and optimistic generalizations about the deregulatory consequences of globalized communications, Julian Thomas offers a biting critique of the assumption that Internet use cannot or should not be the object of national regulation and cultural policy. Public computer networks are often regarded as tools of freedom, challenging for national governments with their aging systems of cultural regulation, but liberating for individual users. But are national regulatory systems and their cultural policy objectives really so irrelevant to the Information Age? Thomas argues that the libertarian expectations of digital networks have so far been disappointed and that the historical tasks of liberal government have not been forsaken, although their reformulation for a new technological context is proving difficult. Traditional forms of national cultural regulation, such as intellectual property and content regulation, are the focus of a new period of public debate and policy review. These processes disclose a shift toward information policy: a new alignment of commercial, cultural, and technological governance. Such a transition is a fateful moment for the complicated arrangements devised to settle public and private interests in analogue cultural policy.

Summing up, editors are well advised to resist the temptation to administer too closely how readers will approach their offerings, all of which possess their own stand-alone interest. Our introduction has simply sought to suggest some of the ways in which our contributors' chapters resonate with one another, offer correctives to problems with theoretical treatments of national and international citizenship, and illustrate the dynamism and relevance for citizenship of the increasingly important field of cultural policy studies.

## NOTES

1. For a range of discussions of the cultural policy field, from different perspectives, see Rowse (1985), Bianchini (1991), Bianchini & Parkinson (1993), Cunningham (1992), Lewis (1994), Craik (1996), McGuigan (1996), Crawley (1997), Evrard (1997), Wyszomirski (1998), and Bennett (1998).

2. Even the most realist of political theorists sometimes subscribe to this utopian image of government. Robert Dahl, for instance, identifies government primarily with the actions of a regime, qua representatives of a sovereign people, addressing problems by passing laws or more broadly making "binding decisions" (Dahl, 1989, p. 107) that are (normatively) expected to meet constitutionally, philosophically, or opinion-based tests of public justification.

3. There are, of course, distinct national traditions of political debate on government's responsibility for public culture. For example, the United States has been portrayed as giving "grudging, sporadic, and marginal" public support to the arts (Billington, 1992, p. 101), by comparison with the levels of state support offered by German and French governments, whose semi-independent arts councils have been benefactors of national culture heritage, the fine arts and performing arts, with some commitment to more diverse popular cultural forms (see Harris, 1995; Koning, 1995; Mulcahy, 1998). In light of the neoliberal turn taken in cultural policy in these European countries and others with strong statist traditions such as Canada, these contrasts are apt to be overdrawn (see Zemans, 1997).

4. See also Swanson's (1997) comment on the same report and its construction of the relationship between cultural policy and culture industries.

5. The right to individuality underpinning human rights is also the fulcrum of many philosophical and constitutional definitions of citizen rights. In both cases, the presumption is that no one ought to be in any respect subject to another. There being no middle ground between liberty and servitude in this perspective (Kriegel, 1995)—and this is another way to characterize what Hunter and Meredyth see as the stumbling block of both liberal and antiliberal theory—the relation of political subject to state sovereign and hence the state itself should on this reasoning ultimately be abolished, in conformity with the familiar Kantian ideal of cosmopolitan moral self-governance (cf. Hindess, 1996). What primarily makes us citizens, as distinct from bearers of human rights, seems to be also determined at a less elevated level. It is the fact that we hold a passport issued by a particular state, in relation to which we are in many respects political subjects.

## REFERENCES

Archibugi, D., & Held, D. (Eds.). (1995). *Cosmopolitan democracy: An agenda for a new world order.* Cambridge, MA: Polity.

Balibar, E. (1991). Citizen subject. In E. Cadava, P. Connor, & J.-L. Nancy (Eds.), *Who comes after the subject?* (pp. 33-57). New York: Routledge.

Bammer, A. (1994). *Displacements: Cultural identities in question.* Bloomington: Indiana University Press.

Beiner, R. (Ed.). (1995). *Theorising citizenship.* Albany: State University of New York Press.

Benhabib, S. (1992). *Situating the self: Gender, community and postmodernism in contemporary ethics.* Cambridge, MA: Polity.

Bennett, T. (1995). *The birth of the museum: History, theory, politics.* London and New York: Routledge.

Bennett, T. (1997). Consuming culture, measuring access and audience development. *Culture & Policy, 8*(1), 89-113.

Bennett, T. (1998). *Culture: A reformer's science.* St. Leonards, New South Wales: Allen & Unwin.

Bianchini, F. (1991). *Urban cultural policy.* London: National Arts and Media Strategy Unit, Arts Council.
Bianchini, F., & Parkinson, M. (Eds.). (1993). *Cultural policy and urban regeneration: The West European experience.* Manchester, UK: Manchester University Press.
Billington, J. (1992). The intellectual and cultural dimensions of international relations: Present ironies and future possibilities. *Journal of Arts Management, Law & Society, 22*(2), 101-118.
Bridges, T. (1994). *The culture of citizenship: Inventing post-modern civic culture.* Albany: State University of New York Press.
Burchell, G., Gordon, C., & Miller, P. (Eds.). (1991). *The Foucault effect: Studies in governmentality.* Brighton, UK: Harvester Wheatsheaf.
Caney, S., George, D., & Jones, P. (Eds.). (1996). *National rights, international obligations.* Boulder, CO: Westview.
Carens, J. H. (1997). Liberalism and culture. *Constellation, 4*(1), 35-47.
Casey, B., Dunlop, R., & Selwood, S. (1996). *Culture as commodity? The economics of the arts and heritage in the UK.* London: Policy Studies Institute.
Castles, S. (1997). Multicultural citizenship: A response to the dilemma of globalisation and national identity? *Journal of Intercultural Studies, 18*(1), 5-22.
Chartrand, H. H. (1992). International cultural affairs: A fourteen country survey. *Journal of Arts Management, Law & Society, 22*(2), 134-155.
Christie, A. (1999). *Arts administration: A hybrid ethical field.* Unpublished doctoral dissertation, Griffith University, Brisbane, Australia.
Clarke, P. (1996). *Deep citizenship.* East Haven, CT: Pluto Press.
Cleveland, G. (1996). *Good citizenship.* Bedford, MA: Applewood.
Clinton, B. (1994). Remarks to the President's Committee on the Arts and the Humanities. *Weekly compilation of Presidential Documents, 30*(38), 1815-1819.
Colbert, F. (1997). Changes in marketing environment and their impact on cultural policy. *Journal of Arts Management, Law & Society, 27*(3), 177-185.
Commen, T. K. (1997). *Citizenship and national identity: From colonialism to globalism.* Thousand Oaks, CA: Sage.
Commonwealth of Australia. (1994). *Creative nation: Commonwealth cultural policy.* Canberra: Australian Commonwealth Department of Communications and the Arts.
Corrigan, P., & Sayer, D. (1985). *The great arch: English state formation as cultural revolution.* Oxford, UK: Basil Blackwell.
Craik, J. (1996). The potential and limits of cultural policy strategies. *Culture & Policy, 7*(1), 177-204.
Craik, J., James Bailey, J., & Moran, A. (Eds.). (1995). *Public voices, private interests: Australia's media policy.* St. Leonards, New South Wales: Allen & Unwin.
Crawley, A. (1997). Canadian cultural policy—bridging the gaps: Or the cultural activist—a laboratory specimen. *Canadian Review of American Studies, 27*(3), 99-110.
Cunningham, S. (1992). *Framing culture: Criticism and policy in Australia.* North Sydney: Allen & Unwin.
Cunningham, S., & Jacka, E. (1996). *Australian television and international mediascapes.* Cambridge, UK: Cambridge University Press.
Dagger, R. (1997). *Civic virtues: Rights, citizenship, and republican liberalism.* New York: Oxford University Press.
Dahl, R. (1989). *Democracy and its critics.* New Haven, CT: Yale University Press.
Dahlgren, P., & Sparks, C. (1991). *Communication and citizenship: Journalism and the public sphere in the new media age.* New York: Routledge.
Daniels, K. (1997). Balancing objectives: The role of the commonwealth in cultural development. *Culture & Policy, 8*(1), 5-24.
Dean, M., & Hindess, B. (Eds.). (1998). *Governing Australia.* Melbourne, Australia: Cambridge University Press.

DiMaggio, P. (1987). *Managers of the arts: Careers and opinions of senior administrators of U.S. art museums, symphony orchestras, resident theatres, and local arts agencies.* Washington, DC: Seven Locks Press.

DiMaggio, P. (1991). Decentralisation of arts funding from the federal government to the states. In S. Carter (Ed.), *Public money and the muse: Essays on government funding for the arts* (pp. 216-256). New York: Norton.

Donzelot, J. (1979). *The policing of families.* New York: Random House.

Donzelot, J. (1988). The promotion of the social. *Economy and Society, 17*(3), 395-427.

Du Gay, P. (1995). *Office as a vocation: "Bureaucracy" but not as we know it.* Brisbane, Australia: Institute for Cultural Policy Studies.

Dunn, A. (1997). Public service broadcasting. The role of ABC Radio in the creation of citizenship models. *Culture & Policy, 8*(2), 91-103.

Everitt, A. (1996). Designer global culture. *New Statesman and Society, 9*(388), 31-33.

Evrard, Y. (1997). Democratizing culture or cultural democracy? (State intervention in culture). *Journal of Arts Management, Law & Society, 27*(3), 167-175.

Featherstone, M. (Ed.). (1990). *Global culture, nationalism, globalisation and modernity.* London: Sage.

Foucault, M. (1978). *The history of sexuality* (Vol. 1; R. Hurley, Trans.). London: Allen Lane.

Foucault, M. (1991). Governmentality. In G. Burchell, C. Gordon, & P. Miller (Eds.), *The Foucault effect: Studies in governmentality* (pp. 87-104). London: Harvester and Wheatsheaf.

Gergen, K. J. (1991). *The saturated self: Dilemmas of identity in contemporary life.* New York: Basic Books.

Hall, S., & Du Gay, P. (Eds.). (1996). *Questions of cultural identity.* London: Sage.

Harris, J. (1995). *Federal art and national culture: The politics of identity in New Deal America.* Cambridge, UK: Cambridge University Press.

Heater, D. B. (1996). *World citizenship and government: Cosmopolitanism ideas in the history of Western political thought.* New York: St. Martin's.

Hindess, B. (1996). *Discourses of power: From Hobbes to Foucault.* Oxford, UK: Blackwell.

Hindess, B. (1998). Governing cultures. *Southern Review, 31*(1), 149-162.

Hirschmann, A. O. (1994). Social conflicts as pillars of democratic market society. *Political Theory, 21*, 203-218.

Hirst, P. (Ed.). (1993). *The pluralist theory of the state: Selected writings of G.D.H. Cole, J. N. Figgis, and H. J. Laski.* London: Routledge.

Hunter, I. (1988). *Culture and government: The emergence of literary education.* London: Macmillan.

Hunter, I. (1994). *Rethinking the school: Subjectivity, bureaucracy, criticism.* Sydney, Australia: Allen & Unwin.

Ivison, D. (1997). *The self at liberty: Political argument and the arts of government.* Ithaca, NY: Cornell University Press.

Jacka, E. (1997). Public service broadcasting in transition: The view from Europe. *Culture & Policy, 8*(2), 115-126.

Jacques, M. (1996). Cultural revolutions. *New Statesman, 126*(4363), 24-27.

Jones, P. (1994). The myth of "Raymond Hoggart": On "founding fathers" and cultural policy. *Cultural Studies, 8*(3), 394-416.

Kaplan, W. (Ed.). (1993). *Belonging: The meaning and future of Canadian citizenship.* Montreal, Canada: McGill's-Queens University Press.

Klusmeyer, D. (1996). *Between consent and descent: Conceptions of democratic citizenship.* Washington, DC: Carnegie Endowment for International Peace.

Koning, H. (1995). A French mirror (civic solidarity in France). *The Atlantic Monthly, 276*(6), 95-105.

Koselleck, R. (1985). *Futures past: On the semantics of historical time.* Cambridge, MA: MIT Press.

Kriegel, B. (1995). *The state and the rule of law* (M. LePain & J. Cohen, Trans.). Princeton: NJ: Princeton University Press.

Kukathas, C. (1992). Are there any cultural rights? *Political Theory, 20*, 105-139.

Kymlicka, W. (1989). *Liberalism, community and culture.* Oxford, UK: Clarendon.

Kymlicka, W. (1995). *Multicultural citizenship.* Oxford, UK: Clarendon.

Kymlicka, W., & Norman, W. (1995). Return of the citizen: A survey of recent work on citizenship theory. In R. Beiner (Ed.), *Theorizing citizenship* (pp. 283-322). Albany: State University of New York Press.

Laitin, D. (1998). Liberal theory and the nation. *Political Theory, 26*, 221-237.

Lemke, C. (1998). Citizenship and European integration. *World Affairs, 160*(4), 212-218.

Lewis, J. (1994). Designing a cultural policy. *Journal of Arts Management, Law & Society, 24*(1), 41-57.

Linklater, A. (1998). *Transformation of the global community: Ethical foundations of the post-Westphalian era.* Sydney, Australia: Allen & Unwin.

Margalit, A., & Halbertal, M. (1994). Liberalism and the right to culture. *Social Research, 61*(3), 491-511.

Mayor, F. (1993, January). Culture and new-found freedoms. *UNESCO Courier,* p. 45.

McGuigan, J. (1996). *Culture and the public sphere.* New York: Routledge.

McNulty, R. (Ed.). (1994). *The state of the American community: Empowerment for local action.* Washington, DC: Partners for Livable Communities.

Mercer, C. (1997). Geographies for the present: Patrick Geddes, urban planning and the human sciences. *Economy and Society, 26*(2), 211-232.

Mercer, C., & Stephens, D. (1997). Navigating the economy of knowledge: Punters, profiles and policies. *Culture & Policy, 8*(1), 133-163.

Miller, T. (1993). *The well-tempered self: Citizenship, culture, and the postmodern subject.* Baltimore, MD: Johns Hopkins University Press.

Miller, T. (1996). Cultural citizenship and technologies of the subject, or where did you go, Paul DiMaggio? *Culture & Policy, 7*(1), 139-156.

Miller, T. (1998). *Technologies of truth: Cultural citizenship and the popular media.* Minneapolis: University of Minnesota Press.

Minson, J. (1985). *Genealogies of morals: Foucault, Nietzsche, Donzelot and the eccentricity of ethics.* London: Macmillan.

Mouffe, C. (Ed.). (1992). *Dimensions of radical democracy: Pluralism, citizenship, community.* London: Verso.

Mulcahy, K. V. (1998). Cultural patronage in comparative perspective: Public support for the arts in France, Germany, Norway, and Canada. *Journal of Arts Management, Law & Society, 27*(4), 247-264.

Mulgan, G., & Worpole, K. (1986). *Saturday night and Sunday morning: From arts to industry—new forms of cultural policy.* London: Comedia.

Nichols, D. (1975). *The pluralist state.* London: Macmillan.

Parekh, B. (1997). Dilemmas of a multicultural theory of citizenship. *Constellations, 4*(1), 54-62.

Pocock, J. A. (1993). A discourse of sovereignty: Observations on the work in progress. In N. Phillipson & Q. Skinner (Eds.), *Political discourse in early modern Britain* (pp. 377-428). Cambridge, UK: Cambridge University Press.

Rabinow, P. (1989). *French modern: Norms and forms of the social environment.* Chicago: University of Chicago Press.

Radbourne, J. (1997). Creative Nation: A policy for leaders or followers? An evaluation of Australia's 1994 cultural policy statement. *Journal of Arts Management, Law & Society, 26*(4), 271-284.

Rorty, A. (1994). The hidden politics of cultural identification. *Political Theory, 22*, 152-166.

Rorty, A. (1995). Rights: Educational not cultural. *Social Research, 62*(1), 161-170.

Rose, N. (1990). *Governing the soul: The shaping of the private self.* London: Routledge.

Rose, N. (1996a). The death of the social? Refiguring the territory of government. *Economy and Society, 23*(3), 327-356.
Rose, N. (1996b). Governing "advanced" liberal democracies. In A. Barry, T. Osborne, & N. Rose (Eds.), *Foucault and political reason: Liberalism, neo-liberalism and rationalities of government* (pp. 37-64). London: UCL Press.
Rowse, T. (1985). *Arguing the arts: The funding of the arts in Australia*. New York: Penguin.
Schensul, J. J. (1990). Organizing cultural diversity through the arts. *Education & Urban Society, 22*(4), 377-393.
Stevenson, N. (1997). Globalization, national cultures and cultural citizenship. *Sociological Quarterly, 38*(1), 41-67.
Stratton, J., & Ang. I. (1994). Multicultural imagined communities: Cultural difference and national identity in Australia and the USA. *Continuum, 8*(2) [On-line]. Available: http://kali.murdoch.edu.au/~continuum/8.2/Stratton.html
Swanson, G. (1997). Cultural industries and cultural development in the international frame: A response to the World Commission on Culture and Development. *Culture & Policy, 8*(1), 37-52.
Taylor, C. (1989). *Sources of the self: The making of the modern identity*. Cambridge, MA: Harvard University Press.
Taylor, C. (1992). The politics of recognition. In A. Gutmann (Ed.), *Multiculturalism and "the politics of recognition"* (pp. 25-73). Princeton, NJ: Princeton University Press.
Throsby, D. (1997). The relationship between cultural and economic policy. *Culture & Policy, 8*(1), 25-36.
Turner, B. S. (Ed.). (1993). *Citizenship and social theory*. London: Sage.
Turner, B. S., & Hamilton, P. (Eds.). (1994). *Citizenship: Critical concepts*. London: Routledge.
Van Steenbergen, B. (Ed.). (1994). *The condition of citizenship*. London: Sage.
Walzer, M. (1997). *On toleration*. New Haven, CT: Yale University Press.
World Commission on Culture and Development. (1995). *Our creative diversity*. Paris, France: UNESCO.
Wyszomirski, M. J. (1998). Comparing cultural policies in the United States and Japan. *Journal of Arts Management, Law & Society, 27*(4), 265-282.
Young, I. M. (1997). A multicultural continuum: A critique of Will Kymlicka's ethnic-nation dichotomy. *Constellations, 4*(1), 48-53.
Zemans, J. (1997). Canadian cultural policy in a globalized world. *Canadian Review of American Studies, 27*(3), 111-127.
Zolberg, V. L. (1994). Art museums and cultural policies: Challenges of privatization, new publics, and new arts. *Journal of Arts Management, Law & Society, 23*(4), 191-277.

# 1. Community, Citizenship, and the Third Way

NIKOLAS ROSE
*University of London*

> *This article analyses recent debates about the Third Way in politics in Britain and the United States. It suggests that what is most significant is the emergence of a new politics of conduct that seeks to reconstruct citizens as moral subjects of responsible communities. The author considers the presuppositions of such a politics and its implications for technologies of government.*

**Are we witnessing the birth** of a novel form of politics?[1] Some, in the United Kingdom, United States, and parts of Europe, answer this question in the affirmative. They give this new politics a name: the Third Way. In this article, I try to draw up an inventory of the little patterns that are emerging in this new way of thinking about politics and diagnose the presuppositions that underpin it. In so doing, I hope to identify some questions that, in the course of these mutations, become more difficult to think.

According to the British Labour Home Secretary Jack Straw (1998), speaking at a recent conference on this theme,

> The Third Way ends the ideological paralysis which so weakened Labour for thirty years. It asserts our mutual responsibility, our belief in a common purpose. And it also asserts that there is no such "thing" as society; not in the way in which Mrs. Thatcher claimed, but because society is not a "thing" external to our experiences and responsibilities. It is us, all of us.

Note this reframing of society—no longer external and constraining, but an aspect of "all of us": It provides a clue to something important. However popular the term is becoming with the New Labour administration of Tony Blair, the Third Way is not exactly a political program. Rather, it is a certain way of visualizing political problems, a rationality for rendering them thinkable and manageable, and a set of moral principles by which solutions may be generated and legitimized:

---

**Author's Note:** *The author would like to thank Risto Eräsaari for the conference invitation that provoked him to think about the issues in this article, and Barbara Cruikshank, Denise Meredyth, Jeffrey Minson, Thomas Osborne, Diana Rose, Michael Shapiro, and Mariana Valverde for advice and comments on earlier drafts of this article.*

> Political theory really does matter. However secular our society may have become, people cannot live by bread alone. They need a framework of belief. Those who govern in their name, in Parliament and the executive need to share that framework—indeed to have marked it out, to have some pretty clear sense of direction, so that there is some template for the scores of individual decisions which they have to make every day. The new Clause 4 [of the Labour Party constitution] is the Third Way—a clear coherent route between the Right . . . and the old, neo-Marxist Left. (Straw, 1998)

The idea of a Third Way in politics is not new (Lukes, 1998). Ever since the debates about individualism and collectivism in Britain, Europe, and the United States at the end of the 19th century, there have been political arguments claiming to have discovered the political principles that could generate a path between these poles, combining the benefits of each while avoiding their reciprocal dangers. The New Liberalism of Graham Wallas, L. T. Hobhouse, and J. A. Hobson represents perhaps the clearest attempt to provide such a politics with a coherent ethical, philosophical, and ideological foundation. Like that earlier project, the current Third Way claims to be more than merely a middle road defined by what it avoids. It aspires to be nothing less than a founding set of moral beliefs for a new politics. What, then, is this Third Way?

Despite its promising title, Giddens's (1998) *The Third Way: The Renewal of Social Democracy* is actually of little help in identifying the key features of a governmentality of the Third Way. For Giddens, reality has changed and politics must respond. This assertion of sociological determinism opens the argument to all the fashionable nostrums of contemporary epochal sociology. Growing globalization is pulling powers away from nation states on one hand and increasing localisms on the other. The historical process of detraditionalization has generated increasing individualism. A "politics of life"—of ecology, of family, of personal and cultural identity and lifestyle—has emerged to join and cross-cut the values of emancipation and social justice. Citizens have lost faith in big government and politics, and a subpolitics has emerged to challenge the conventional spheres of politics and government. Our present—and our future—are structured by the centrality of the problematics of risk and the concomitant rise of a politics of the environment.

As conceived by Giddens (1998), these apparently ineluctable and universal processes of modernization and the new types of subjectivity to which they give rise present themselves to politics fully formed. These new and inescapable realities require a politics of the "radical center" that will "help citizens pilot their way through the major revolutions of our time" (Giddens, 1998, p. 64). Given this slippage between the descriptive and the normative and given that what must be is dictated by what is, it is not surprising that there is so little political inventiveness on display.

For despite its epochal wrapping, Giddens's Third Way is largely a repackaging of political proposals and philosophical themes that have shaped social-liberal thought for much of the 20th century: an admixture of democratization, constitutional tinkering, hopes for a vitalized mixed economy, support for family values, praise for civil society, aspirations to improve the effectiveness of welfare provisions, commitment to equality of opportunity, support for religious and value pluralism, and plans for better international regulation of trade. Not much is new in this politics, apart, perhaps, from the addition of a certain therapeutic individualism (the language of self-realization) and an expansion of the ethic of collective responsibility to include nature as well as humankind. Its techniques of government are minor modifications of those already entrenched, with the infusion of faith in the power of markets (already jettisoned by the former epigones of neoliberalism in the international economy) and a naive enthusiasm for the mantras of managerial gurus. Its objectives are a familiar assortment from the grab bag of liberal democracy, without the utopianism that gave some liberal politics its radical edge.

At first sight, Tony Blair's (1998) recent pamphlet, *The Third Way: New Politics for a New Century*, does not go much further. For Blair, too, the imperatives for a new politics are sociological.

> The growth of increasingly global markets and global culture.... Technological advance and the rise of skills and information as key drivers of employment and new industries.... A transformation in the role of women... offering half the population the chance—in the name of equality of opportunity—to fulfil their full potential according to their own choices.... Radical changes in the nature of politics itself... with twin pressures; from localities and regions wanting more control of their own affairs and from a globalised world in which a growing number of problems depend on international co-operation. (Blair, 1998, p. 6)

Blair's vision of the Third Way similarly includes conventional objects of social-liberal programs, such as revitalizing the economy through investment in education and infrastructure, supporting families, moving away from big government though decentralization and partnership with other sectors, and stricter targeting of welfare resources on those who most need them. Although these may be significant, even desirable emphases within liberal social democracy, they hardly amount to a new politics.

Among these well-worn stratagems, more significant symptoms recur: references to civil society, civic activism, strong communities, rights, duties, and responsibilities. These may be dismissed as warm words, but they point to the way in which the Third Way grounds itself in values.[2] "Our mission," Blair (1998) writes, "is to promote and reconcile the four values which are essential to a just society which maximizes the freedom and potential of all our people—equal worth, opportunity for all, responsibility and community" (p. 3). The first pair of values harks back to the obligations of left-of-center political governments down the ages (and partly justify presenting this politics as a renewal of social democracy). The second pair, however, identifies the reciprocal obligations of the subjects of government in a way that is distinctive even if it is not novel. In linking these pairs of values, the Third Way aspires to a contract between those who exercise power and those who are obliged to be its subjects. Although the former must provide the conditions of the good life, the latter must deserve to inhabit it by building strong communities and exercising active responsible citizenship.

## THE POLITICS OF BEHAVIOR

In this community-oriented aspect of the Third Way, we can discern an attempt to create some novel links between the *personal* and the *political*. Human beings are no longer considered social in the way in which they were within the forms of social government that took shape in the first six decades of the 20th century. Nor are they considered rational as proposed in the discourse of classical economics and all those neoliberal ways of thinking and governing that modeled themselves on such ideas of individuals as maximizers of self-interest. Nor, even, are they considered psychological, mobilized by unconscious forces and desires. Human beings are now considered to be, at root, ethical creatures. The problems that human societies are undergoing are increasingly made intelligible as ethical problems, and new ways are emerging for governing the behavior of individuals through acting on this dimension of ethics.

Although contemporary proposals for governing behavior through ethics differ, each seeks a way of acting on the ethical formation and self-management of individuals to promote their engagement in their collective destiny, in the interests of economic advancement, social stability, and even justice and happiness. It is no longer sufficient, they suggest, to give citizens a political stake through their vote in representative elections. It is not enough to give them a stake through social citizenship, the social wage, and the public ownership of the commanding heights of the economy as was hoped by postwar social democracy. Nor is it enough to give them an economic stake through home ownership or the development of a share-owning democracy as proposed in the privatization programs of neoliberal governments in the 1980s. The stake has to be generated in the community-based ethic that shapes the values that guide each individual. This is to be accomplished through building a new relation between ethical citizenship and responsible community fostered, but not administered, by the state.

A particular territorialization of life dominates these contemporary discussions of the politics of behavior. The person whose conduct is to be governed is believed to desire personal autonomy as a right, but autonomy does not imply that individuals live their lives as atomized isolates. They are understood as citizens, not of societies as national collectivities, but of neighborhoods, associations, regions, networks, subcultures, age groups, ethnicities, and lifestyle sectors—in short, communities. It is from these communities that autonomous, freedom-aspiring individuals are thought to derive the guidelines, techniques, and aspirations by which they think about and enact their freedom. If political strategies are to depend on the enactment of individual freedom, they can and must act on this freedom indirectly. They should try to intensify and redirect the forces that bind individuals into such groupings and relations—shame, guilt, responsibility, obligation, trust, honor, and duty. This, it is thought, will intensify the virtuous consequences of such bindings—reciprocity, mutuality, cooperation, belongingness, and identity. In these ways, perhaps, free and autonomous individuals can be governed through community.

I term this new politics of behavior *ethopolitics*. Foucault, of course, identified the rise of disciplinary power, focusing on maximizing the utility and docility of individuals, and biopower, focusing on maximizing the health and welfare of the population. If discipline individualizes and normalizes and biopower aggregates and socializes, ethopower works through the values, beliefs, and sentiments thought to underpin the techniques of responsible self-government and the management of one's obligations to others. In ethopolitics, life itself, in its everyday manifestations, is the object of adjudication. I think that this political deployment is related to a new diagram of power or a new game of power: the community-civility game. It involves new conceptions of those who are to be governed and the proper relations between the governors and the governed.

In particular, contemporary ethopolitics reworks the government of individual and aggregate souls in the context of the increasing role that culture and consumption mechanisms play in the generation, regulation, and evaluation of techniques of self-conduct. Politically organized and state-directed assemblages for moral management no longer suffice. Schools, asylums, reformatories, workhouses, washhouses, museums, homes (for the young, old, or the damaged), unified regimes of public service broadcasting, housing projects, and the like have been supplemented and sometimes displaced by an array of other practices for shaping identities and forms of life. Advertising, marketing, the proliferation of goods, the multiple stylizations of the act of purchasing, cinemas, videos, pop music, lifestyle magazines, television soap operas, advice programs, and talk shows—all of these partake in a civilizing project very different from 19th-century attempts to form moral, sober, responsible, and obedient individuals, and from 20th-century projects for the shaping of civility, social solidarity, and social responsibility.

Of course, ethopolitics merely names a space of political debate, strategy, and technique. It can take many forms. Following Foucault's distinction between ethics and morality, one can discern two broad configurations of such a politics. The first seeks to govern the ethical self-regulation of the individual in terms of fixed moral codes justified by relation to some external set of principles or concepts of human nature. The second emphasizes the aesthetic elements in the government of ethics: the self-crafting of one's existence according to a certain art of living, whether this concerns friendship, domesticity, erotics, or work. In contemporary ethopolitical debates, one can see elements of each of these configurations.

## FROM SOCIETY TO COMMUNITY

Castel (1995) has pointed out that the idea of the social state that underpinned welfare regimes in the 20th century was grounded in the presupposition that political government could achieve the gradual and simultaneous betterment of the conditions of all forces and blocs within society—employers, laborers, managers, and professionals. Political strategies could ameliorate the hardship of the worst off without destroying the principle of productive labor. They would cushion the harshness of capitalism within the workplace. They would lessen the fear of unemployment by supporting those outside the labor market. They would put in place state-centered networks of personnel, devices, and resources for the production and maintenance of solidarity, sociality, and citizenship. The social state would thus contain the dangers posed by the worst off and reinforce the security and individual freedoms of the better off. It would also make it legitimate to confine and reform the mad, the criminals, the delinquent, the work shy, and the socially inadequate: They had refused this social contract or were unable to give assent to it. Hence, it appeared that all strata of society could be bound into an agreement for social progress guaranteed by the state. This image of social progress through civility, solidarity, and security won out over both the image of social revolution on one hand and that of unfettered competition on the other.

During the last two decades, this social mentality of government has come under challenge from all sides of the political spectrum. Another image of the state is coming to the fore: that of the facilitating state, the enabling state, or the state as animator (Donzelot & Estebe, 1994). It is this image that infuses Third Way politics, as well as the other postsocial politics and antipolitics that took shape in the final decade of the 20th century. Political government was to be relieved of its powers and obligations to know, plan, calculate, and steer from the center. The state was no longer required to answer all society's needs for order, security, health, and productivity. Individuals, firms, organizations, localities, schools, parents, hospitals, and housing estates would take on a portion of the responsibility for resolving these issues—whether this be by permanent retraining for the worker or neighborhood watch for the community. This involves a double movement of autonomization and responsibilization. Populations that were once under the tutelage of the social state are to be set free to find their own destiny. Yet, at the same time, they are to be made responsible for their destiny and for that of society as a whole. Politics is to be returned to society itself, but no longer in a social form: in the form of individual morality, organizational responsibility, and ethical community (see Rose, 1996).

Increasingly, it is the language of community that is used to identify a territory between the authority of the state, the free and amoral exchange of the market, and the liberty of the autonomous, rights-bearing individual. This space of community appears as a kind of natural, extra-political zone of human relations; this is not merely an ontological claim but implies affirmation, a positive evaluation. Yet, simultaneously, community is identified as a crucial element in particular styles of political government, for it is on its properties and activities within it that the success of such political aspirations and programs depends. Hence, community must become the object and target for the exercise of political power while remaining, somehow, external to politics and a counterweight to it. Community, that is to say, names a transactional reality: It consists of multiple objectifications formed at the unstable and uncomfortable intersections between politics and that which should and must remain beyond its reach.

Of course, the theme of community and its incipient loss, the need to remake it or substitute for it, is one of the traditional themes of constitutional thought (Tully, 1995). It emerges with remarkable regularity in critical reflections on the state of the nation from the 19th century onwards. Today, community is not primarily a geographical space, a social space, a sociological space, or a space of services, although it may attach itself to any or all such spatializations. Etzioni's (1997) following definition is exemplary:

> Community is defined by two characteristics: first, a web of affect-laden relationships among a group of individuals, relationships that often crisscross and reinforce one another (rather than merely one-on-one or chainlike individual relationships), and second, a measure of commitment to a set of shared values, norms and meaning, and a shared history and identity–in short, to a particular culture. (p. 127)

Community is thus an affective and ethical field, binding its elements into durable relations. It is a space of emotional relationships through which individual identities are constructed through their bonds to microcultures of values and meanings. It is through the political objectification and instrumentalization of this community and its culture, through strategies for the government of autonomy through acting on sentiments, values, identities, allegiance, trust, and mutual dependence, that a Third Way for politics is to be found.

The reinvention of community is linked to new conceptions of the ways in which subjects of government are collectivized. Debates about social citizenship concerned the ways in which equal rights could be accorded to all members of a single national territory with a uniform common culture. The shift from the image of the melting pot to that of the rainbow illustrates the way that the politics of recognition stresses the existence and legitimacy of incommensurable—or at least distinct—domains of culture, values, and mores. These are no less significant, it appears, because they are not unified across a nation but localized, fragmented, hybrid, and activated differently in various arenas. The uniform social citizenship that was the objective of the citizen-forming and nation-building strategies of the 19th and 20th centuries is now challenged by diverse forms of identity and allegiance that are no longer deferential to such a territorialized image of national and civic culture. The question now is not one of national character but of the way in which multiple identities receive equal recognition in a single constitutional form (cf. Tully, 1995).

We have moved then from *culture* to *cultures*, including fusions of culture and commerce. Many of the new practices of generation, regulation, and evaluation of techniques of self-conduct fuse the aim of manufacturers to sell products and increase market share with the identity experiments of consumers. Commerce and self-culture are mediated by highly developed techniques of market research into finely calibrated and segmented consumer target groups. Advertising images and television programs interpenetrate in the promulgation of images of lifestyle and narratives of identity choice. These images and narratives typically highlight the ethical aspects of lifestyle choices. Styles of aestheticized life choice that were previously the monopoly of cultural elites have been generalized in this new habitat of subjectification; that is to say, the belief that individuals can shape an autonomous identity for themselves through choices in taste, music, goods, styles, and habitus (cf. Osborne, 1998). These new practices have contributed to a pluralization of the moral order. Contemporary identity formation involves a subtle process in which the imagined wants and hopes of every conceivable type of individual (e.g., as categorized by age, gender, region) are calibrated with the promises of products in images, narratives, and designs that locate them within recipes and routines for the conduct of life. Individuals and groups then manipulate, use, or subvert these recipes for purposes they take to be their own. Hence, these practices both presuppose and intensify a shift of emphasis from morality to ethics. The shift is from compliance with an externally imposed code of conduct and values in the name of the collective good to the active and detailed shaping by individuals of their daily lives in the name of their own pleasures, contentments, or fulfillments.

Within these new spaces of lifestyle and culture and no longer integrated in a total governmental field, it is possible for subjects to distance themselves from the cohesive discourses and strategies of the social state (schooling, public service broadcasting, municipal architecture, etc.) and access resources of subject formation in order to invent themselves, individually and collectively, as new kinds of political actors (cf. Patten, 1995, p. 226; see also Hardt, 1995). This fragmentation of the social by the new commercial technologies of lifestyle-based identity formation has produced new kinds of collective existence lived out in milieus that are outside the control of coherent norms of civility or powers of political government. The politics of conduct is faced with a new set of problems: acting on the ethical self-government of human behavior in this new plural field.

## IN TERMS OF COMMUNITY

It is important to note the variety of forms in which this new politics of community can be articulated. Communitarian thinkers in the United States aligned with neoconservatives and the religious Right claim that liberal education policies, family policies, welfare policies, and crime control policies have bred illegitimacy, crime, illiteracy, and more poverty (cf. Cruikshank, 1997; see, e.g., Himmelfarb, 1994). In the face of this collapse of values, political government was presumed to be the only force powerful enough to carry out the culture war that was necessary if America was to be remoralized and responsible autonomy and civic virtue were to be recreated. Other American communitarian thinkers problematized their present in very similar ways, but their solutions were different. Bellah, Madsen, Sullivan, Swidler, and Tipton (1985) suggest that the "habits of the heart" of which de Tocqueville wrote have undergone a profoundly individualist shift leading to the decline, perhaps even the collapse, of civic engagement (cf. de Tocqueville, 1835/1969). Putnam (1995a, 1995b) and Etzioni (1997) both paint a familiar picture of drugs, crime, alienation, family breakdown, loss of good neighborliness, and so forth, with Putnam conceiving this breakdown in moral order in terms of the decline of *social capital*: cultural networks of civic trust.[3] The communitarian answer to the crisis of values, however, differs from that proposed by neoconservatives. What was necessary was not strong government but the recreation of civic engagement. Moral order cannot rest on legal codes enforced and upheld by guardians; it is embodied and taught through the rituals and traditions in the everyday life of communities. Hence, a strategy to recreate civic morality cannot succeed if it seeks to articulate and enforce a fixed set of virtues, but must seek to recreate community engagement, to foster moral dialogue within and among diverse communities around a minimum set of core values shared by all. The moral voice of the community "is the main way that individuals and groups in a good society encourage one another to adhere to behavior that reflects shared values and to avoid behavior that offends or violates them" (Etzioni, 1997, p. 124).

The communitarian emphasis in Third Way politics is strong. Etzioni (1997) refers to a speech by Tony Blair (then leader of the British Labour Party and now Prime Minister) on the stakeholder society to support his view that

> for a society to be communitarian, much of the social conduct must be "regulated" by reliance on the moral voice rather than on the law, and the scope of the law itself must be limited largely to that which is supported by the moral voice. (p. 139)

In the Thatcher years, the government of the United Kingdom frequently condemned the church for failing to assert its traditional moral authority. In fact, the Church of England was pursuing a different, perhaps communitarian path, as in its influential report *Faith in the City* (Archbishop of Canterbury's Commission on Urban Priority Areas, 1985). Tony Blair chose to mark the 10th anniversary of this report in a speech in Southwark Cathedral in 1996, later published under the title "The Stakeholder Society," where he posed the reinvention of community as an alternative to individualistic conceptions of human conduct which he felt infused thinking on both right and left.

> People are more than separate economic actors competing in the market-place of life. They are citizens of a community. We are social beings nurtured in families and communities and human only because we develop the moral power of personal responsibility for ourselves and each other.... Our relations with and commitments to others are not add-ons to our personalities: they make us who we are. (Blair, 1996a, pp. 299-300)

And, as he put it in the simultaneous newspaper article titled "Battle for Britain," "the search is on to reinvent community for a modern age, true to core values of fairness, co-operation and responsibility" (Blair, 1996b, p. 12). Individuals needed to be given a stake that generated that

> wider synthesis of community and individual... is the essential underpinning of Labour's new approach.... Successful communities are about what people give as much as what they take, and any attempt to rebuild community for a modern age must assert that personal and social responsibility are not optional extras... we owe duty to more than self. (Blair, 1996a, p. 304)

Thus, what would later be termed the *Third Way* would suture community and citizenship, collective belonging, and individual responsibility.

## THE POLITICAL TECHNOLOGIES OF THE THIRD WAY

The politics of the Third Way recasts public ills in terms of ethical and cultural subjectivity. The technologies of the Third Way are intimately linked to that vision. As Straw put it in 1997, speaking to a National Neighbourhood Watch conference, "the government's vision is, put simply, the recreation of a civic society" (quoted in Hargreaves, 1998, p. 70). The Old Left, it appears, confused the principle of individual freedom with the idea of license to do anything one wants and confused the principle of collective responsibility with the idea of the state as "some sort of universal great provider, which made no moral judgements regardless of the merits of those who were dependent upon it" (Straw, 1998). This reinforced the natural tendencies of human beings toward selfishness; it made rights seem like consumption goods dispensed by the state to its inhabitants and pictured individuals as mere consumers, bundles of wants: "the citizen, perceiving himself in like fashion, loses sense of his duties, as a citizen, to himself, his fellows, and the civic order, at worst without sense of honour or shame" (Straw, 1998, quoting Selbourne's [1995] *Principle of Duty*, p. 70). Duty, honor, shame—these relations of reciprocal obligation are framed by Straw (1998) within Titmuss's notion of the gift relationship.

> In many ways the most important example of our approach is our commitment greatly to extend the idea and practice of volunteering—of people doing something for each other rather than having the State doing it for them and *so diminishing them*. We have described this voluntary activity as "the essential act of citizenship."...

We are trying to develop the concept of "the Active Community" in which the commitment of the individual is backed by the duty of all organisations—in the public sector, the private sector and the voluntary sector—to work towards a community of mutual care and a balance of rights and responsibilities. (Straw, 1998, emphasis added)

Although the proponents of the Third Way tend to agree with Straw that individuals are diminished by the support of the state, they do not therefore view civil society as an entirely self-generating phenomenon. Giddens (1998), for example, attributes to neoliberals the view that the state can only be destructive to civil society: "We can't blame the erosion of civility on the welfare state," writes Giddens, "or suppose that it can be reversed by leaving civil society to its own devices. Government can and must play a major part in renewing civic culture" (p. 79). But this part is not to be played through the traditional apparatuses of representative democracy (a professional bureaucracy, Town Hall politics, elected political representatives, and all the paraphernalia of municipal socialism). The legitimacy granted to public services by the democratic process has proven to be ineffective, unnecessary, and even harmful. Instead, we need new techniques of legitimation such as focus groups, citizens' juries, boards of directors chosen to represent different sectors and interests, partnerships of all sorts between the public services and those wanting to make profits, between public, profit-making and not-for-profit organizations, between professionals and lay persons, between political institutions and voluntary organizations, and much more. These new hybrid mechanisms, more flexible and closer to local needs than the bureaucratized organs of the central or local state will, it seems, ensure accountability, reconcile competing interests, and transcend the harmful split between state and society (Hargreaves & Christie, 1998).

This is apparently what is meant by the recreation of civil society. On one hand, the term refers to that amalgam (of not-for-profit organizations, nongovernmental agencies, residents' associations, and other enterprises whose purpose is social rather than for the pursuit of profit) that is often termed *the third sector* (Rifkin, 1995). In the politics of the Third Way, suggests Hargreaves (1998), such third-sector activities are accorded a key role in the reform of welfare, health care, education, and in civic revival more generally. On the other hand, as I have suggested, the Third Way is as much an ethical as a practical program. Civil society as seen by Hargreaves (1998) is a veritably bucolic zone of liberty, "a place where citizens freely act together to consolidate and express their freedoms, to solve problems, to provide services to each other or simply to enjoy each other's company" (Hargreaves, 1998, p. 68). For it is "morally desirable for citizens to be able to express their instincts to help others, rather than contracting out all of these actions to 'professional' or 'state' services." Moreover, "effective and affordable care of children and the elderly demands that a substantial level of responsibility be accepted within the family and the wider local community on a voluntary basis" (Hargreaves, 1998, pp. 71-72).

Similar themes run through other proposals for Third Way programs, for example, in the lifelong "learning society" to be created by educational reform (Bentley, 1998), in proposals for strengthening and preserving marriages and families to build social capital, and in drugs and crime-prevention schemes (Wilkinson, 1998, pp. 115, 121). Most significant, the Third Way is linked to proposals for new technologies of welfare.

The character of these welfare technologies is captured most precisely in the opposition of exclusion and inclusion running through the proposals. This transforms the problem of poverty into one that has less to do with material or cultural resources than with a lack of belongingness and of the responsibility and duty to others generated through connection to the responsibilizing circuits of moral community. Exclusion is the absence of the stabilization of conduct and self-control provided by work, family, housing, and so forth, whereas inclusion—or even, for Giddens, equality itself—is a matter of reattachment (Giddens, 1998, pp. 102-103). Although exclusion may refer also to the revolt of the elites as more affluent groups withdraw from public life into fortress communities, its prime focus is the suggestion that a culture is taking shape in the inner cities characterized by growing economic, physical, and cultural detachment from the mainstream—what Blair (1996a) referred to in his stakeholder society speech as "the *Blade Runner* scenario" (p. 308).

Exclusion codes a way of thinking that paradoxically—and despite its sociological take up—is more concerned with describing the damaging and dangerous effects of these fragmentations on the individual and the community than with seeking to grasp the political and economic processes that generate such phenomena and that are, indeed, dependent on them. The unequal distribution of material resources, which had been a target of Left politics since the end of the 19th century, gradually blurs as an object of investigation and political action. In its place, a sector of problematic persons comes into view—a sector that the social liberalism of the early decades of the 20th century also classified as the residuum, the unemployables, and the social problem group. The excluded are characterized as failures, lacking personal skills and competencies. In the Third Way, these are to be addressed through practices of control targeted at the excluded themselves—principally those that seek to foster or coerce the development of the personal capacities thought to enable access to the workplace though the labor contract. Although it increasingly frames itself in the economic vocabulary of human capital, what is at stake here is actually the work ethic. Everyone within the ghetto, every member of the underclass, each excluded person should be given the opportunity to achieve full membership in a moral community through work and to adhere to the core values of honesty, self-reliance, and concern for others. Their willingness to do so is to form the object of scrutiny of new moral authorities in the benefits agencies and elsewhere.

Giddens (1998), for example, suggests that conventional poverty programs should be replaced with community-focused approaches, which emphasize "support networks, self-help and the cultivation of social capital as a means to generate economic renewal in low-income neighbourhoods" (p. 110). These welfare-to-work programs presume that existing benefit and welfare systems demoralize their recipients; rob them of their pride, self-esteem, and self-reliance; mire them in financial and psychological dependency; and exacerbate their exclusion. Hence, the technologies of welfare-to-work deploy a mixture of remoralizing therapies, pedagogies for inculcating citizenship competencies, and punitive measures. Threats of public shaming and withdrawal of support are supposed to cajole or coerce welfare recipients into the responsibilities of employment, no matter how menial, in order to reap the disciplining and moralizing benefits thought to flow from wage labor. The wage, it seems, is a mechanism for reattachment to moral community, with its external responsibilities, its norms of comportment, and its psychological concomitants of identity, stability, commitment, and purpose.

Through ethical reconstruction, the excluded, demeaned, and failing quasicitizen is to be reattached to a virtuous community and the civility it engenders. The measures for the reform of criminal justice proposed by the British Labour Party, which are analogous to those supported by many communitarians in the United States, take a similar form. Here we see slogans such as zero tolerance, "naming, blaming, and shaming," and parental responsibility for the crimes of their children. This is tough love, or to use the phrase currently popular with the Labour government in Britain, "compassion with a hard edge." Thus, Jack Straw (1998), Home Secretary, remarks in the speech quoted earlier, that although statist responses to rising crime presume that external engineering of police numbers and powers would do the trick, this misleadingly implies that

> the police by themselves can make orderly those communities hit by crime. Instead what we are doing is to bind communities into fighting crime through, for example, the statutory partnership in the Crime and Disorder Bill and the empowerment of local communities through measures like the Anti Social Behaviour Orders and the Child Area Curfews.

Those who refuse to become responsible and govern themselves ethically have also refused the offer to become members of our moral community. Hence, for them, harsh measures are entirely appropriate. Three strikes and you are out. Citizenship becomes conditional on conduct. The counterpart to the moralism of these community-based programs is the enhancement of the powers of the penal and psychiatric complexes and the transformation of social workers and other caring professionals into agencies of control concerned with risk management and secure containment.

Of course, this political strategy can parody itself and nowhere is this more frequent than in its attempts to generate attachment and inclusion through acting directly on the conduct of domestic existence. Take for instance this little text, a headline on the front page of the British newspaper *The Guardian*, which appeared on July 29, 1997, 3 months into the term of the New Labour government headed by Tony Blair:

Parents Told to Sign Reading Pledge
Primary school parents will be asked to sign an undertaking to read with their children at home for at least 20 minutes a day under government proposals for improving literacy published yesterday. The parental reading pledge will be included in home-school contracts setting out teachers' responsibilities and parents' contribution towards the good behaviour, attendance and punctuality which will be expected of the children. (p. 1)

In what other politics would elected politicians seek to use the apparatus of the law to require parents to read to their children for a fixed period each day? Ethopolitics here can incite and justify a will to govern that imposes no limits on itself. Here one can identify the threat of governing too much, which haunts the current administrations of Bill Clinton and Tony Blair: This is a Third Way that would seek to govern a polity through the micromanagement of the self-steering practices of its citizens. Beyond such examples, what conclusions can we draw from this provisional inventory of some of the presuppositions and practices of the Third Way?

## AN INVENTION IN POLITICS?

There is, of course, not much new about the specific elements of this ethopolitics of community. But, articulated together, they do make up some new little patterns and logics of political thought and action. The novelty, such as it is, is not provided with its coherence sociologically as Giddens suggests, although clearly an appeal to sociology plays a part in the rhetoric and truth claims of this new govern-mentality. Rather, it consists in small mutations along four axes of government: its objects, its subjects, its explanatory regimes, its techniques and technologies. Each of these reconfigures the relation between state, society, and individual that once lay at the heart of the social politics of welfare. New territorializations of politics are involved in the emergence of community as an object of government. New specifications of political subjects are involved in the framing of moral responsibility in terms of identity, values, and belongingness in the new politics of conduct. New conceptions of economic and moral processes are entailed in the take up of the terms *human capital* and *social capital* in this politics, and new moralizing explanations of individual and collective pathologies underpin political strategies to regulate crime, enhance individual competencies, and administer security through activating the responsibilities of communities for their own well-being. Novel techniques of subjectification are being incorporated into technologies for the reactivation of civil society, for the management of risk and security, and the regulation of pathological conduct.

To the extent that it links politics and ethics, ethopolitics offers the opportunity to escape from all those attempts to translate ethical judgments into apparently more objective terms: normal and pathological, social and antisocial, natural and unnatural, productive and unproductive, progressive and reactionary, feminist and patriarchal, oppression and liberation. Although each of these oppositions derives from a different account of conduct, each seeks to close off ethical debate by appealing to the authority of a true discourse and to the authority of those who are experts of this truth. To the extent that it escapes this will to truth in the field of behavior, ethopolitics thus allows the possibility of opening up the evaluation of forms of life and self-conduct to the business of debate and contestation, but this opening up is fragile and closure is easy.

In the politics of the Third Way, as in the varieties of communitarianism that are flourishing in the United States, the shift toward community as a means of moral reformation for lone parents, feckless idlers, drug addicts, and so forth gives civility a definite shape, that of a civil religion, a secular and civic Christianity of respectability, moderation, charity, probity, fidelity, and the like. Although it purports to govern while respecting the autonomy of individuals and associational life, this strategy to sustain civility through community actually seeks to inscribe the norms of self-control more deeply into the soul of each citizen than is thought possible through either disciplinary technologies such as mass schooling or through social technologies such as those of welfare states. Rather than recognizing the possibilities and ethical dilemmas presented by the contemporary pluralization of cultures and ethics, this version of the politics of community seeks to foreclose the problems of diversity by propagating a moral code justified by reference to values that purport to be timeless, natural, obvious, and uncontestable. In operating at this moral pole of ethopolitics, the Third Way sets itself in opposition to the very autonomy it purports to respect (cf. Shapiro, 1997).

Perhaps, at a time when technological change makes our capacities more malleable than ever before and promises the possibility of radically novel stylizations of existence, we should try to reactivate an earlier hostility to the bourgeois, Christianized values of charity, compassion, moderation, manners, discipline, duty, work, self-improvement, and self-fulfillment. Although the political activism of the elite youth of Europe and North America in the 1960s is much derided, at least those micropolitical movements recognized the structural hypocrisy of appeals to obedience, fidelity, continence, normality, humility, and care for others at a time of systematic political and economic violence, of gross commercial exploitation of those deliberately rendered weak and powerless. They questioned the virtue of sanctimonious but disingenuous sexual rectitude and mocked the myths that one might work one's way to security or buy one's way to happiness. In doing so, with whatever limited practical results, they forced us to recognize that the values of normality and civility that we have come to take for granted in the West in the late 20th century are only one version, neither the oldest nor the best, of all the ways in which human beings might shape an individual and collective existence for themselves. However unrealistically, they dreamed that we might have a real choice about the imagined communities of which we might become citizens, and they discomforted us by demanding that, for such experiments in living, our slogan should be "If Not Now, When?"

## NOTES

1. Some of the arguments in this article are derived from Rose (1999).
2. In this sense, of course, like the bourgeois do-gooders of the second half of the 19th century and the social liberals of the early decades of the 20th century, these would be the people that Marx and Engels warned us against in the *Communist Manifesto*: "economists, philanthropists, humanitarians, improvers of the condition of the working class, organisers of charity, members of societies for the prevention of cruelty to animals, temperance fanatics, hole-and-corner reformers of every possible kind" (Marx & Engels, 1968, p. 58; cf. Clarke, 1978, p. 1).
3. For the original, less normatively conceived conception of social capital, see Coleman (1990).

## REFERENCES

Archbishop of Canterbury's Commission on Urban Priority Areas. (1985). *Faith in the city: A call for action by church and nation*. London: Church House.
Bellah, R., Madsen, R., Sullivan, W. M., Swidler, A., & Tipton, S. M. (1985). *Habits of the heart: Middle America observed*. Berkeley: University of California Press.
Bentley, T. (1998). Learning beyond the classroom. In I. Hargreaves & I. Christie (Eds.), *Tomorrow's politics: The Third Way and beyond* (pp. 80-95). London: Demos.
Blair, T. (1996a). *New Britain: My vision of a young country*. London: 4th Estate.
Blair, T. (1996b, January 1). Battle for Britain. *The Guardian*, p. 1.
Blair, T. (1998). *The Third Way: New politics for a new century*. London: Fabian Society.
Castel, R. (1995). *Les métamorphoses de la question sociale* [The metamorphoses of the social question]. Paris, France: Fayard.
Clarke, P. (1978). *Liberals and social democrats*. Cambridge, UK: Cambridge University Press.
Coleman, J. (1990). *Foundations of social theory*. Cambridge, MA: Harvard University Press.
de Tocqueville, A. (1969). *Democracy in America* (J. P. Maier & G. Lawrence, Eds.). Garden City, NY: Anchor. (Original work published 1835)
Donzelot, J., & Estebe, P. (Eds.). (1994). *L'Etat animateur: Essai sur la politique de la ville* [The animator state: Essays on the politics of the city]. Paris, France: Esprit.
Etzioni, A. (1997). *The new golden rule: Community and morality in a democratic society*. London: Profile.
Giddens, A. (1998). *The Third Way: The renewal of social democracy*. Cambridge, MA: Polity.
Hardt, M. (1995). The withering of civil society. *Social Text, 14*, 27-44.
Hargreaves, I. (1998). A step beyond Morris dancing: The third-sector revival. In I. Hargreaves & I. Christie (Eds.), *Tomorrow's politics: The Third Way and beyond* (pp. 65-79). London: Demos.
Hargreaves, I., & Christie, I. (Eds.). (1998). *Tomorrow's politics: The Third Way and beyond*. London: Demos.
Himmelfarb, G. (1994). *The demoralization of society: From Victorian virtues to modern values*. New York: Vintage.
Lukes, S. (1998, September 25). Left down the middle [Review of the book *The Third Way: The Renewal of Social Democracy* by A. Giddens]. *Times Literary Supplement*, pp. 3-4.
Marx, K., & Engels, F. (1968). *Selected works of Marx and Engels*. London: Lawrence and Wishart.

Osborne, T. (1998). *Aspects of enlightenment: Social theory and the ethics of truth.* London: UCL Press.
Patten, C. (1995). Refiguring social space. In L. Nicholson & S. Seidman (Eds.), *Social post-modernism: Beyond identity, politics* (pp. 216-249). Cambridge, MA: Cambridge University Press.
Putnam, R. (1995a). Bowling alone: America's declining social capital. *Journal of Democracy, 6*(1), 65-78.
Putnam, R. (1995b, December). Tuning in, tuning out: The strange disappearance of social capital in America. *Political Science and Politics*, pp. 664-683.
Rifkin, J. (1995). *The end of work: The decline of the global labor force and the dawn of the post-market era.* New York: Tarcher/Putnam.
Rose, N. (1996). The death of the social? Refiguring the territory of government. *Economy and Society, 25*(3), 327-356.
Rose, N. (1999). *Powers of freedom: Reframing political thought.* Cambridge, UK: Cambridge University Press.
Selbourne, D. (1995). *Principle of duty.* London: Abacus.
Shapiro, M. (1997). Bowling blind: Post-liberal civil society and the worlds of neo-Toquevillean social theory. *Theory and Event, 1* [Online serial]. Available: http://128.220.50.88/journals/theory-&-event/v001/1.1shapiro.html
Straw, J. (1998, July). *Building social cohesion, order and inclusion in a market economy* [Online]. Paper presented to the Nexus Conference on Mapping Out the Third Way. Available: http://www.netnexus.org/
Tully, J. (1995). *Strange multiplicity: Constitutionalism in an age of diversity.* Cambridge, UK: Cambridge University Press.
Wilkinson, H. (1998). The family way: Navigating a Third Way in family policy. In I. Hargreaves & I. Christie (Eds.), *Tomorrow's politics: The Third Way and beyond* (pp. 111-125). London: Demos.

# 2. Acting on the Social

## Art, Culture, and Government

**TONY BENNETT**
*Open University*

> *The cultural turn in sociology tends to merge the realms of the social and the cultural into one another. In two case studies on cultural governance, it is suggested that these realms are more usefully regarded as distinct in order to understand how culture has been shaped into a historically distinctive means for acting on the social. The first case study examines how art was enlisted as a means of acting on what were deemed problematic class behaviours in the reforming programs of mid-19th century English liberalism. The article then considers the varied roles accorded art as a means of acting on communities in contemporary programs of advanced liberalism. Consideration is also given to the implications of this perspective on the relations of art, government, and the social for the status of the work of art.*

**One of the most distinctive** recent tendencies in sociology has been the influence of the so-called "cultural turn."[1] This has consisted less in the renewed significance that has been accorded the study of culture when compared with, say, industrial sociology or political sociology than in the new place that has been organized for culture in relation to the social. The most obvious casualty of this development has been the marked decline in the influence of earlier Marxist topographical conceptions of the relations between culture and the social.[2] Within these, culture, no matter how much its relative autonomy might be stressed or how much emphasis is placed on the mediated nature of its relationship to the social, is always accorded a relay role in which its action is accounted for as an effect of the social on itself. This is evident in theories of hegemony in which culture appears as an effect of the structure of class relations, but one endowed with a capacity to react back on those relations. When this capacity is looked at more closely, however, the scope for culture's action is usually limited to its role in moderating the ways in which forces and relationships arising out of the organization of the social are able to react back on themselves. This might be to reinforce the relations of class power arising from the social relations of production or, when the underlying movement of the economy generates moments of crisis, to contribute to the undoing of prevailing relations of class power. Either way, what is not in question in these conceptions is the existence of the social as a realm of conduct and interrelationships that exists independently of culture.

It is in challenging this assumption that the cultural turn in sociology has fashioned a new place for culture and a new form of action for it in relation to the social. This consists, in essence, in the importation of culture into the fabric of the social as a consequence of the role that is accorded it in organizing the identities of social agents and the forms of their interaction. The social, as a consequence, is denied any existence independently of the cultural forms in which it is constituted, whereas the action of culture consists in the role it plays in structuring the discursive ground on which social interaction takes place. There is little doubt that this has been a productive move: Its role in disabling earlier hierarchical conceptions in which the action of culture is always secondary and derivative in relation to the social is especially to be welcomed. There is, however, a potential downside to the cultural turn that, in some formulations, renders the realms of culture and the social so permeable in relation to one another that it runs the risk of making them virtually indistinguishable.[3] Where this is so, the result is, so to speak, a "culturalization of the social" in which both terms of the equation tend to lose any distinctiveness of character and effect.

Therefore, the move I want to propose here is one in which, by adding a historical twist to the cultural turn, culture, far from being imported into the social, is explicitly distinguished from it but in a manner that stresses the historically specific and artefactual character of both. The 19th-century emergence of the social as a historically formed surface, comprising a realm of problematic conducts and interrelationships to which remedial action of varying kinds is to be applied, has been examined in detail in the literature that has followed in the wake of Donzelot's (1980) *The Policing of Families*.[4] Somewhat less attention has been paid to the ways in which, during roughly the same period, hitherto dissociated forms of cultural activity were cohered together as a sphere of activity with an identifiably separate identity as *culture*, or to how these were fashioned into a means for acting on the social through the capacity attributed to them of being able to transform ways of life.[5] It is the second aspect of this historical process that I want to explore here. I shall do so by looking at some of the different programs in which art has been enlisted for the purposes of governing during the past 150 years and at how, in the process, it has been shaped to act on the social in different ways.

The role that was accorded art as a means of curbing drunkenness in the reforming programs of Henry Cole offers an appropriate point of entry into these concerns. In 1867, in the context of the extension of the suffrage to significant sections of the male working classes, Cole urged the need to "get these people who are going to be voters, out of the public-house," saying that he knew no better way of doing so than "to open museums freely to them" (Select Committee: para. 808, p. 730). In 1875, in an address to the Liverpool Institute, he proposed that museums should "go into competition with the Gin Palaces" (Cole, 1884, p. 363), reflecting his confidence that the museum would prove an efficient moral reformatory, one among many forms of action—cultural and sanitary —that governments needed to take in order to lead the workingman away from a life of drunkenness and imprudence. In the closing image of his address, Cole evokes a scene in which—if they were allowed to open on Sundays—museums would help make God's day of rest "elevating and refining to the workingman." They would lead him to wisdom and gentleness, bonding him with his wife and family while also detaching him from the life of brutality and perdition that would remain his lot if he were left "to find his recreation in bed first, and in the public-house afterwards" (1884, p. 368).

Cole was by no means alone in entertaining expectations of this kind. They formed a part of the terms in which the benefits to be derived from opening art museums to the public were regularly posed and debated in the second half of the 19th century. When the Sheepshank Gallery of the Victoria and Albert Museum was opened in 1858, a contemporary magazine was in no doubt that this would be of immediate benefit to the working-class household.

> The anxious wife will no longer have to visit the different taprooms to drag her poor besotted husband home. She will seek for him at the nearest museum, where she will have to exercise all the persuasion of her affection to tear him away from the rapt contemplation of a Raphael. (cited in Physick, 1982, p. 35)

There is also a longer history to the advocacy of museums as a possible antidote to vicious and demoralizing entertainments. This was, however, usually as part of a tactics of diversion, in which the museum was to provide the workingman with an alternative way of spending his free time rather than as part of a strategy of reform. The difference I have in mind here is evident in the assessment (quoted above) of the good that the Sheepshank Gallery would do. What is envisaged here is not merely that the art gallery will supply an alternative form of entertainment to the taproom. Rather, the scene that is conjured for our contemplation is that of a workingman who is not only not drinking but who has been so transported to a higher plane of existence that he has lost the desire to do so. This was, for 19th-century liberal reformers such as Cole, the acid test of art's reforming capacities. As such, it rested on a belief in art's capacity to bring about an inner transformation of a kind whose more general effect would be that of changing the workingman into a self-regulating moral agent capable of managing and subduing his passions in developing a commitment to a way of life based on prudential principles of self-restraint.

To us now, of course, it seems improbable if not downright fanciful to expect that art might induce the workingman (or anyone else for that matter) to shun the demon drink. My first concern, then, will be to perform an act of historical recovery that will help make the benefits that were sought through creating new public contexts for art's exhibition intelligible rather than a historical curio. My second concern will be with the more lasting effects of this—to my mind—formative moment in the development of a distinctively modern set of relations between art and liberal forms of governance. This consisted in the construction of art as an instrument for acting on the social whose mechanism depended on its ability to effect an inner moral transformation that would give rise to changed forms of behavior. The specifics of this mechanism have long since fallen by the historical wayside as have the conceptions of the social as a problematic set of working-class conducts that are to be regulated—in a gendered logic that will become clear—by enhancing the self-regulatory capacities of the workingman. Nonetheless, the view that art can be fashioned as a means of acting on the social remains very much a part of contemporary art and art-museum practice. This is true of what is now the most distinctive nexus of relations between art and liberal forms of government. This consists in the proliferation of programs that construct the social in the form of a set of differentiated communities that, when acted on by art (seen now as a means of community empowerment) are to be rendered self-managing and self-sustaining as collectivities while also functioning as important sites for the identity formation of their individual members. My concern here, then, is with the respects in which the enlistment of art for such purposes constitutes a mutation within, rather than a departure from, the relations of art, government, and the social that were developed in the context of the reforming programs of 19th-century liberalism.

My third concern will be to identify the implications of these perspectives on the relations between art, government, and the social for the terms in which the history of the modern art museum should be written. The most influential tradition here, in a line that runs from Adorno (1967) to Crimp (1993), views the modern art museum as an institution that, in bringing together works of art that originally had their roots in a diversity of social contexts, abstracts art from life, disconnecting it from any effective attachments to, and involvement in, the world. There can be little doubt regarding the productivity of this tradition and the richness of the insights it has generated. It is at best, however, only half the story. The history of the modern (by which I mean post-Enlightenment) art museum has also been one in which the works of art collected together in the art museum have been reconnected back to the social world in a diversity of ways in the very process of being wrenched from the earlier social contexts in which they had earlier been set.

These worldly connections have comprised the programs—of artists, curators, education officers, and arts bureaucrats—in which works of art have been deployed with a view to acting on the social by involving a range of agents (the workingman, communities) as voluntary participants in their own management and regulation. In this aspect of its practices, moreover, the modern art museum has constituted the very model of the new forms of cultural administration required by liberal forms of government. For, in eschewing the impositional logic of earlier forms of rule based on the principle of *raison d'état*, these have typically relied on means of acting on the social that respect the freedom and autonomy of individuals (or communities), seeking to govern them at a distance, and indirectly, by involving them as active agents in the processes of their own transformation and self-regulation.[6] The construction of art as a means of self-reform has provided government with a means of intervening in the regulation of social life while also keeping its distance from it. I shall suggest, in arguing this point, that such relations of art and government compose a form of culture's action on the social that can best be understood from the perspective of the historical twist to the cultural turn within sociology that I have outlined.

## GOVERNING AT A DISTANCE: ART AND THE WORKINGMAN

Let us go back to Cole. The concern to find a way of influencing the conduct of the workingman in a manner that would respect his autonomy and freedom is clear from the alternatives that he rehearses before alighting on the art museum as an appropriate cultural means for the task of combating male drunkenness. Whereas the poor had previously had access to the fine arts—"the handmaidens of religion and gentle culture"—through churches, abbeys, and cathedrals, Cole (1884) warns his Liverpool audience that it is no use looking to religion as a cure for drunkenness as the "millions of this country have ceased to be attracted by our Protestant churches and chapels, and the law cannot compel them to attend" (p. 368). Similarly, the experimental town of Saltaire, where public houses were banned by the simple dictate of its owner, did not offer a generalizable solution to the problem of drunkenness precisely because it depended on the exceptional and arbitrary power of a despotic individual. "But Sir Titus Salt," as Cole puts it, "is a burly despot, as his very name proves, and he makes his people healthy, happy, and godly without drink" (p. 366). That Cole is in search of an inner mechanism that will avoid the need for exterior forms of compulsion is clear when he goes on to say that his aim is "to make every place more attractive than the public-house, and to encourage the feeling of responsibility among all classes that it is a disgrace to get drunk, even in a public-house" (p. 366). The desirability of intervening directly in the working-class home, by passing the male head of household, is also entertained. Cole clearly believes that the circumstances warrant such intervention even though it would be at odds with the principles of liberal government. At the same time, however, he recognizes that, in fact, it would exceed the scope of action granted the liberal reformer.

> I have little hope for the class of people, forty years of age, that lay on straw drunk. I do not know what can be done with them; but if I were potent enough, I would take from their wages something for their wives and children before they had spent all, though that would be interfering with the liberty of the subject. (Cole, 1884, p. 365)

The limits that government must not trespass beyond are clear. It may go so far as the workingman's front door, but no further; it may provide contexts in which behaviour will be changed through the voluntary actions of free and sovereign individuals, but it cannot compel any specific change of conduct. If this much is clear, we shall need to look elsewhere to explain why, for Cole and other liberal reformers, the workingman was consistently singled out for such special attention. This was attributable, ultimately, to the influence of Malthusianism and the unique focus this brought to bear on the morality of the workingman in the new forms for the administration and relief of the poor that were introduced by the 1834 Poor Law Amendment Act.[7] Directly inspired by Malthus's work, this act aimed to establish a close connection between morality and poverty in tying the provision of material support for the poor to measures that were intended to bring about the moral transformation of the workingman. Within the merciless logic of Malthusianism, forms of pauper support that allowed the improvident poor to breed without restraint merely aided the geometric growth of population. The prospect of an accelerating increase in numbers, always outstripping the arithmetic growth of the means of subsistence, transformed 18th-century utopian conceptions of progress into the dystopian visions of a society destined for misery, mass starvation, and civil strife that dominated 19th-century thought (see Young, 1985).

The only way of avoiding this seemingly inexorable fate that Malthus left open was the possibility that the exercise of prudential restraint in the conduct of conjugal relationships might avoid the threat of overpopulation. However, this was a demand that, as Dean (1991) has shown, bore uniquely on the male head of household. For given an economic theory that still took the household as its basic unit and a legal context in which, with some exceptions, the head of household was male, the male head of household served as the sole point of connection between the household, the market, and beyond that, the unremitting scarcity of nature. Only he, accordingly, was in a position to interpret the effect of nature's scarcity—mediated via the market—and to translate this lesson into a voluntary and self-imposed program of prudential restraint that would rescue the household from a remorseless descent into brute poverty and starvation. This was reinforced, of course, by the legal entitlement to the exercise of their conjugal rights that men still enjoyed.

For a complex conjunction of reasons, then, the morality of the workingman was placed on the line in a manner that was not true previously and that has not been paralleled since. The new poor laws sheeted home this responsibility inexorably in denying able-bodied males, their wives, and their children—whether living with him or not—any forms of poor relief outside the disciplinary alternative of the workhouse. In the midst of these pressures, the morality of the workingman was opened up as a new zone of individualized responsibility. Whether or not the specter of overpopulation, and of the vice and misery that would be attendant on it, could be averted was seen to depend on whether the workingman could develop a capacity for self-restraint in his conjugal relationships. This, in turn, was connected to his ability to develop a capacity for self-regulation in all the other areas of his life. Male drunkenness occupied a special place within this nexus of concerns. It was related to fears of working-class promiscuity as drunkenness decreased the likelihood of restrained male sexuality. The public nature of drunkenness also meant that it functioned as the most visible sign of the limitations of the workingman's moral capacities when compared with what was asked of them. Male drunkenness also posed a threat to the moral economy of the new forms of poor relief through its association with improvidence and carelessness for family obligations. Women and children, who were ineligible for any direct forms of public support so long as they were married to an able-bodied male, were entitled to receive such support in their own right on the death of their husbands. Those who drank themselves to death would therefore impose a burden on the public or philanthropic purse even in departing the world. Cole (1884) makes the problem graphically clear:

> Now, if you want to see sights in Liverpool that reduce men to the nature of aborigines, you will see people that are allowed to get as drunk as they can, starve their wives and children, looking to others in the end to find coffins for themselves and feed them in the workhouse beforehand. (p. 364)

It was because Malthusianism and the new systems for administering the poor to which it gave rise made the inner life of the workingman an object of attention in new ways that art and culture came to occupy an important role in the newly emerging strategies of liberal government. "The evil attendant upon the principle of population," Dean (1991) argues in summarizing the cultural logic of Malthusianism, "is thus the force which promotes civilizing conduct and institutions" (p. 89). Of course, the ways of life of the laboring classes had been an object of concern in association with earlier forms of poor relief administration. The ale-house, in 18th-century debates, was seen as a threat to the requirements of a productive economy and there was no shortage of proposals for legislative mechanisms and forms of surveillance that would rescue the laborer from the ale-house and save his unwasted body, spared the ravages of alcohol, for a life of productive industry. There was also—and this is a part of Cole's argument, too—a ready appreciation of the need to provide alternative and attractive forms of popular entertainment to help lure the workingman away from the temptations of drink. However, this was a tactic of diversion that lacked a strategy of reform that either sought to effect or relied on an inner mechanism of moral restraint. Just as important, it provided no opportunity for practicing a capacity for ethical self-regulation that would be of more general use. Yet, as we have seen, the concern to encourage thrift and self-reliance while leaving improvidence unrewarded that characterized the post-1834 system of poor relief placed considerable stress on the cultivation of just such a capacity. If, then, in the liberal programs of cultural reform that, in the mid-century period, are most conspicuously symbolized by the development of the South Kensington museum complex, the accent is placed on art's role in helping form a workingman who will not *want* to drink, this is because it was also important to help cultivate those capacities that would make the workingman *want* to save, *want* to practice sexual restraint, and *want* to work.

If Malthusianism supplied the need, Romantic aesthetics promoted the belief that the work of art might serve as a means of meeting that need. Yet, Cole's relationship to Romanticism was a complex one. On one hand, his conception of the South Kensington Museum as the centre of a national system of schools of art and design that would help improve the standards of British design and manufacturing constituted an instance of the very kinds of practicalization and commercialization of art that Romanticism pitted itself against. Ruskin, for example, thought that Cole "corrupted the system of art-teaching all over England into a state of abortion and falsehood from which it will take twenty years to recover" (cited in Alexander, 1983, p. 152). Cole was also at odds with many of his contemporaries in stating that any art, not necessarily of the highest quality, would assist the purposes of reform so long as it started the workingman off on a course of aesthetic and, thereby, social self-cultivation.[8] On the other hand, his belief that exposure to art might help the workingman to acquire powers of self-inspection and self-regulation depended on the ways in which romanticism had fashioned a space within the artistic text in which the subject could be inserted and initiate a program of self-improvement in contemplating the distance between the ideal forms of perfection embodied in the art work and the imperfections and inadequacies of the empirical self. It was in the perception of this gulf that the individual might be prompted to commence a program of self-cultivation designed to bridge the gap between the two.[9]

Thus, it is in opening up a moral surface within the individual as the interface through which art acts on the social that the distinctive accomplishment of Cole's rich and complex mixture of liberalism, Malthusianism, utilitarianism, and romanticism consisted. The view that art might serve as a "moral technology" (Levin, 1982, p. 54) was a central perception of the Enlightenment and one that was put into effect in the aftermath of the French Revolution by the use of art in festivals (see Ozouf, 1988) and museums (see McClellan, 1994) as a means of cultivating civic virtue. The mechanisms at work here, however, were mainly emulative as the citizen was invited to model his conduct on the exemplars of national and civic virtue that the art museum, in its republican conception, was to make visible and commemorate. What the mid-19th-century mix I have been concerned with added to this was a mode of relation between the individual and the work of art that made it possible for the latter to act on ways of life, thereby vastly expanding the orbit of its possible activity.

## COMMUNALIZING THE SOCIAL

This concern to use cultural resources as a means of acting on the social was not restricted to the aesthetic sphere. The second half of the 19th century witnessed a profusion of schemes for, in one way or another, enrolling the newly enfranchised citizens of Western democracies as active participants in the task of managing themselves by bringing them into contact with the lessons of nature (whether those of a benign and harmonious Paleyism or those of a Darwinian nature, red in tooth and claw) or the lessons of evolution (whether inscribed in the history of the rocks, the development of species, or the progress of human societies from the primitive to the complex). A significant (although by no means the only) site for these endeavors was that composed by the new collecting institutions—museums of natural history, geology, and ethnology—that were developed in this period. Together with public art museums, these constituted a highly distinctive set of contexts in which a new class of experts (specialist curators in anthropology, natural history, and art history) contrived to manage a range of cultural resources (paintings, sculptures, bones, costumes, stuffed species, tools, rocks, minerals) in such a way as to enable them, when exhibited publicly, to function as the props and occasions for various forms of civic or moral self-management.

It would be wrong to attribute any unity of design or purpose to these. The reforming schemes of this new class of scientific showmen varied according to the particular positions they took up within the scientific controversies of the period (Darwinists vs. Owenites, liberal Darwinists vs. eugenicists) as well as the configuration of the field of the social in different national contexts. The migrant child was an obsessive object of attention in the United States in ways that had no ready parallels in Britain, whereas in Australia, fears centred on the Australian-born or larrikin child. That said, these reforming programs had in common a conception of the social as a field of conducts defined principally in class terms. In being put to work to act on the social, art and culture were envisaged as means for bringing about changes in working-class ways of life to avert whatever catastrophe otherwise threatened: the Malthusian nightmare of overpopulation if the workingman carried on drinking to excess, revolution if the political implications of Darwin's message of evolutionary gradualism were not heeded, degeneration if the unfit continued to outbreed the fit. It is also true that in most cases these programs aimed to achieve their effects through the mechanism of the individual, acting on the social indirectly through changes in ways of life that were to be brought about as a result of individuals having learned to act on themselves and regulate their own conduct, in new ways.[10]

The legacy of the ways in which 19th-century liberalism brought art (and, indeed, culture more generally), government, and the social into new forms of contact with one another is still a part of the horizon in which cultural resources are managed. The belief that ways of life can be acted on through the governmental deployment of artistic and cultural resources still informs the practices of both public and private cultural institutions as well as the policy agendas of governments. The most obvious difference, however, is that it is no longer the classed individual that is targeted as the primary surface to which the actions of art and culture are to be applied. Rather, art's object, the surface on which it is to act, is now more typically that of community as it is increasingly assigned the task of empowering communities. This involves the use of artistic resources as a means of building strong, self-reliant communities that are capable of managing themselves and producing a strong, but not exclusive, sense of identity and belonging for their members while contributing to the resolution of social problems at the community level. The Artskills project at Merseyside provides a convenient example. In offering a training in arts skills, it aims to bring disaffected young people back into the mainstream through the route of community involvement while using arts training as—in the words of its coordinator, Fiona Cameron—a means of "raising young people's awareness of the different ways they can help themselves in every aspect of their lives" (cited in Hilpern, 1998, p. 8).

This change of focus had its first dress rehearsal in the Community Art Center program of the New Deal whose initiatives were often resurrected, albeit in different form, in the postwar cultural policy initiatives of the United States, Britain, and Australia (Gibson, 1997). The formative role of these initiatives is also acknowledged in the title of the Blair government's "New Deal for Communities" program. The Community Art Centre program was, however, very much a transitional form in promoting the cultures and values of specific communities (sometimes identified in regional terms and sometimes in racial terms) as the route through which to rebuild what was seen as a fragmented community at the national level. Its purpose was to reconstitute American society as the sum of a set of nonantagonistic differences in which identification with the national whole was routed through its, ideally, harmoniously constituent communities (see Harris, 1995). Today, the purposes for which art, culture, and community are most distinctively brought together are different. The focus is now typically on the organization of self-regulating and self-managing communities that are, in some respects, disconnected from the larger wholes of nationally defined societies or, in the case of diasporic communities, cut across them.

This is not, however, a development restricted to the cultural sphere. The project of governing through community is, in the assessment of Rose (1996), part of a significant mutation in the forms and methods of liberal governance. There are two issues here. The first concerns the relationships of government, individuals, and communities. These have been significantly transformed in the respect that it is now no longer the freedom and autonomy of individuals as such that is to be respected, but the freedom and autonomy of individuals, only in so far as they are members of communities. The second issue concerns the relationships between community and nation. These, too, have been transformed to the extent that the primary surface that government is called to act upon is no longer that of a nationally unified society but the differentiated and often deterritorialized field of communities. Rose's concern here is to chart the effects of the criticisms of earlier forms of liberal government that have been mounted, since the 1960s, by civil rights activists, libertarians, and new social movements in the context of the emergence of new forms of identity politics and empowerment. These criticisms questioned earlier understandings of the role of the subjects of government as "a relation of obligation between citizen and society enacted and regulated through the mediating party of the State" (Rose, 1996, p. 330).

Emphasizing instead the need to involve individuals more actively in their own governance, they substituted "a relation of allegiance and responsibility to those one cared about the most and to whom one's destiny was linked . . . one's family, one's neighbourhood, one's community, one's workplace" (Rose, 1996,

p. 331) for the formal bonds of civic obligation. In their critique of earlier identification projects centred on organizing an unmediated relationship involving the socially identified citizen as a member of a single integrated national society, these critical movements, Rose (1996) suggests, have resulted in a new conception of the forms of identification into which individuals should be enlisted.

> The subject is addressed as a moral individual with bonds of obligation and responsibilities for conduct that are assembled in a new way—the individual in his or her community is both self-responsible and subject to certain emotional bonds of affinity to a circumscribed "network" of other individuals—unified by family ties, by locality, by moral commitment to environmental protection or animal welfare. Conduct is retrieved from a social order of determination into a new ethical perception of the individualised and autonomised actor, each of whom has a unique, localised and specific tie to their particular family and to a particular moral community. (p. 334)

Much of this is familiar ground. Rather more important for my concerns here is the spin Rose puts on these observations when he goes on to suggest that these communitarian and libertarian arguments should be seen as parts of a process through which the norms, forms, and strategies of government—far from having been abandoned—have been reconfigured.

> ...community is now something to be programmed by Community Development Programmes, developed by Community Development Officers, policed by Community Police, guarded by Community Safety Programmes and rendered knowable by sociologists pursuing "community studies." Communities became zones to be investigated, mapped, classified, documented, interpreted, their vectors explained to enlightened professionals-to-be in countless college courses and to be taken into account in numberless encounters between professionals and their clients, whose individual conduct is now to be made intelligible in terms of the beliefs and values of "their community." (Rose, 1996, p. 332)

This is a veritable swarming of new forms of expertise based on new objects of knowledge and connected to strategies of governing that work, essentially, by organizing communities as points of emotional investment and identification in order that they might become self-governing as collectivities and capable of managing the activities of their members. This embodies a redistribution of responsibilities from the centralized mechanisms of the state and their dispersal across and through the overlapping networks of community. This is so whether these are defined as territorial communities grounded in a particular place, as diasporic communities in networks that span national boundaries and encompass territorially displaced populations, or as virtual communities based on a shared lifestyle or common political interests: gay and lesbian communities, for example. At the same time that it is central to this new conception of governing, however, community has constantly to be rescued from its imminent disappearance or, because the perceived need for community often precedes its existence, to be organized into being.

> Each assertion of community refers itself to something that already exists and has a claim on us: our common fate as gay men, as women of colour, as people with AIDS, as members of an ethnic group, as residents in a village or a suburb, as people with a disability. Yet our allegiance to each of these particular communities is something that we have to be made aware of, requiring the work of educators, campaigns, activists, manipulators of symbols, narratives and identifications. (Rose, 1996, p. 334)

Here, then, is a broader context in which to place the various forms in which art and community have been brought together during the past quarter of a century or so: in community arts, community cultural development, cultural diversity, and cultural maintenance programs; in community museums or ecomuseums or in the community galleries of larger museums.[11] These new spaces and forms in which art has been made active have also, of course, been accompanied by new forms of knowledge and expertise. These typically focus on organizing and managing community-based processes of dialogue and consultation. The forms of expertise associated with community arts and development officers are the most obvious case in point. So, too, are curators being increasingly called on to act as cross-cultural mediators managing—in the terms proposed by Clifford (1997)—the "contact zones" between "settlers" and indigenous communities or, in different contexts, other cross-cultural boundaries. No single unifying purpose underlies these new relations of art, government, and the social: The objectives to be achieved may range from the empowerment of specific communities through the promotion of cross-cultural dialogue between differentiated communities to the role of art in ensuring the cultural survival of particular communities. Nor is there a single politics in play here. Rather, the political values invested in community may range from those of radical identity politics through social-welfare constructions of community to the understanding of community as a force for moral and religious reformation that characterizes conservative forms of neoliberalism. The community renewal strategies of the Third Way in which culture is to play its role in reviving lost forms of civility provides yet another variant of the community theme (see Giddens, 1998, p. 87). Whichever the case, what is at issue is the role that artistic and cultural resources are able to play through the manner in which they are organized to act on the social by organizing, maintaining, and developing community-based ways of life. That this is not Cole's world is clear. It is equally clear, though, that the contemporary articulation of the relations between art, government, and community is an adaptation of, rather than a total departure from, the coordinates for deploying works of art as instruments within a liberal program of governance that Cole and his generation established.

## ART, MUSEUMS, AND WALLS

How we might most usefully view the modern art museum in light of the perspectives outlined above will depend, ultimately, on how we see the relationships between art, museums, and walls. The critique of the museum that sees it as responsible for disconnecting art from the world interprets the museum's walls as essentially enclosing in their function, separating art off from the museum's outsides so that it might become an object of cultic veneration. This tradition, as I have already suggested, is not without point, especially when viewed in the light of the tendency—undeniably still with us—for art museums to function as socially exclusive institutions in which their habitués accumulate marks of distinction by virtue of the social distance that participation in the art museum establishes for those whom it includes from those whom it excludes. Even so, this is not the truth and nothing but the truth so far as the history of the modern art museum is concerned. This consists in the pull between this tendency, in which the museum's walls function as an impermeable divide, and the countervailing tendency in which the museum's walls are viewed as surfaces on which to so arrange art that its effects—however they might be construed—will be carried back out into the world and enabled to act on it.

This tension may be present in many ways. It may exist within the space of a single institution in the tugs-of-war that often characterize the relationships between specialist curators and education departments. It may take the form of a different set of priorities between, on one hand, major metropolitan museums, and regional galleries and their relations to community arts projects on the other. It may also, in some contexts, take the form of a tension between the professional staff of art museums and the representatives of the local elites, who often dominate their boards of trustees. The complex and contradictory nature of these institutions—when looked at not just singly but as parts of a network— comes to light, however, only when we keep both aspects in view.

There's another point at issue here, too. If it is important to restore to the art museum that aspect of its history in which it has, so to speak, constantly striven to breach its own walls—to devise a means for art to connect with the world outside so that it might be effective in and on the world—this is because this tendency always dethrones art, always embroils it in a muddy and tangled set of realities, in a manner that disavows the special status that is required for it to function as the marker of a privileged zone of social exclusivity. When Cole (1884), in his address to the Liverpool Institute, discussed the reformatory role he envisaged for art museums, he did so alongside a discussion of many other things (efficient sewerage systems and supplies of clean water) that might have contributed to the same end of combating male drunkenness. This was a general characteristic of the speeches and writings of liberal reformers: At the same time that the reforming capacity derived from art's Romantic idealization was extolled, art was also brought down to, and discussed on a par with, a series of practical remedies tending to the same end. The enlistment of art in the service of community has the same effect: It *practicalizes* art, placing it on the same footing as a series of other initiatives (community development programs, AIDS awareness programs, the promotion of cultural diversity, the maintenance of indigenous communities) with similar characteristics.

These, I think, are the debates that matter. That is how, through the contexts of its deployment, art can be brought into contact with the social in order to have good and useful effects. How these are to be defined, however, is of course a matter for political struggle and contestation—struggles that, today, revolve in good part around the meaning that is to be given to the politics of community in both civil life and public policy. If, in its relationships to identity politics, to community empowerment, to cultural diversity, and to social and political movements, art is connected to community through its *good* side, we can also see how, in the new Right's attempts to reconstitute an authoritarian moral or virtuous community, art can be attached to community through its *bad* side. In these respects, the cultural wars of our times are very much about the ways in which cultural resources are to be deployed and managed—how they are to be socially harnessed—in the context of these, and other, competing versions of community. These struggles will be more effectively engaged in, however, when it is acknowledged that the art museum has not been solely a place of art's seclusion "where art was made to appear autonomous, alienated, something apart, referring only to its own internal history and dynamics" (Crimp, 1993, p. 13). There needs also to be an active recognition of, and engagement with, the ways in which the art museum has, at various times in a range of contexts, been tied—discursively and institutionally—to a variety of governmental programs aimed at bringing about changes in ways of life.

It is equally clear, however, that a cultural politics of this kind requires that the action of art and culture, and the nature of their relationships to the social, should be reviewed along the lines proposed at the beginning of this article. From the perspective of Adorno or Crimp, the work of art is disabled if it is detached from the social and historical conditions in which it originated or if it does not remain connected to them by an effective continuity of tradition. When deprived of these anchoring points, it is unable to connect with and act on the social except in ways that are axiomatically negative. From the perspective of the cultural turn in sociology, the work of art is compressed into the social as one among many signifying practices helping to constitute the identities of social actors and the discursive ground of their interactions. When the cultural turn is given a historical twist along the lines I have suggested, however, works of art emerge as being successively connected to the social in different ways. Their relation to the social does not have a general theoretical character but depends on different discursive and institutionalized forms of culture's action on the social within which they come to be inscribed and through which their historically varying forms of effect are organized. Culture, rather than being superimposed on the social as a relation of meaning in a general manner that reflects, ultimately, the influence of linguistics, has rather to be thought of as standing off from the social in a manner that allows us to see the historically variable ways in which it is then connected to it in different strategies of governing.

## NOTES

1. This is a general tendency evident, *inter alia*, in the work of Hall (1997); the project of the journal *Theory, Culture and Society*, and, more recently, the work of Jameson (1998).

2. I draw here and in other parts of this opening discussion on an earlier engagement with related issues (see Bennett, 1997).

3. Hall (1997) recognizes the difficulties here clearly enough when he notes the danger that the cultural turn can become a new form of cultural idealism in which the sense of any distinction between what is, and what is not, culture is lost (1997, p. 225). However, Hall's response to these difficulties is different from the one I want to pursue here.

4. The literature here is now abundant. However, the editorial program of *Ideology and Consciousness* was perhaps the most influential early route through which these ideas connected with English-speaking debates, although the role of *Economy and Society* in this regard has proved more enduring.

5. See, however, Brewer (1997) for a suggestive account of the respects in which earlier courtly practices of culture were reassembled, alongside emerging forms of commercial culture, in new relations of use and effect in the course of the 18th century. Brewer suggests that it was as a consequence of these developments that culture, as a distinctive and separate sphere, first became recognizable as such. Therborn's (1976) account of the relations between Marxism and sociology and the role accorded cultural and moral factors within the latter as a means of acting on the social is also instructive as an example of the late-19th-century tendency to harness the cultural sphere to governmental tasks. Therborn's discussion is also a useful reminder that aspects of the cultural turn in sociology embody a return (but in different theoretical and political form) to the stress on the role of culture that characterized the classical period of sociology. Hall (1997, p. 224) also makes this point.

6. My arguments here are derived from Foucault's comments on liberal government and the now extensive literature that has developed in their wake. For two central sources of reference, see Burchell, Gordon, and Miller (1991) and Barry, Osborne, and Rose (1996).

7. I draw here on a discussion of these matters in an earlier article (see Bennett, 1995, republished in Bennett, 1998).

8. See, for example, Cole's testimony to the 1867 Select Parliamentary Committee report on the Paris Exhibition. I have discussed this aspect of Cole's position elsewhere (see Bennett, 1992).

9. The apparent contradiction between Romantic constructions of art and the use of art as an instrument of government is, I would argue, akin to that which Bourdieu notes in suggesting that it was the organization of an aura for art that established the conditions for its commercial circulation (see Bourdieu, 1993, pp. 113-14). In both cases, aesthetic conceptions that seem to provide for art's distancing from the world in fact provide the necessary conditions for specific forms of its worldly deployment.

10. The major exception was that comprised by eugenic programs that often proposed direct forms of intervention directed at specific social groups that were defined, usually, in racial terms.

11. For examples of different forms of the art-community relationship, see Fuller (1992) for an account of the use of art in an ecomuseum community empowerment program and Hawkins (1993) for an account of the community arts programs of the Australia Council. I have also addressed these issues elsewhere (see Bennett, 1997).

# REFERENCES

Adorno, T. (1967). Valéry Proust Museum. In *Prisms*. London: Neville Spearman.

Alexander, E. (1983). *Museum masters: Their museums and their influence*. Nashville, TN: The American Association for State and Local History.

Barry, A., Osborne, T., & Rose, N. (Eds.). (1996). *Foucault and political reason: Liberalism, neo-liberalism and rationalities of government*. London: UCL Press.

Bennett, T. (1992). Useful culture. *Cultural Studies*, 6(3), 395-408.

Bennett T. (1995). The multiplication of culture's utility. *Critical Inquiry*, 21(4), 861-889.

Bennett T. (1997). Museums and their constituencies. *New Zealand Museums Journal*, 26(2), 15-23.

Bennett, T. (1998). *Culture: A reformer's science*. Sydney, Australia: Allen & Unwin.

Bourdieu, P. (1993). *The field of cultural production: Essays on art and literature*. Cambridge, MA: Polity.

Brewer, J. (1997). *The pleasures of the imagination: English culture in the eighteenth century*. London: HarperCollins.

Burchell, G., Gordon, C., & Miller, P. (Eds.). (1991). *The Foucault effect: Studies in governmentality*. London: Harvester Wheatsheaf.

Clifford, J. (1997). *Routes: Travel and translation in the late twentieth century*. Cambridge, MA: Harvard University Press.

Cole, Sir H. (1884). *Fifty years of public work of Sir Henry Cole, K.C.B., accounted for in his deeds, speeches and writings*. London: George Bell and Sons.

Crimp, D. (1993). *On the museum's ruins*. Cambridge, MA: MIT Press.

Dean, M. (1991). *The constitution of poverty: Toward a genealogy of liberal governance*. London: Routledge.

Donzelot, J. (1980). *The policing of families: Welfare versus the state*. London: Hutchinson.

Fuller, N. J. (1992). The museum as a vehicle for community empowerment: The Ak-Chin Indian Community ecomuseum project. In I. Karp, C. M. Kreamer, & S. D. Lavine (Eds.), *Museums and communities: The politics of public culture* (pp. 327-66). Washington and London: Smithsonian Institution Press.

Gibson, L. (1997). Art, citizenship and government: "Art for the people" in New Deal America and the 1940s in England and Australia. *Culture and Policy*, 8(3), 41-56.

Giddens, A. (1998). *The Third Way: The renewal of social democracy*. Cambridge, MA: Polity.

Hall, S. (1997). The centrality of culture: Notes on the cultural revolutions of our time. In K. Thompson (Ed.), *Media and cultural regulation* (pp. 207-38). London: Sage.

Harris, J. (1995). *Federal art and national culture: The politics of identity in New Deal America*. Cambridge, UK: Cambridge University Press.

Hawkins, G. (1993). *From Nimbin to Mardi Gras: Constructing community arts*. Sydney, Australia: Allen & Unwin.

Hilpern, K. (1998, August 26). Arts and soul. *The Guardian Society*, pp. 8-9.

Jameson, F. (1998). *The cultural turn: Selected writings on the postmodern, 1983-1998*. London: Verso.

Levin, M. R. (1982). The wedding of art and science in late eighteenth-century France: A means of building social solidarity. *Eighteenth Century Life*, 7(3), 54-73.

McClellan, A. (1994). *Inventing the Louvre: Art, politics, and the origins of the modern museum in eighteenth-century Paris*. Cambridge, UK: Cambridge University Press.

Ozouf, M. (1988). *Festivals and the French Revolution*. Cambridge, MA: Harvard University Press.

Physick, J. (1982). *The Victoria and Albert Museum: The history of its building*. London: Victoria and Albert Museum.

Select Committee of the House of Commons on the Paris Exhibition. (1867). Report of the Select Parliamentary Committee of the House of Commons on the Paris Exhibition.

Rose, N. (1996). The death of the social? Re-figuring the territory of government. *Economy and Society, 25*(3), 327-356.
Therborn, G. (1976). *Science, class and society: On the formation of sociology and historical materialism*. London: New Left Books.
Young, R. M. (1985). *Darwin's metaphor: Nature's place in Victorian culture*. Cambridge, UK: Cambridge University Press.

# 3. The National Endowment for the Arts in the 1990s

## A Black Eye on the Arts?

TOBY MILLER
*New York University*

> *This article seeks to explain the battering sustained by the United States' National Endowment for the Arts (NEA) during the ongoing culture wars over federal subsidies, by situating the NEA in the conjoined histories of both U.S. cultural policy and contemporary debates about citizenship. On the basis of this analysis, it is suggested that the policy options of leaving culture to the market, base, or existing systems of support all lack a base in democratic politics.*

**When he signed the legislation** that birthed the United States' National Endowment for the Arts (NEA) in 1965 as an agency dispensing public money for the production and distribution of art, President Lyndon Johnson explained that "it is in our works of art that we reveal to ourselves, and to others, the inner vision which guides us as a nation" (quoted in Martin, 1998, p. 90). Three decades later, the public face of that interior had taken a battering: Representative Dick Armey referred to the Endowment as the "single most visible and deplorable black eye on the arts in America." This article seeks to explain what happened to Johnson's vision during the intervening years, and the implications for the future, by situating the NEA in the history of U.S. cultural policy and contemporary debates about citizenship. In the 1990s, the Ford, Carnegie, and Rockefeller Foundations, themselves modeled on ancient regime aristocratic patronage but in a demotic vein, are setting the trend for Europe and the other Americas, whereas the rise and decline of the Endowment mirrors Europe's state socialist, national socialist, and welfare-state systems of cultural provision in a telescoped form. What does this history tell us about citizenship and U.S. cultural policy, both "cultural and artistic activity" fostered by the state and "the production of social relations and identities" (Volkerling, 1996, p. 191), that derived from such art? I come down against the current fashion for civil society and in favor of a radical-democratic culture. This article argues that the options of leaving culture to the market, foundations, or existing systems of support lack a base in democratic politics.

## THE HISTORY OF U.S. CULTURAL SUBVENTION

The ethos of democracy identified by de Tocqueville in his eulogy to early 19th-century America forcefully rejected European ruling-class accounts of civilization and how to stimulate it.[1] de Tocqueville identified a belief that equality militated against artistic transcendence: There could be few patrons in an economic democracy, and so profoundly utilitarian a country as the United States would not recognize the value of aesthetics. So from the first, the issue of migration and a new kind of citizenship were critical to the relationship between government and art. An egalitarian philosophy supposedly flattened tastes through cultural relativism, denying the age-old route to artistic distinction provided by a socially hierarchical rank order. Ennoblement was in the eye of the ennobled rather than a universal quality. Practicality was preferred to artistry in a New World driven by market pressures to manufacture large amounts of product at cheap cost as opposed to satisfying a single, discriminating paymaster-patron. de Tocqueville's account is more than a description of its time. It has become a touchstone of U.S. folklore and political culture (Filicko, 1996).

This utilitarian faith in the market allocating cultural resources was evident early on: The relationship of the U.S. federal government and the arts began with copyright provisions authorized by the Founding Parents as a means of encouraging innovation (Van Camp, 1996). However, in 1825, when President John Quincy Adams asked Congress for money to start a national university, observatories, and related programs, this led to accusations of centralization from Martin van Buren and John C. Calhoun. There is continuity in this distaste for connecting culture to the state. The U.S. government's paper at the United Nations Educational, Scientific and Cultural Organization's (UNESCO) 1969 Monaco Round Table on Cultural Policies began with the famous line: "The United States has no official cultural position, either public or private" (cited in Kammen, 1996, pp. 795, 798). Put another way, a profound American commitment to keeping the state separate from the production and restriction of meaning, notably evident in the First Amendment, meant that the federal government supposedly declined to elevate, discriminate, or even differentiate artistically.

Despite all the rhetoric and its international image, one might argue that the United States actually invented modern cultural policy in a federal frame. In 1872, Congress purchased Thomas Moran's painting of the Grand Canyon, which so engaged spectators that the area depicted was later secured for conservation. In 1917-1918, the United States was the first nation to permit tax deductions for gifts to nonprofit organizations. National parks were first established in the United States, which was also the nation that pressed for the United Nations to have a cultural organization. There is nothing in any democracy to compare with the Works Progress Administration's arts projects of the 1930s, and the 1973 Comprehensive Employment and Training Act also had an important influence through its Artists-in-Residence program, which provided income security to artists, unintentionally fostering social critique (Dubin, 1987; French, 1997; Kammen, 1996).

This has been a tale of uneven development, however. In the 1950s, U.S. conservatism took a turn against what was variously termed *rationalism, statism,* and *collectivism*: legacies of the Roosevelt Administration's use of government money and agency to stem the ideological tide and social misery of the Great Depression. Republicans in the 1950s reacted against the subsequent consolidation of centralized governmental authority in the Second World War, but were themselves divided as a movement between libertarians (collective was bad, individual was good) and those reasserting the character of the United States as a Christian nation (collective was bad, familial was good) (Himmelstein & Zald, 1984). This was the era when the egghead professor developed a plural form (the little-remembered "eggmass"), not to mention some horns. Anticommunism continued in the 1960s, but it produced additional divergences. Many on the Right concurred with liberal Democrats in favoring massive internal and external federal action to counter the resources of state socialism. The aim was to best the Soviet Union in every sphere, in a way that was homologous, analogous, and aetiological—battles on all fronts, from book bounties to bomb ballistics.[2]

In the 1960s, U.S. not-for-profit foundations, principally Carnegie, Ford, and Rockefeller, helped generate an infrastructure of artistic diversity at the same time as the federal government and state and private colleges stimulated development. This transformation was legitimized by economic studies of the time, which established that the performing arts were inherently prone to cost overruns, unlike mechanically or electronically reproducible art. The very values of live performance—its mutability and uniqueness—set limits on its profitability. Expenses were high with no prospect of economies of scale through increased production or adjusted inventory (Hirsch, 1997; Zolberg, 1996). So the market would not be sufficient to ensure a wide range of cultural production.

From 1960, John F. Kennedy, Johnson, and Richard Nixon were all worried that Nelson Rockefeller's wealth might buy him the Presidency, and Rockefeller's support for the arts was an important means of product differentiation from his competitors. So they smiled on the public subvention of culture until Nixon muttered to H.R. Haldeman, after years of abuse from liberals, "the arts are not our people. We should dump the whole culture business" (cited in Kammen, 1996, p. 796).[3] Despite Nixon's anxieties, the 1960s and 1970s were a time of burgeoning faith in immigration and government cultural policy, mutually reinforcing signs that the U.S. model of free traffic in persons and ideas could generate better, as well as fairer, outcomes than command economies could (Dittgen, 1997). On the other side, the liberal foundations certainly feared both polarities, of market-driven and government-driven systems, so they sought a third way, pouring millions into making partnerships across the three sectors. This was equally a response to another impetus to federal arts funding: the chaos of American inner cities in the mid-1960s. The Business Council for the Arts and the Rockefeller Foundation argued for arts infrastructure as an alternative to the grave peril of "leisure" in these areas (Martin, 1998, p. 90).

The result was enormous growth. In 1965, when the NEA was enacted, the United States had a total of 100 orchestras and dance, theatre, and opera companies. Today, the number is 800. Six hundred local arts agencies then have turned into 3,800 now, and equivalent state arts bureaux have increased from 6 to 56 (NEA, n.d.). In the first 20 years of the endowment, professional arts organizations grew by 700% (Bayles, 1995). It has been estimated that each dollar of NEA money provides a 20-fold return in contracts, services, and jobs (American Arts Alliance [AAA], n.d.-a). Given this economic interdependency, we might ask what the loss of this financial and political multiplier effect would be, acknowledging that prior to 1965, the United States already housed, no thanks to federal funds, more museums than Western Europe, more libraries than any other country, and half the world's symphony orchestras (Moen, 1997).

## THE PROBLEM

How did the NEA become a problem? The answers lie in four adjacent domains: party politics, constitutional law and lore, the function of art, and debates about sex and race. Each one is interlaced with the notion of what constitutes Americanness: private enterprise versus centralized power, the separation of the state from the generation and suppression of meaning, and changes in national citizenship occasioned by migration, public sexual subjectivity, and their expression in cultural forms.

Because their leader had scored zero on political morality, post-Watergate Republicans proclaimed the need for a return to traditional Christian standards of personal morality. In the name of this morality, they attacked the Left and social movements, notably civil rights and feminism. Areas of symbolic power, such as cultural products, attracted particularly intense criticism. Corporations were major supporters of the growth of right-wing think tanks from the 1970s, as arguments from *Commentary* and other periodicals about a Left elite "using" government grew in appeal. Coors, the Scaife family, and the Hearst Foundation funded antiarts groups (Himmelstein & Zald, 1984, p. 179). "Defund the Left" was on the letterhead of the conservative caucus by the late 1970s. Immediately upon its election, the Reagan Administration's 1981 budget proposed a 50% cut in the NEA's vote. Reagan's faction of the Republican party had long opposed UNESCO in a move that was simultaneously ideological and an instance of realpolitik: a belief in the wrong-headedness of state support to culture coalesced with a belief that left-liberal forces were entirely dependent on government funds to do their work, and hence could be destroyed by organizing the Right to get at these reserves. Pressure from a Democrat-dominated Congress saw half the NEA cuts restored that year and again in 1983 (Himmelstein & Zald, 1984). The way was clear, however, should the Republicans gain control of the legislature.

As this ideological buildup developed with the dismantling of the Cold War, aesthetic forms of life were attacked in a manner homologous to assaults on ethnic and sexual minorities. Many such groups had found public representation in the arts, which simultaneously increased their visibility and vulnerability (Yudice, 1990). These minorities were largely opposed to Republican politics.

At the same time as the Republicans geared up to shut down the NEA, there was a gathering philosophical and aesthetic anxiety over the issue of disinterestedness. The idea of supporting art for selfless motives in a sphere cordoned off from profit making or politics was strong (Zolberg, 1996). Whenever cultural organizations appeared to be building themselves as institutions rather than allocating resources to art, or were engaged in social critique, they became vulnerable. In constitutional law, art has generally been regarded, at least since 1952, as a source of social commentary that can be translated into political speech. Protection of free expression is given to it on the basis that art can embody the social criticisms designed to be encouraged by the First Amendment. This disturbs those conservative libertarians who see art as a mystical form of life that beggars communicative norms and rationality. Neither mimetic nor counterfactual, art is claimed as a beneficial "condition for imaginatively living" that, like religion, may subvert the state in the interests of liberty (Hamilton, 1996). But it suits those who maintain that the capacity of art to speak with *truth* and *purity* (and so influence public affairs to the good) is the very reason why it should not be subject to funding from governments. Hamilton (1996) argues that "the inconsequential size of the NEA budget" clouds a "coercion of culture" behind "benign assistance" (p. 116). She claims that "AIDS awareness and multiculturalism" have been favored by the endowment. Such social goals serve to chill original artistic expression, with the result that avant-garde art is subordinated to art that fits policy priorities. The argument follows that governments should not promote speech, but simply permit its free expression, which would logically entail an end to the Government Printing Office, the Congressional Record, campaign financing, and virtually all education (AAA, n.d.-b).

From a slightly different angle, but one that is more agnostic about social amelioration, consider the words of David Boaz, Executive Vice-President of the right-wing think tank the Cato Institute, addressing Delaware's Center for Contemporary Arts in 1995:

> There are only two basic ways to organize society: coercively, through government dictates, or voluntarily, through the myriad interactions among individuals and private associations. . . . Because art has power, it deals with basic human truths . . . it must be kept separate from government. . . . Take a typical American taxpayer. She's on her feet eight hours a day selling blue jeans at Wal-Mart. She serves spaghetti twice a week because meat is expensive, and when she can scrape together a little extra she likes to hear Randy Travis or take her daughter to see Mariah Carey. Now what gives us the right to tax her so that lawyers and lobbyists can save a few bucks on Kennedy Center tickets? (Boaz, 1995, p. 541)

Such talk combines common-folk demotics with anti-elitism. It assumes that government has nothing to do with democracy, while consumption has nothing to do with boardrooms; or put another way, that citizens have no power over the state, and that company directors have no power over corporations. Other figures are in control: in the case of the state, shadowy bureaucrats and rent-seeking politicians, in the case of business, sovereign consumers. Some adherents of this argument also claim that the arts and their appreciation are part of individual human capital at both supply and demand ends of the relationship. Arts laborers elect to work in the industry, foregoing accumulation elsewhere, and so are voluntarily offering discounted labor for their nonfinancial benefit. Arts audiences add to their utility through aesthetic improvement; so if they truly value culture, they will pay for it directly rather than through subsidies that burden others. Either way, there is no need for state funds. This human capital argument (Becker, 1993) sometimes merges with libertarian discourses.

Many conservative figures dispute such neoliberal logic: They believe that values are partly instilled through high culture in a process that is not supported by pure market structures. Excellence is beyond the collective grasp of the great unwashed, and the higher calling of the arts will be debased if it is left to the tastes of the American public. The NEA is misguided in seeking to broaden the audience for art and in encouraging politicized topics, but governments are right to fund the maintenance of a civilization's memory (Dworkin, 1985; Himmelstein & Zald, 1984). This thinking follows Friedrich Schiller's dictum that "to please many is bad" and Victor Cousin's "l'art pour l'art." Their anxiety is that the federal arts budget has a perverse multiplier effect, instilling conservatism (in the sense of constraints on artistic innovation) because corporate and foundation buyers look to the NEA's systems of peer review as a guide (Schiller & Cousin quoted in Cargo, 1995, pp. 215-216; see also Benedict, 1991; Hamilton, 1996; Smith & Berman, 1992).

We come now to the 19th-century romanticism of the solitary artists who reject the Old World of Europe in favor of transcendence through a self unfettered by social standing or origin, a potent U.S. myth via the Puritan ethos of self-reliance. The myth can work both ways: It can be antigovernmental and foster nostalgia for individualism, or it can provoke laments for the impoverished intersubjectivity of electronic commodification and governmentality. This line emphasizes the loss of face-to-face community produced by the spread of microelectronic communication. The loss of community is held to be a reason to have a NEA because "live events will begin to seem like some of the few authentic experiences we have. . . . That is really what the Arts Endowment is all about—helping people connect with their families, their culture and their community" (Alexander, 1996, pp. 210-211). This recalls the comments of Representative Frank Thompson, an early NEA advocate, who urged that it was essential to ensure that "our supply of humanists is large enough so that in future years machines remain the servant of mankind, and not vice versa" (quoted in Moen, 1997, p. 186). Consider also another anecdote about arts funding—populist and mythic like Boaz's story. A few weeks after Boaz braved the arts rentiers, NEA Chair Jane Alexander talked with bourgeois rentiers: the Economic Club of Detroit. Her story is of being escorted through the city by two policemen "since I had such a tight schedule and wanted to see as much as I could."

> One of the last places we visited was the Detroit Institute of the Arts which has a fine collection of African and Egyptian art and does significant outreach to the community, and one of the police officers became more and more interested in the collection as we went through it. As we said our goodbyes at the airport, he said, "You got to me today. I'm taking my kids to the Mosaic Youth Theatre tomorrow night. I think they'll really like it, and the Museum, there's a lot there for them! I haven't been there since I was a kid, and it's changed. I can see my face and those of my kids reflected there now." (Alexander, 1996, p. 210)

The anecdote echoes two centuries of government-sponsored cultural elevation and moral improvement, delivering opportunities for citizens to improve their lives (Bennett, 2000 [this issue]).

Today, of course, it is argued that the state has an obligation to maintain the variant identities that compose its citizenry. We currently confront claims that there is such a thing as cultural citizenship (Miller, 1998). Proponents argue that social identity is developed and secured through a cultural context where collective senses of self are more important than individual ones. Rights and responsibilities therefore ought to be determined in accord with cultural membership rather than in terms of the general category of the singular human subject (Fierlbeck, 1996). For some, this flexibility can be achieved through a doctrine of cultural rights. For opponents of cultural rights, however, this flexibility is a by-product of universal access to education, a "primary condition of free and equal citizen participation in public life" (Rorty, 1995, p. 162). The latter oppose public funding to sustain specific cultural norms of familial or religious origin (norms that are often contestable even within the cultures in question). Instead, they emphasize cosmopolitanism: People should be able to learn about their own country's public life and their "global neighbors" without having cultural identity prescribed for them in terms of their culture of origin and in a manner that does not adjudicate between a range of roles and forms of life (as worker, believer, etc.) that they inhabit (Rorty, 1995, p. 164). Such a position is the flip side to the human capital argument in that it is concerned about social practice in the aggregate rather than in the atom.

The cultural rights argument draws heat when it touches on the politics of identity. During the summer 1997 congressional debate, Representative Duncan Hunter offered on the floor of the House the comment that NEA money goes to "aging hippies . . . to desecrate the crucifix." He was referring to 1989 controversies surrounding Piss Christ by Andrés Serrano and to a posthumous exhibition of homo- and autoerotic photographs by Robert Mapplethorpe (Bolton, 1992). The resulting debate gave rise to the NEA's Jesse Helms Amendment, which prohibited the endowment from supporting "obscene or indecent materials."

The amendment passed with very few senators present and was upheld by the Supreme Court in 1998 (Moen, 1997; Plagens, 1998).[4]

These conservative voices claim to speak in the name of most Americans. Yet, public opinion is solidly behind some form of relationship between government and the arts. A 1981 poll showed that 26% of Americans said that government should not be involved in the arts, 24% approved participation by local government, 19% expressed support for the states being in on it, and 14% supported involvement from Washington. In both 1980 and 1992, about half the people polled were prepared to pay an extra $25 in taxes annually to help the arts. In 1990, 76% of the U.S. population thought that the NEA directed money to appropriate organizations, 69% disagreed that it was wasting tax dollars, and 83% felt that it served "a useful purpose for American society" (all this at the height of the so-called culture wars) (Filicko, 1996, pp. 230, 237, 238). There was great controversy about the National Museum of American Art's 1991 display of Western art and the 1994-1995 cancellation of The Last Act, an exhibition about World War II in the Pacific Theatre planned for the Smithsonian's National Air and Space Museum. Taken together, these debates, which raised issues about both taste and heritage, indicate a strong level of popular concern about representations of a unitary heritage now seen as compromised by revisionist history from below and by demographic transformations in American life.

## THE CRISIS

The 1994 congressional elections saw Republican takeovers of both Houses for the first time in decades. The Grand Old Party (GOP) swept to power in an antipolitical, antiprofessional wave of reactionary sentiment hailed and codified by the Contract With America. Since that time (predictably, given the history outlined above), federal cultural policy has been in crisis, with the GOP voting in the House of Representatives in the summer of 1997 to reduce the NEA's 1998 appropriation to $10 million, which would be used to close down operations. Representative Armey called on his Republican allies to "vote for freedom, vote for the children, vote for the parents, and vote against elite control of Art in America," and they did (Association for Theatre in Higher Education, n.d.). The score was 217 to 216 to include the endowment in a point of order that wound up agencies that had not been reauthorized. Congress had previously cut the 1996 budget by almost 40%, from $162.4 million to $99.5 million, on top of 15 years of declining purchasing power (Alexander, 1996).

Some Republican members of Congress proposed that an amount equivalent to the NEA's 1996 disbursements should go to the states in block grants: $80 million, 40% to arts agencies and 60% to school districts. At the same time, 28 GOP Congresspeople wrote to then House Speaker Newt Gingrich, indicating their support for the NEA in light of the $3.4 billion in revenue given back to the federal government by the arts each year in federal taxation. They were also acknowledging the $37 billion a year generated by the industry in externalities. The Clinton administration threatened to veto the Interiors Bill, an omnibus supply package that included the NEA's wind-up vote, and the Senate wrote an alternative bill restoring $100 million to the endowment. The upper house, long more favorable to the NEA, made it safe with an eventual budget of $98 million, and that figure was retained during the summer 1998 appropriations vote, as many Republicans in the House of Representatives changed their minds (it being an election year). The NEA was supported by 253 votes to 173 votes. It remains to be seen whether this is a temporary, psephological reprieve, or a seriously rethought response to the endowment's promise to cut the New York liberal art scene's hold on 25% of all funds. It was assuredly a major reversal for the Christian Coalition and a source of pleasure to those Republican funders who are patrons of the arts or associated with businesses that thrive on art exhibits and theatrical shows (Seelye, 1998).

During the 1994 campaign, promises were made on the GOP side (quickly borrowed by the executive branch) to balance the federal budget. How was this to be achieved? Once Congress was under its control, the far Right established what were called "Conservative Action Teams," loose groupings of about 60 Congresspeople. The NEA was a purely symbolic target: Despite its perceived multiplier effects, defunding it would not have sufficiently affected the deficit.[5] The other three aims (abolishing affirmative action, cutting taxes, and balancing the budget) were both substantive and symbolic, involving vast sums of money and immense implications for a diverse workforce (Gee, 1997). Although welfare reform was the principal item for discussion, high-profile minor cuts, such as those to the NEA, were also a priority. Cuts to the endowment represented easy delivery of a Contract With America item, one that posed no threat to the corporate welfare that underwrites companies, which in turn underwrite Republican (and Democrat) electoral expenditure.[6]

We are seeing a coalition at work here between two wings of the Republican party. One is composed of fiscal conservatives who want reductions in public expenditure and regulation. They are barely ideological, more accumulationist. The other wing defines the country's problems in expressly ideological terms. Cutting budgets meets defunding the Left in a way that does not hurt right-wing pork barreling (Himmelstein & Zald, 1984). Virtually since its inception, the endowment has had problems with Republicans and southern Democrats in the House of Representatives, where opposition to government participation in culture matches a desire for expenditure patterns that assist constituents. House conservatives routinely recommend winding up the NEA when Democrats are in the White House (Moen, 1997; for concerns about returns to constituents, see Gilmore, 1993, p. 138). By contrast, Senate Republicans are much more positive about the endowment, recognizing both the multiplier effect and the appeal, for their statewide electorates, of boosterism in federal arts expenditure (Moen, 1997). Sometimes, attempts to cater to this diverse Republican reaction produce their own problems. The recent shift by the NEA away from discipline-based review panels such as dance to issue areas such as heritage, education, creation, and stabilization (a shift designed to answer charges of revolving-door rent seeking) simply adds to the Right's accusations of cultural engineering.

In 1996, Alexander, then chair of the NEA, spoke of a tripod of arts institutions. The civil society of volunteerism and localism was one leg, a disinterested but concerned business community the second, and committed legislatures the third. With the global waning of governmental solutions to social issues, this civil-society model of philanthropic and corporate underwriting is increasingly popular both in the United States and overseas. This distinctive partnership of the private and the public, driven by tax exemptions and plutocrats in search of cultural capital (Ostrower, 1997), has become internationally revered to the point where it is now proliferating throughout Europe and Latin America. In the case of Latin America, the neoliberal push for reduced governmental expenditure merges with a democratizing influence that associates state-driven cultural engineering with the totalitarian dictatorships of the 1960s-1980s period. The United States is increasingly developing and exporting a notion of corporate citizenship, essentially unaccountable and yet supposedly principled. The most powerful export is the idea that U.S. private philanthropy and corporate support generate at least as much diversity and quality in the arts as taxation revenue does (Zolberg, 1996). Instead of an uplift model in which welfarist doctrines prompted governments to give money to the arts to improve their citizenry, the model is a cultural-industry one. The state underwrites new market infrastructures, such as art fairs, where consumer preferences determine the canon (Ardenne, 1995). But at the same time as this neoliberal/industry policy rapprochement was under way, there were dirigiste pressures as well. The United States saw repeated assaults on migrants, ranging from the denial of benefits to legal residents to crackdowns on employed workers without papers. Meanwhile, Europe saw a renewed nationalism that merged anti-immigration rhetoric on the Right with the Left's call for national cultural policy (Ingram, 1998).

## CITIZENSHIP

Traditionally conceived as a means of instilling loyalty in citizens, cultural policy is now thought of by the Left as related to citizen rights, as a means of realizing the aspirations of social movements by translating them into actionable policy. On the Right, culture is subject to privatization pressures. Citizens and consumers continue their uncertain dance in the rhetoric of political philosophy, neoclassical economics, and neoliberal policy mandarinism (Miller, 1993; Zolberg, 1996). The new Democrats and the *New York Times* subscribe to a form of communitarianism, whereas the radical wing of the Republicans and the *Wall Street Journal* adhere to a form of liberalism. On the Right, the division in crude terms is between those who hold that there are responsibilities beyond the self and those who do not. On the Left, citizenship is regarded as a newly valuable form of entitlement that transcends the category of class and provides protection from the excesses of both the market and state socialism.

Such traditional antinomies have been thrown into confusion, however, by immigration and multiculturalism (Feldblum, 1997). Where Republican doctrines of citizenship figure a subject who throws off prior loyalties in order to become a citizen, or nationals of the same country who put aside social divisions in the common interest, multiculturalism blurs the lines between liberal individualism (part of the transcendence promised by identity politics) and collaborative communitarianism (part of the recognition procedures of identity politics). This new form of citizenship does not locate fealty in the sovereign state nor does it necessarily articulate with democracy, because subjects of the trade in labor lack the access to power of native-born sons and daughters (Preuss, 1998). Liberalism assumes, with neoclassical economics, that people emerge into citizenship fully formed as sovereign individuals with personal preferences. Multiculturalism assumes, with communitarianism, that group loyalties override this notion. But where communitarianism assumes that people find their collective identity through political participation, multiculturalism assumes, with liberalism, that this subjectivity is ordained prior to politics (Shafir, 1998). In this way, U.S. cultural policy has seen a series of debates in which apparently polar opposites—the Republican Right and multicultural arts—seem to be logocentrically interdependent. Each group dismisses traditional aesthetics in favor of a struggle to use art to represent identity and social purpose (Yudice, 1990). Multiculturalism stresses the need for a grassroots and marginal arts activism focused on civil rights and a combination of demographic and artistic representation or representativeness. Conservatism calls for an arts practice that heralds Western values and progress while obeying the dictates of Christian taste.

Orthodox histories of citizenship (cf. Hindess, 1998) postulate it as the Western outcome of "fixed identities, unproblematic nationhood, indivisible sovereignty, ethnic homogeneity, and exclusive citizenship" (Mahmud, 1997, p. 633). This history ignores the fact that theories of citizenship were forged in relation to the imperial and colonial encounters of West and East as a justification of extraterritorial subjugation, followed by incorporation of the periphery into an international system of labor (Mahmud, 1997). These conditions led in turn to cultural policy concerns with language, heritage, and identity, expressed by both metropole and periphery as they exchanged people and cultures. In the postcolonial states of Southeast Asia, the generation of a discourse about Asian values became a distinctive means of policing the populace in the name of an abiding idea of personhood that is in fact a reaction to the growth of capitalism and participation in international cultural exchange (Birch, 1998).

As Honig (1998) has shown, immigrants have long been the limit-case for loyalty, back to Ruth the Moabite in the Bible. Such figures are both perilous for the sovereign state (where does their fealty lie?) and essential (as the only citizens who make a deliberate decision to swear allegiance to an otherwise mythic social contract). In the case of the United States, immigrants are crucial to the foundational ethos of consent, for they represent alienation from elsewhere and endorsement of the New World. This makes a national culture all the more fraught, for just as memory of what has been lost by choice is strong, so is the necessity to shore up the preference expressed for U.S. norms. In Europe, the creation of supranational citizenship in 1992 problematized the coupling of citizenship with national culture. At the same time that this recognized a new international division of labor, there were equivalent, powerful moves to limit the rights of guest workers. In each case, it is clear that citizenship has ceased to be based on soil, blood, or culture. With the impact of new nationalisms and cross-border affinities and of pressures on the international labour market that no single governmental apparatus can contain, the sovereign state is no longer the key frame of reference for citizenship (Feldblum, 1997). This has had significant effects on those who, like Asian Australians since the 1970s, have been transformed by changing socioeconomic conditions into officially acceptable migrant citizens. For most of the 20th century, excluding and brutalizing Asians had been critical to Australian national identity, so Asian Australians' latter-day take on citizenship is, not surprisingly, instrumental (Ip, Inglis, & Wu, 1997). Of course, many migrant workers around the world are neither citizens nor immigrants. Their identity is quite separate from their domicile and source of sustenance, with equitable treatment guaranteed not by a sovereign state, but through the supranational discourse of human rights and a notion of everyday custom and belief superintending the legal obligations of conventional citizenship (Shafir, 1998).

Activists in these areas frequently turn to cultural policy to assist in the maintenance and development of collective identities and their expression in artistic form. However, the warm, fuzzy Whiggishness of Marshall's (1964) teleology of Western European citizenry (in which the state is an ever-expanding womb of security that progressively grants civic freedoms, political representation, and welfare) is clearly inadequate to the new models derived from U.S. experience and applied across the globe (Shafir, 1998).

In the art world, the new international division of labor and associated racism has meant that the NEA has found it difficult to attract minority applicants for grants, so profound is their alienation from organs of governance, which are seen to police them and service others (Gilmore, 1993). Dominant doctrines of citizenship and the arts have largely ignored such people. The discourse on culture and citizenship has seen a right-wing split between those, like Bill Clinton, who see a small role for government in the arts (to provide for the public what the market cannot), and those who think that all art should be dictated by consumption. The Left sees the arts in a far more transformative way, harking back to the ideals of socialist man as a new being. Somewhere in between resides Hughes (1996), who favors the NEA because it gives a "sense of community with other citizens... the creation of mutuality, the passage from feeling into shared meaning." That is a nice sentiment, but it appears to be at odds with much of the art world's allergic reaction to such talk as nationalistic and imperialist (Plagens,

1998). The precise nature of this mission has also varied by genre. Whereas the major U.S. museums, for example, foster blockbuster shows and free admission days as a way of avoiding charges of elitism, NEA-assisted performing organizations have done little for the general public. When classical music orchestras hold free or accessible events, these are cordoned off from the norm and are one-off affairs that do not inflect typical offerings and structures of power (Zolberg, 1996).

The NEA's reaction to such pressures has been to call for citizenship by artists and the public that is about collaborative endeavor outside politics—a renewal of volunteerism that has always been the nation's response to the damage of market capitalism (Larson, 1997). This folksy notion of people muddling through their troubles together, without the powerful forms of expertise, technology, and compulsion available to corporations and governments, is little more than emotionally appealing. In the arts field, its impact is laughable. Money holds art together, and voluntary grassroots associations do not have those resources. Citizenship is the way to go, but not this kind of citizenship.

## CONCLUSION

What does the gradual erosion of the NEA portend, and how should citizenship be framed within the associated debates? There has been lower direct corporate support for culture since the end of the art-market boom in the late 1980s and subsequent recessions. In 1991, about 12% of corporate giving went to the arts; in 1994, the proportion was 9.5%. Total donations to the humanities and the arts declined by $270 million in the 3 years to 1995 (Alexander, 1996; Policy.com, 1997). They can hardly be expected to step into the breach. From the other side, Gingrich was sent a letter from 114 business leaders, including the Xerox Corporation and John Brademas, a Congressional sponsor of the NEA's enabling legislation, stating that "the corporate world is not able to carry the entire burden of the cost of cultural access, awareness and education." As Mulcahy (1997) suggests, without the NEA, state and community arts agencies might increase in importance, but would struggle with the still-unclear outcome of the general devolution of welfare payments to the states. (For example, will the disemployed leave poor states for rich ones once federal assistance is no longer available?). The focus of new art forms on everyday life may be left to the market, as NEA supporters rally around "distant and difficult" art that transcends the quotidian in search of difference and newness (Danto, 1997, p. 6), appealing to an elite.

We will probably see heightened cultural commodification, shrinkage of arts organizations, and a decrease in assistance to minorities unless the growing Black, Hispanic, and Asian middle class funds cultural diversity through philanthropy or corporate giving. Business support will increasingly require product placement: The NEA announced a record-tied grant in 1996 for school arts education from H.J. Heinz. The trade-off was that Mr. Heinz announced a contest for school children to redesign the firm's ketchup label during class, and Alexander proudly referred to ketchup as "the nation's favorite condiment." During her tenure, the NEA also welcomed and publicized tiny contributions from Grand Marnier and Borders Books—not to the arts, but to the NEA itself—through its new Office for Enterprise Development (Association for Theatre in Higher Education, 1996; Alexander quoted in Winer, 1996). Perhaps we will move to a federal cultural policy that focuses on its own agencies such as the Kennedy Center for the Performing Arts, the Library of Congress, the Smithsonian Institution, and the National Gallery of Art, leaving indirect assistance to its continued subvention of bourgeois taste (Cargo, 1995). Other possibilities include block grants to the states, national grants to large organizations, or merging the NEA with the National Endowment for the Humanities. It is a time of great flux. Renewed American world economic power may be built on cultural export, but domestic policy flails about in that very area.

Does the future of the NEA matter for democratic culture? The NEA has assuredly assisted official, institutional culture, whether at the level of the Metropolitan Museum of Art or local galleries, but its criteria for funding require incorporation, boards of directors, and auditable books. Schedules must be made a year in advance, and a range of nominated communities addressed: "In short, be co-opted or lie" (Schechner, 1996, p. 8). Schechner (1996) suggests that American performance has lost its vibrancy because of such bureaucratization and reportage. ACT UP, the best avant-garde around, gets no money from Philip Morris or the state.

> Now we are in the final act of *Death of a Salesman* and Willy is realizing he's been had. It's not just that the NEA is shutting down or redefining itself, it never was that big a deal in the first place. (Schechner, 1996, p. 9)

The relationship of citizenship to culture needs redefinition. To go on as we are would be to permit multicultural and neoconservative forces to push citizenship further into the unaccountable realm of civil society. This is straightforwardly implausible as a means of ensuring a devolved, plural, and equitably distributed public culture. Consider these statistics about the work of U.S. philanthropy. First, 40% of arts money comes from 0.07% of foundations. Second, 1% of arts organizations receive 32% of philanthropic money. Third, 65% of that money goes to just five states (Larson, 1997). The NEA also has a poor record of granting money outside the major arts areas (Rice, 1997). Why? Private agencies are only accountable to civil society—their shareholders and boards of governance decide where money is allocated. For its part, the NEA is caught up in a form of cultural capital that appeals to upholders of Old World norms as superior to U.S. immigrant and popular culture.

This is no way to democratize the arts. It is no way to make expenditure sensitive to the will of the people. Put simply, that will is concretely expressed in either purchasing (markets) or political preferences (government subvention). The NEA's decision-making panels should be selected from among local politicians, artists' unions, Congress, academics, small popular-culture businesses, and community groups, and these people should decide what happens to foundation funds derived from tax revenue foregone. The largesse of 19th- and 20th-century plutocrats may be liberal or conservative, but under existing arrangements it will never be democratically arrived at or dispersed. I recognize that the notion of transforming the state into a major source of direct cultural funding will not fly in the United States, and that it is increasingly regarded as outmoded in the rest of the developed world, as neoliberal economic ideology rolls back the state from participation in the everyday. We can at least hope, however, for a model of cultural provision that acknowledges ideals of publicness, inscribed in social-movement organization, as a return.

## NOTES

1. Thanks to the editors for comments.
2. My favorite instance of this is an occasion when hearings of the House Committee on Education and Labor in 1954 found a New Jersey Democrat anxious lest the Union of Soviet Socialist Republics "picture our citizens as gum-chewing, insensitive, materialistic barbarians" (cited in Kammen, 1996, p. 801). Of course, we should not go overboard in stressing the significance of culture within the State Department. For many years, cultural diplomats were apparently selected from those in the foreign service who suffered from mental illness or severe physical disorders—also a feature of decolonizing powers, such as France, where intellectual enfeeblement and chronic professional failure were qualifications for cultural governance (Ingram, 1998; Wieck, 1992).
3. Nixon might have been happier with covert CIA arts funding, exemplified in Cold War assistance to the Congress for Cultural Freedom, which brought together anti-Communists of every hue to push the value of culture created without state interference.
4. Of course, the numerous sex scandals involving U.S. military personnel these past few years have had no discernible impact on funding in that area. Incidents of rape do not see an end to the military, but a particular artistic representation of consensual sex is imagined by religious mavens, anxious critics, and cultural politicos to threaten the arts community.
5. In 1995, the NEA cost each taxpayer 64¢; in 1996, 38¢ per person. Its budget has never exceeded the amount the Defense Department spends each year on military bands and is currently half that figure (Plagens, 1998; Schechner, 1996). In 1996, Congress approved the purchase of 80 C-17s costing $300 million each (240 times the annual NEA appropriation) and voted the Pentagon $7 billion more than it had requested (Alexander, 1996; Hughes, 1996).
6. In addition, the Right's populist side argues that removing the NEA would save the equivalent to the total tax bill for more than 400,000 working-class families (Policy.com, 1997).

## REFERENCES

Alexander, J. (1996). Our investment in culture: Art perfects the essence of our common humanity. *Vital Speeches of the Day, 62*(7), 210-212.
American Arts Alliance (AAA). (n.d.-a). *Economic impact of arts and cultural institutions in their communities* [On-line]. Available: http://www.tmn.com/Oh/Artswire/www/aaa/fact.html

American Arts Alliance (AAA). (n.d.-b). *Myths & facts about national support of the arts & culture* [Online]. Available: http://www.tmn.com/Oh/Artswire/www/aaa/myth.html

Ardenne, P. (1995). The art market in the 1980s. (M. Vale, Trans.). *International Journal of Political Economy, 25*(2), 100-128.

Association for Theatre in Higher Education. (n.d.). *Arts-alert-usa* [Online]. Available: http://www2.hawaii.edu/athe/ATHEWelcome.html

Bayles, M. (1995, May 28). Bad art, bad politics [Book review]. *New York Times*, p. 9.

Becker, G. (1993). Nobel lecture: The economic way of looking at behavior. *Journal of Political Economy, 101*(3), 385-409.

Benedict, S. (Ed.). (1991). *Public money and the muse: Essays on government funding for the arts.* New York: Norton.

Bennett, T. (2000). Acting on the social: Art, culture, and government. *American Behavioral Scientist. 43*, 1412-1428.

Birch, D. (1998). Constructing Asian values: National identities and "responsible" citizenship. *Social Semiotics, 8*(2-3), 177-201.

Boaz, D. (1995). The separation of art and state. *Vital Speeches of the Day, 61*(17), 541-543.

Bolton, R. (Ed.). (1992). *Culture wars: Documents from the recent controversies in the arts.* New York: New Press.

Cargo, R. A. (1995). Cultural policy in the era of shrinking government. *Policy Studies Review, 14*(1-2), 215-224.

Danto, A. C. (1997, November 17). "Elitism" and the N.E.A. *The Nation*, pp. 6-7.

Dittgen, H. (1997). The American debate about immigration in the 1990s: A new nationalism after the end of the Cold War? *Stanford Humanities Review, 5*(2), 256-286.

Dubin, S. C. (1987). *Bureaucratizing the muse: Public funds and the cultural worker.* Chicago: University of Chicago Press.

Dworkin, R. (1985). *A matter of principle.* Cambridge, MA: Harvard University Press.

Feldblum, M. (1997). "Citizenship matters": Contemporary trends in Europe and the United States. *Stanford Humanities Review, 5*(2), 96-113.

Fierlbeck, K. (1996). The ambivalent potential of cultural identity. *Canadian Journal of Political Science/Revue Canadienne de Science Politique, 29*(1), 3-22.

Filicko, T. (1996). In what spirit do Americans cultivate the arts?: A review of survey questions on the arts. *Journal of Arts Management, Law & Society, 26*(3), 221-246.

French, S. (1997). Letter to the editor. *Policy Review: The Journal of American Citizenship, 84*, 4-5.

Gee, C. B. (1997). Four more years—so what? *Arts Education Policy Review, 98*(6), 8-13.

Gilmore, S. (1993). Minorities and distributional equity at the National Endowment for the Arts. *Journal of Arts Management and Law, 23*(2), 137-173.

Hamilton, M. A. (1996). Art speech. *Vanderbilt Law Review, 49*, 72-122.

Himmelstein, J. L., & Zald, M. (1984). American conservatism and government funding of the social sciences and arts. *Sociological Inquiry, 54*(2), 171-187.

Hindess, B. (1998). Divide and rule: The international character of citizenship. *European Journal of Social Theory, 1*(1), 57-70.

Hirsch, S. (1997). Letter to the editor. *Policy Review: The Journal of American Citizenship, 84*, 4.

Honig, B. (1998). Immigrant America? How foreignness "solves" democracy's problems. *Social Text, 56*, 1-27.

Hughes, R. (1996, May 27). The case for élitist do-gooders. *New Yorker.*

Ingram, M. (1998). A nationalist turn in French cultural policy. *The French Review, 71*(5), 797-808.

Ip, D., Inglis, C., & Wu, C. T. (1997). Concepts of citizenship and identity among recent Asian immigrants to Australia. *Asian and Pacific Migration Journal, 6*(3-4), 363-384.

Kammen, M. (1996). Culture and the state in America. *Journal of American History, 83*(3), 791-814.

Larson, G. O. (1997). *American canvas: An arts legacy for our communities.* Washington, DC: National Endowment for the Arts.

Mahmud, T. (1997). Migration, identity, & the colonial encounter. *Oregon Law Review, 76*(3), 633-690.

Marshall, T. H. (1964). *Class, citizenship, and social development: Essays by T. H. Marshall* (S. M. Lipset, Ed.). Chicago: University of Chicago Press.

Martin, R. (1998). *Critical moves: Dance studies in theory and politics.* Durham, NC: Duke University Press.

Miller, T. (1993). *The well-tempered self: Citizenship, culture, and the postmodern subject.* Baltimore, MD: Johns Hopkins University Press.

Miller, T. (1998). *Technologies of truth: Cultural citizenship and the popular media.* Minneapolis: University of Minnesota Press.

Moen, M. C. (1997). Congress and the National Endowment for the Arts: Institutional patterns and arts funding, 1965-1994. *The Social Science Journal, 34*(2), 185-200.

Mulcahy, K. V. (1997). *Public support for the arts in the United States, Western Europe and Canada: Polities, policies, politics* (Commissioned by the American Assembly). New York: Columbia University Press.

National Endowment for the Arts (NEA). (n.d.). *Question & Answer* [Online]. Available: http://www.cco.caltech.edu/~ope/nea.html

Ostrower, F. (1997). *Why the wealthy give: The culture of elite philanthropy.* Princeton, NJ: Princeton University Press.

Plagens, P. (1998, July 24). Squishy defenses by its supporters don't help the Endowment. *Chronicle of Higher Education,* pp. B4-B5.

Policy.com. (1997). Issue of the week: Defunding the NEA. *Policy Information Service, 1-3* [Online]. Available: http://www.policy.com/issuewk/0721/072197b.html

Preuss, U. K. (1998). Migration—a challenge to modern citizenship. *Constellations, 4*(3), 307-319.

Rice, W. C. (1997). I hear America singing: The arts will flower without the NEA. *Policy Review: The Journal of American Citizenship, 82,* 37-45.

Rorty, A. O. (1995). Rights: Educational, not cultural. *Social Research, 62*(1), 161-170.

Schechner, R. (1996). Bon voyage, NEA. *The Drama Review, 40*(1), 7-9.

Seelye, K. Q. (1998, July 22). For election year, House approves arts financing. *New York Times,* pp. A1, A14.

Shafir, G. (1998). Introduction: The evolving traditions of citizenship. In G. Shafir (Ed.), *The citizenship debates: A reader* (pp. 1-28). Minneapolis: University of Minnesota Press.

Smith, R. A., & Berman, R. (Eds.). (1992). *Public policy and the aesthetic interest: Critical essays on defining cultural and educational relations.* Urbana: University of Illinois Press.

Van Camp, J. (1996). Freedom of expression at the National Endowment for the Arts: An opportunity for interdisciplinary education. *Journal of Aesthetic Education, 30*(3), 43-65.

Volkerling, M. (1996). Deconstructing the difference-engine: A theory of cultural policy. *European Journal of Cultural Policy, 2*(2), 189-212.

Wieck, R. (1992). *Ignorance abroad: American educational and cultural foreign policy and the Office of Assistant Secretary of State.* Westport, CT: Praeger.

Winer, L. (1996, June 28). So what's next, a mustard ballet? *Newsday,* p. B3.

Yudice, G. (1990). For a practical aesthetics. *Social Text,* (25-26), 129-145.

Zolberg, V. (1996). Paying for art: The temptations of privatization à l'Américaine. *International Sociology, 11*(4), 395-408.

# 4. Participatory Policy Making, Ethics, and the Arts

JANICE BESCH
*Australia Council*

JEFFREY MINSON
*University of Technology, Sydney*

> *The ethic of community participation is dominated by the ideal of the self-governing community of reflective citizens. This article suggests the need to focus on some of the more down-to-earth ethical attributes of a responsible participant that tend to be overshadowed by that ideal. The authors look at the disciplinary, rhetorical, and role-specific demands of participatory styles of governance. Implications of this perspective are drawn out in an examination of how the challenges of community participation are or might be played out in an arts policy field that is currently under the sway of neoliberal approaches to government and anti-elitist political challenges to the arts.*

**Enthusiasm for community participation** in decision making has of late spread to many different walks of life, from central government initiatives to the most hierarchical private organizations, from social movements of the new Left to those of the new Right, and from childrearing to parental intervention in "the school community." Radical political theorists and management gurus alike can be found arguing that the locus of social and organizational power should move away from central government and its sitting armies of professional experts and bureaucrats.

At the more idealistic end of the spectrum, community participation in public policy making figures as a theoretical sine qua non of a truly democratic republic. In the neo-Kantian ideal of a society of reflective, morally self-governing citizens espoused by Barber (1982), for example, politics is envisaged as a strictly amateur affair: "a direct encounter between citizen and citizen without the intermediary of expertise" (p. 152). In talk of the third sector, political and social theory and their ideals of citizenship meld into public management theory. In a "community-owned government," states Osborne (1994), entrepreneurial public sector organisations "push control out of the bureaucracy" (p. xiii). Previously

---

**Authors' Note:** *The authors would like to thank Denise Meredyth for editorial suggestions, Ann Freadman for rhetorical advice, and Glyn Davis and Patrick Bishop for sharing their views on contemporary participatory governance. The views expressed by the authors are their own and do not reflect official or even unofficial philosophical or policy positions attributable to the Australia Council or to previous employers.*

passive recipients of directives, benefits, and opportunities, for example, must be empowered to become active partners in self-governing, livable communities (McNulty with Page, 1994). Neighborhoods are assigned the role of mediating structures between the state and the individual (Berger & Neuhaus, 1977). Equally, and often in the same breath, terms such as *ownership* and *empowerment* form part of a more amoral rhetoric and technique of governance, enjoining governments to give organisations what they say they need in order to do their own thing while carrying out the work of government, for example, by delivering services to the community that are cheaper and more effective than those that government can provide.

Given this profusion of practices that appeal to the participatory imperative, it is hardly surprising that such appeals evoke mixed responses. There is no end of good (ethical) reasons to refuse an invitation to participate oneself or to be unenthusiastic about certain activist expressions of communities' concerns. Even the most enthusiastic advocates of citizen participation as a recipe for progressive social and economic change must blanch at some of the monsters created by the craze for inclusiveness. (Think of the Southern Californian suburban homeowner movement bonded by perceived threats to property values and hatred of racially mixed schools and neighborhoods, which spearheaded the epochal 1978 tax revolt; see M. Davis, 1992).

Faced then with the prestige of the participatory imperative and this superabundance of different participatory norms and practices, the following question arises: How should we relate ourselves ethically to this imperative when it impinges on us? We do not propose to be critical of trends to a more participatory style of policy making. Rather, treating these trends as a political fact, we map out the ethical contours of participatory governance, drawing particular attention to the more worldly personal capacities that citizens and government officials alike need to acquire if the community participation component of public policy is to contribute to competent government.

Our contribution combines two very different sorts of intellectual resources: unofficial empirical and operational observations drawn from the field of Australian arts and cultural policy, and academic explorations across the disciplines of political science, government ethics, and the history of ethics. The intention is to direct attention away from the moral high ground of collective self-determination in order to spotlight the moral low ground of participatory governance—especially the neglected self-disciplinary and rhetorical conditions, procedural devices, and the plurality of role-based ethical mindsets—needed for responsible participation.[1] We then move to a discussion of how the current participatory imperative is, or might be, played out in an arts policy field currently dominated by neoliberal approaches to government and political challenges to the arts. By contrast with the critical/self-acting-citizen focus of so much discussion of participation, we look at the challenges of participation in arts policy development for interested parties in particular roles: professionals in the cultural sector, arts administrators, and politicians in government. Our general point is this: Idealizing participation makes it harder to find a place for a conception of democracy as in part entailing an expansion as much as a contestation of the expertise available to government.

## ACTIVE PARTICIPATION AS MORAL PROGRESS?

The participatory imperative is a formidable cocktail. As exemplified in the multiple resonances of catch phrases such as *owning the process*, it combines elements of religiosity backed up by promises of material powers that may or may not impose moral burdens and by suspicion of expertise, bureaucracy, and state sovereignty.[2] These antiauthoritarian suspicions are sometimes linked to a cheerfully amoral association of democracy with freedom in the sense of negative liberty. They are also linked to a more religiose worry about any exercise of power that seems to detract from the ideal of moral self-determination: moral agents being (on this view) only subject to restraints they have in some sense reflectively given or consented to themselves. It is easy to understand why so many humanities-trained critical intellectuals are drawn to the view that community participation so understood; that is, where the will of communities has a suitably morally thoughtful form represents the perfection of democracy. What more is there then to the ethics of democratic participation than the right to participate and the obligation to shape one's participation around commonly reiterated principles such as equal respect, preparedness to revise one's own views, and openness to differences of outlook that are matters of reasonable disagreement?

Among the many morally and politically relevant considerations excluded by this evaluative grid is the fact that, in a liberal democracy, uncivil communities such as the Southern Californian homeowners' associations, which are certainly irrational by these intellectualist standards, cannot conceivably be barred from exercising their citizen rights on that account (Kymlicka & Norman, 1995).[3] Moreover, despite their sensitivity to power wielded by others, advocates of community participation also have to be reminded that active participation itself is always necessarily shadowed by an element of elitism.[4] Community activists, particularly today, are always vulnerable to charges of constituting an unrepresentative oligarchy.

This is not to suggest that there is anything inherently problematic about the fact that "any system which favors more than minimum participation favors the active over the passive" (Lucas, 1974, p. 230). On the contrary, we will be arguing that in the case of the arts there are good reasons why activists should be trying harder to have a disproportionate say in shaping public policy. A sure sign of the need for a political ethics that does not privilege community activism is governments' recent and increasing reliance on direct polling of sections of the electorate in developing public policy.

The emergence of this technique is linked to the familiar fact that political democracy and politicians have been compelled to become more demotic. In contrast to the process-driven consultations or negotiations with community organisations that provide vehicles for sustained active citizen participation, direct polling is supposed to allow the wider community who might be disconnected from policy communities or sectoral interest groups to have a bigger influence. In this era of audience democracy (Manin, 1997), neoliberal government programs tend to begin with market research, tailoring initiatives in response to needs discovered, with community ownership processes feeding in through advertising campaigns that pick up on community responses to issues and sell them the initiative.[5]

Needless to say, these programs can be plausibly represented as also entailing a deduction from democracy. In the familiar purchaser-provider model of public service delivery, for instance, government as purchaser, after polling and coming up with palatable solutions, buys the product from the department concerned and does not expect the department to involve the community beyond client service surveys postdelivery. The mechanism of participation sits outside of the service delivery itself, which must to an extent be "top down" if the elected government is to earn a reputation for responsiveness. Yet, from this neoliberal perspective, dialogue between community organisations and government agencies may indeed pose the threat of governments being captured by some sectional interest. Consultation and negotiation can also be seen, again not always unreasonably, as just another level of bureaucratic process (meetings, etc.).

We are not about defending direct polling for policy settings as a superior form of democracy. That would be to idealize the voice (and above all the capacities) of the citizenry, no less so than does the insistence on embedding reflexive participatory processes within the policy development and program delivery continuum. A more promising way to argue the limits of poll-driven policy development might be to headline not so much the will or rights of citizens who might contribute to a policy consultation process as the various kinds of expertise, including moral and political capacities, which they may either bring to it or acquire as a result of such involvements.

## ETHICS AND THE ARTS OF PARTICIPATION

To do justice to these moral and political capacities means setting aside the propensity to think of the expression "community participation" as first and foremost encapsulating a moral demand for change addressed to a democratically deficient reality in the name of an ideal of self-governing community. The alternative is to think about participation as itself a reality, one that is too widespread, messy, and complicated to be weighed on any single scale of values and that imposes moral demands on participants. The question then becomes, What ethical attributes are required for responsible participation and how are they acquired? Participationist theorists such as Rousseau, Mill, and Cole have all along stressed participatory processes' morally educative, indeed trans- formative, effects on the character of citizens (Pateman, 1970). However, we will argue that many of the character-forming dimensions of participation are rather more mundane and circumscribed.

How do procedures of democratic participation induce participants to modify the way they conduct themselves in particular political or organizational settings? Consider the banal kinds of capacities for self-discipline fostered by staple ingredients of deliberative assemblies and meetings such as the quorate rule or the advance circulation of agendas and written materials relating to them. These institutions both promote and rest on the display of personal qualities such as dependability. Responsible participants have to be minimally competent at time management. They have to acquire habits of attendance and reading up on matters for discussion in advance of meetings.

They also have to be civil, but this requires more than being committed to democratic ideals such as equal respect. It is no exaggeration to say that maintaining patience in the face of the tedium and frustrations that are inseparable from participatory processes calls for a measure of bodily "ethical labor" or "ascesis" (Foucault, 1992, pp. 27-28, 72-77): a habitual mastery of body language. It is through a decidedly nonspiritual mastery of mind over matter (the moulding of facial musculature, our sitting posture, etc.) that we practise respect for fellow committee members or political opponents. They may be long-winded or hold views bitterly opposed to ours, but they are entitled not only to their say but also, as a general rule, to a show of interest on the part of their listeners.

Along with patience, the responsible participant needs tact. Which is to say that the concomitant of "keeping a civil tongue" in negotiations is very often the necessity to restrain oneself from uttering humiliating home truths that could undo the taxing work of finding common ground (Kingwell, 1998). Democratic participation is supposedly synonymous with openness. Yet, step down from the plinth of principle to the level of the manner(s) prerequisite to practising participation and you begin to appreciate why, in a pluralistic polity, unrestrained "public sincerity . . . would ruin democratic civility" (Shklar, 1984, p. 78).

Finally, in some contexts, responsible participation depends on one's ability to provisionally adopt an attitude of indifference towards one's cherished moral or political commitments, or to use the more precise Renaissance term, to treat them as adiaphora (Minson, 1993, 1998). To illustrate its contemporary applicability, consider the delicate balancing act required of those whom Yeatman and others have recently dubbed policy activists located in government agencies (Yeatman, 1998). Insider activists of this kind are distinguished by a reforming zeal that, whatever its source (preexisting social/community commitments or a more professionally informed passion) goes beyond the normal requirements of bureaucratic office. These advocates for sectoral interests are scattered throughout bureaucracies, pushing some public good–oriented policy directions, seeking access to strategic decision-making forums, winning cross-agency support, or animating wider debate and helping to coordinate and temper contributions to these initiatives from sections of the relevant policy community. Their contribution to the division of activist labor is based on a mixture of idealism and an intimate and pragmatic understanding of how and where to frame, interpret, and operationalize policy ideas (Dugdale, 1998).

To be a policy activist within government, one must be, morally speaking, "a hybrid creature" (Dugdale, 1998, p. 109). Policy activists must be able to respect the moral limits to their activist ethos, which are set by other requirements of their job, from helping ministers implement election promises to which the activist is personally averse to refraining from pushing other programs or routine tasks for which they are responsible to others. As governments extend their mechanisms for input to polling the citizenry, policy activists will need to position themselves much more directly as experts who have the capacity to interpret these needs and aspirations into actionable ideas. This is to say that they must both lay aside their own assumptions that they know what action should be taken and be able to apply their expertise and give life to ideas that have popular support, but that might seem to them personally uninformed and second best.

These mundane disciplinary moral capacities and comportments needed for responsible and civil participatory governance set limits to the more high-minded moral concomitants of participatory democracy. Our earlier example of practising equal respect suggests that they also help to materialize such principles. So it is not our intention to suggest that a participant's official obligations, say, as a committee member, always ought to override their principled commitments. Focusing on the mundane yet ethical person-forming dimensions of participation merely allows us to discern the ethical value of things such as compromise and economizing on frankness and the corresponding irresponsibility of those who spurn them.[6]

## RHETORIC AND ETHICAL LABOR-SAVING DEVICES

These examples of the disciplines of participation also help to pinpoint its rhetorical dimensions. There is a well-known connection between political performance and rhetoric as an art of composition (e.g., Lincoln's Gettysburg Address, Burke's parliamentary speeches, and so on), but rhetoric's political importance is not restricted to winning arguments or inspiring an audience. Rhetorical skills are indispensable tools of negotiation through which people with different views or priorities find common ground in the formulation of mutually acceptable terms of moral redescription (Minson, 1998; Skinner, 1996). In addition, rhetoric, institutionalized in ancient Greek and Roman elite education and under the name of *paedeia*, has also always been a theatrical art of self-fashioning. One reason why this history is more than a matter of passing historical interest for ethics is the fact that the *self* that had to be *fashioned* through paedeia was always something that had to be defined relative to some official identity or role (orator, lawyer, diplomat, statesman, wife, friend, and so on) (Condren, 1997).

Similarly, where the kind and extent of contemporary moral self-shaping required for responsible participation is concerned, it is important to emphasize the limited nature of the self-scrutiny and self-modification at stake here. Curbing a propensity to dominate discussion hardly requires acceding to a higher level of consciousness, and contrary to a widespread modern connotation of the words *role* or *office*, the appropriate demeanor required for civil and productive discussion cannot be reduced to a finite set of formally determined tasks of behavior. It takes practice to acquire an intelligent feeling and judgment for what is appropriate. Contemporary reflection in ethics, which has sought to rehabilitate the Ciceronian conception of moral responsibility and agency as an accumulation of roles or offices, has hitherto mostly been confined to the sphere of elected and unelected public officials or professional ethics (Weber, 1948). Citizen involvement, too, can only take place by participants assuming different roles, each of which "has its own dynamic and is capable of influencing the policy development process in different ways" (Considine, 1994, p. 141).

We have already noted this plurality of roles in the case of the office of committee member or policy activist. Perhaps, then, there is an alternative to conceiving the figure of the citizen or activist in the image of an authentic self-determining individual, defined by their irreducibility to any given role. *Role* does not only refer to an inventory of functional duties. It also possesses a dramaturgical meaning, whence the relevance of a rhetoric of personal composure to participatory roles. Offices or roles can be embodied in one or more role-specific personae, a personal manner that is the product of orchestrating habits of mind, passional dispositions, and forms of conscience required by the role(s) in question. The question of what to do in cases of conflicts between role responsibilities cannot be determined by appealing to general citizenship values, equality, justice, and so forth because these do not form a consistent set and may be overridden by responsibilities internal to particular role responsibilities.

Having talked about the person-forming effects or preconditions of participatory-democratic arrangements, we should also, finally, acknowledge the existence of rules and procedures that avoid the need to make onerous ethical demands on participants. A perfect example, as the procedural equivalent of adiaphorism or indifference (see above), would be the diverse precepts of avoidance or self-censorship sometimes known as *gag rules*. These are the means by which deliberative bodies delimit the range of subjects they permit themselves to consider in the interests of preserving civil peace.[7] *Gagging* our moral desires can be every bit as demanding as restraining nonmoral ones. Gag rules save us from agonizing where it is impossible to give effect to moral convictions. Other kinds of democratic/participatory rules work in the same way; for instance, the device that keeps dissenting members of an enquiry committee from resigning or dropping out of a wider participatory relationship with governments by permitting them to publish a dissenting minority report (Office of Multicultural Affairs, 1994). Such rules protect us from ourselves, including our higher selves. In so doing they also help to make the institution of a varied array of practices of participatory governance feasible.

To summarize, it has been the purpose of this section to illustrate the yield of a pluralistic, prudential, historically minded and office-based ethical approach to how one goes about conducting oneself within actually existing participatory mechanisms. We have touched on some of the ethical and rhetorical comportments that are necessary for responsible participation, its mundane purposes, and its mechanical but ethically efficacious devices. We now cross to the terrain of arts and cultural policy to see how our emphasis on the disciplinary and rhetorical moral low ground of the ethics of participation bears on the central problem of how to equip those in the arts with more supple and effective approaches to advocacy and policy intervention.

## CULTURAL SECTOR PARTICIPATION IN POLICY MAKING

We begin by asking why there is so little input by cultural sector professionals as professionals into the public policy process and so little appreciation of what they have to offer and where they could be making these contributions. This involves consideration of the relationship between cultural sector professionals and arts bureaucrats, who also often perform the role of sectoral advocates. We also need to consider the standpoint of the government of the day—the techniques that governments can and do use in ensuring that their programs are palatable to, and deliver results for, the electorate. To what extent do these techniques of government either engage or unplug both sectoral expertise and advice from the bureaucracy? What moral and rhetorical abilities do cultural sector professionals need to cultivate if elected representatives are to be persuaded to draw down on their expertise and if participatory processes such as peer assessment, consultation, and negotiation are to be made more viable as means for establishing the overall policy settings for the arts in Australia?

Australia is a country in which the arts have long relied on government support to an extent that contrasts starkly with the situation in the United States (T. Miller, 2000 [this issue]), but which is not particularly high by European standards. So, although the concerns of arts policy extend well beyond funding issues and private corporate sector support is not negligible, participation by cultural sector professionals in arts policy has a history in Australia of consistently focusing on advocacy designed to increase government support for the arts.

Today, the future shape and extent of that support is uncertain. The current climate is on the whole one of static or declining public funding for the arts across the Australian federation. This is in part a consequence of the application of so-called neoliberal or economic rationalist microeconomic reform principles across all three tiers of government, in conjunction with elements of what we have been calling the audience democracy dimension of modern government (polling of community preferences, client satisfaction surveys, and so on).[8] Even if we see the trend to neoliberal governance in arts policy as a double-edged sword, the current political climate for the arts remains a potentially hostile one. To Australian governments generally, the arts are either a nonissue or, more recently, appear as a potential source of voter backlash due to alleged public associations of the arts with privileged elites (partly as a consequence of the recent resurgence of extreme right-wing populism).

For many in the cultural sector, the neoliberal turn in public policy is a barrier to participation in regard to policy questions, yet it has had diverse impacts on the cultural sector. We should note that, in the Australian case, cultural policy has been implicated in neoliberal economic arguments at least since the release of the first national cultural policy, *Creative Nation*, in 1994. This template for Australian national cultural policy argued the arts, including strong state support for them, almost entirely in terms of their economic significance and concentrated its recommendations on new initiatives for cultural industry development in growth areas such as information technology. Policy priorities to emerge more recently maintain a focus on the economics of the arts but add to this focus a distributional concern (in the current government's electoral policy statement *For Arts Sake: A Fair Go* [Liberal and National Coalition, 1998]) and a concern about the efficiency and effectiveness of current arts infrastructure.[9] Current cultural policy is partly a creature of neoliberal governance, not an exception to it.

As arts bureaucrats are well aware, governments of all persuasions are concerned not to overspend or overgovern. Despite the antistatist doctrines associated with them, neoliberal strategies of government are also pragmatic exercises in statecraft and party-political self-preservation, means to keep the ship of state afloat and catch the international trade winds, or to enhance the standing of the country, for instance, by supporting artwork of international standard and repute. It is important for arts bureaucrats to see governments' concerns with fiscal restraint, responsiveness to clients, and electoral approval as bipartisan preoccupations. Furthermore, the "economic focus" trend in public policy is not always inimical to the cultural sector's capacity to serve the public good. The demands it places on cultural organisations to focus more on the business of the arts are not entirely unreasonable and have the potential to lead to greater sectoral stability.

Arts bureaucrats have a role to play in policy making that is distinct from that of artsworkers—even though many actually move between employment in the bureaucracy and work in their own arts practice or in administrative roles within funded arts organizations, adopting different roles and managing shifting collegial relationships. As policy activists, many arts bureaucrats have more than a modicum of concern for their sector. This can be both an aid to advocacy for the arts and an impediment. On one hand, arts bureaucrats carry with them a great deal of sectoral expertise that can assist them in channeling a sectoral voice and developing measures to meet sectoral needs. On the other hand, the bureaucracy can only do so much in terms of arguing the arts. Policy settings are not made by public servants, but by the government of the day that they are there to serve. Sometimes cultural sector professionals fail to acknowledge this difference of role, assuming that their colleagues in government agencies are in a better position than they are to fight the good fight.

Further distancing from policy making for both professionals and bureaucrats is provided in the trend to a more demotic style of government, where politicians privilege first the voice of their electorate and then effective lobby groups. More than ever, in the name of *empowering the community*, states are unplugging their experts. Powers and resources are being devolved in some cases to private or third sector organizations or ever smaller and more local bodies, irrespective of whether the competencies are really out there or how self-determining citizens might acquire them. There is a virtual freezing over of the earlier relationships that might have existed between professionals and policy makers.

What are the barriers to more effective advocacy from the cultural sector? First, limited opportunity, as in Australia, there are comparatively few entry points to policy, and fewer opportunities for people to take up their role as experts and apply this at crucial times. Policies have more to do with party-political processes being played out by the government in power than they do with ongoing commentary in public or private fora. Outside these party-political processes, there are no solid syndications of view. In the United States, by comparison, public policy fields are relatively fluid, influenced by informal links between professional lobbyists, politicians scouting around for initiatives on which to make their reputations, bureaucrats turned consultants, academics, journalists, and community leaders (G. Davis, 1998).[10] This contrast may be useful when searching for new forms of application of cultural sector expertise in policy. On the positive side, however, the arts bureaucracy here in Australia is so small that artsworkers are closer to the decision-making process than they might think. In their capacities as practitioners, grantees, and peers on funding panels, artsworkers have some opportunities to join the policy debates and argue the "public good" case for the arts.

Arguably, other barriers to effective inputs into arts policy emanate from attitudes within the sector itself: arts professionals' reluctance to engage with economic rationalist agendas, the tendency to rely on general claims about the public benefits of the arts, and a reluctance to combat arguments about the elitism of the arts. In these instances, the *ethics of role* can provide a resource for more effective dialogue if participants are willing to exercise the discipline of role, refrain from poor rhetorical tactics, and assert their case as experts with more calculation.

To begin with, when putting the case for funding, the sector needs to avoid the conspicuous bad form of special pleading, anticipating the objection that public subsidy for the arts draws funds from areas of greater social need, such as health, welfare, education, and housing. Recent populist agitation about the elitism of the arts has increased the pressure to make policy development more cognizant of possible electoral reactions to expenditure decisions. In any case, arguments that appear as pleas for special treatment are likely to be seen by some government officials and politicians as evidence of the public choice theorists' dogmas about publicly funded systems' will to self-perpetuate and grow, in defiance of fiscal restraint and public opinion.

Advocates also need to be more articulate in challenging anti-elitist sentiments, both in the broader community and in academic commentary. Take, for example, some of the contentious interpretations coming out of cultural studies, purporting to expose the specialist and elite character of the arts and their audiences through the sociological analysis of arts consumers in terms of cultural capital. The primary social function of the arts, runs a now classic argument, is to provide a means for its patrons and audiences to create and reinforce social distance (Bourdieu, 1984). In a climate hostile to public spending on the arts, those within the sector itself need to be more robust in responding to such generalizations, which reinforce the populist allegation that public dollars are being wasted on elite tastes. Rather than letting the assertion that the arts is an accomplice to the class distinctions stand, other explanations for the correlation between arts participation, high-education levels, and high incomes should be put forward. Arts educators are aware of the research into the correlation between arts education and learning ability, for example, which implies a very different causal relationship between the arts and social standing.

The charge of elitism challenges the sector to draw on its expertise and experience to direct attention away from elite consumers at the top of the social ladder and toward the broad range of individuals and organisations who have a stake in the arts. These include producers, performers, technical support personnel, presenters, publishers, the businesses that prosper in arts precincts, and the variety of communities whose lives are enriched through engagement with the arts. Artsworkers know the importance of the less commercially viable work they do. They can show that successful productions feed off experimentation. They can explain that the greatest successes have often proved to be the ones initially greeted by audiences with consternation and outright hostility. They can identify the links between theatre, creative writing, and film and across the visual and performing arts and into architecture, design, and advertising. In short, they know about the ecological interdependencies within the arts world and they know the importance of artsworkers to that world. The challenge is to ensure that decision makers make use of this experience and expertise.

Finally, the sector needs to scale down the long-standing historical barriers between government and experts. Since the birth of public patronage for the arts, the primary form of connection between artsworkers and governments has been that of supplicant to patron. The frequently expressed hostility generated between the two during the period from the mid-20th century is hardly surprising given that the majority of artsworkers' grant applications are turned down.[11] This antagonism is not overcome by the existence of arms-length, peer-based funding mechanisms—quite the reverse. The process itself is so fraught with taboos on active dialogue about the actual basis for decisions that the effect is to seal off the arts community's expertise from the funder, the applicants, and the public.[12] Those involved in grant decisions have a real opportunity here to contribute to the development of measures to assist their artform area, at the moment when they advise politicians and the community of the quality of applications received in that funding round. Yet, this advice more often than not comes in the form of a merit list, the detail of which is suppressed from fear of offending those whose projects were not funded. The act of participation in government via the peer process seems to generate an equal and opposite effect of distancing governments from the controversial business of the arts. The much celebrated transfer of control over to communities (in this case, a community-of-interest defined by artform practice) places governments in a position of being blinded to their broader responsibilities to that very constituency—even if we think of those responsibilities in terms of an animating and facilitating rather than a controlling role (Donzelot, 1991; Rose, 1996, 2000 [this issue]). The participatory moment manages to conceal more knowledge than it reveals.

How could cultural sector professionals break the seal over their expertise in matters such as peer feedback to government? Perhaps making the grant process somewhat more transparent and publicly articulated could help. The expert criteria used in the process could be publicized and made more recognizable to both the general community and the government of the day. The specialist peer judgments of the sector must not be compromised, but publicizing the criteria (and to some extent making them contestable) might be one way of combating the charge of elitism, abstruseness, and perversity so often attributed to the arts.

Above all, cultural sector professionals must learn to wear different hats in different circumstances. They need to be open to ideas that might at first seem anathema and they need to adopt languages while playing an advocacy role that they might be uncomfortable using at any other time. Arts policy advocacy might be thought of as a performance role; after all, nobody should make a better advocate than a professional performer or a writer able to turn a phrase to pinpoint a problem.[13]

## CONCLUSION

The models of effective and responsible advocacy suggested here do not correspond to the morally prestigious conception of community participation as the political or collective equivalent of moral self-governance. We repudiate the blanket suspicion of expertise so often associated with this conception. The challenges facing the cultural sector illustrate our point that pushing control away from the bureaucracy and out into the community is far from empowering, either for the arts or for citizens in general. There is a place for arguments about the link between the cultural sector and the public good, but it is unlikely to be articulated by those who speak in the voice of the community or citizens in general. Hence, our emphasis on the need to develop models of the democratic role of expertise in government.

We have put the case that responsible participation in arts policy development might require those in the sector to develop some stronger rhetorical and strategic skills as advocates and as experts. The currently worsening climate for arts support has many contributing factors, some of which only the sector itself can work to correct. If political parties and governments of the day have become more responsive and even demotic in their style, then the sector must find ways of taking a more public-spirited seat at the policy table, as well as in wider forums of public debate. The intellectual work must be done by cultural sector professionals in every instance of policy formulation to ensure that politicians have the information available to make the right decision in the light of historical and contextual considerations. This is no mean task. It requires not only discipline but also the capacity to think in a disinterested way (as determined by the offices of participation, not by philosophy) about whether attention to the arts should be favoured above other challenges confronting the government of the day. A more calculated use of the ethical and rhetorical arts of professional self-presentation can help those in the arts to become more worldly about the workaday moral heterogeneity of these environments. Rather than stranding themselves on the high moral ground, as elitist and self-interested critics of political programs, arts bureaucrats, artsworkers, and advocates may be able to position themselves as experts between public opinion and politics.

## NOTES

1. The perspective on the ethics of participation offered here extends and qualifies arguments developed in Minson (1993, 1998, 2000). The latter will present a synthesis of the three very different intellectual traditions or disciplines that provide resources for raising questions along the following lines: (a) the genealogy of ethics and related historical and comparative studies of the formation of moral and political personhood (Foucault, 1992; Hunter, in press; Minson, 1993); (b) role ethics, especially as developed at the intersection of applied ethics and public administration (Condren, 1997; Rohr, 1978, 1994; Uhr, 1990, 1994); and (c) certain realist political science–based approaches to democracy (Di Palma, 1990; Sartori, 1987).

2. On the religious-fundamentalist lineage of participatory democracy, see J. Miller (1991), Shain (1994), Clark (1993), Phillips (1993), and Minson (2000).

3. Commitment to rational ideals is no guarantee of civility: *vide* Barber's (1982) egregious comparison between "the public rites of voting" in national elections and "using a public toilet" (p. 188).

4. See Manin (1997) on the historical presumption and the logical inevitability that the elected must be in some respects superior to those who elect them.

5. *Audience democracy* is an ideal-typical category that takes its meaning from Manin's (1997) argument that representative government, historically defined through a contrast with democratic self-rule, has had to become more demotic as mainstream parties struggle to maintain their traditional support base in volatile electorates, as broadcast and print media have become a more

important component of the political system, and as politicians' self-images rival party affiliation as a determinant of voting behavior.

6. See Minson (1993) on the implications of the ethical dimension of compromise for how we think about moral pressure to be public spirited, or the "laundering of preferences" effect (Goodin, 1986) in public discussion.

7. On the variety of purposes served by gag rules, see Holmes (1995, pp. 208-209).

8. We take these terms to refer to a diverse swag of structural reform processes aimed at shifting the role of government from providing services for the community to facilitating and stimulating competition within the marketplace in the name of improved services to the public and better value for the taxpayer's investment.

9. This is the subject of a current federal inquiry.

10. G. Davis (1998) describes the American policy dynamic as a "Heraclitean flux, the constant making and remaking of choices, in a system where change can embrace everything: the policy, the policy makers and the institutions they inhabit" (p. 37). The cultural sector's biggest impact is currently most notable in connection with voting on appropriations bills and during the now annual Arts Advocacy Day held in Washington, DC. Advocates corner Congressmen, draw their attention to pro-arts "opinion-editorials," and generally push home the vote for the arts in the most extraordinarily organized manner.

11. The strike rate for grant applications usually ranges from 1 in 4 to 1 in 8 applications. For example, in the Australia Council's 1996-1997 grant round, its Funds Board considered 5,225 formal applications (out of approximately 24,000 inquiries) from individual artists and organisations, seeking $158 million in funding. Altogether, 1,678 applications were successful (Australia Council, 1997).

12. These taboos arise from the difficulty of explaining to unsuccessful applicants the lack of relative merit of their artistic endeavors in a context where every recorded comment is subject to Freedom of Information legislation. Angst over this problem has arguably stifled opportunities to generalize about the current state of health of any artform sector as revealed through the submissions received.

13. Slogans, for instance, are a legitimate means of communicating complex problems to the general community and therefore to the government of the day. Speaking of the impact of festivals and musicals on local companies as the "suck out factor" (a term used in the Western Australian arts community) is a simple and compelling way of describing the negative effects that the blockbusters recently funded by government and the private sector have had on the audiences of local productions.

## REFERENCES

Australia Council. (1997). *Annual report* [Online]. Sydney: Australia Council. Available: http://www.ozco.gov.au

Barber, B. (1982). *Strong democracy: Participatory politics for a new age*. Berkeley: University of California Press.

Berger, P., & Neuhaus, R. (1977). *To empower people: The role of mediating structures in public policy*. Washington, DC: American Enterprise Institute for Public Policy Research.

Bourdieu, P. (1984). *Distinction: A social critique of the judgement of taste* (R. Nice, Trans.). Cambridge, MA: Harvard University Press.

Clark, J. (1993). *The language of liberty, 1660-1832: Political discourse and social dynamics in the Anglo-American world*. Cambridge, UK: Cambridge University Press.

Condren, C. (1997). Liberty of office and its defence in seventeenth century argument. *History of Political Theory, 18*(3), 460-482.

Considine, M. (1994). *Public policy: A critical approach*. Melbourne, Australia: Macmillan.

Davis, G. (1998). Policy from the margins: Reshaping the Australian Broadcasting Corporation. In A. Yeatman (Ed.), *Activism and the policy process* (pp. 36-55). St. Leonards, New South Wales: Allen & Unwin.

Davis, M. (1992). *City of quartz: Excavating the future in Los Angeles*. New York: Vintage.

Di Palma, G. (1990). *To craft democracy: An essay on democratic transitions*. Berkeley: University of California Press.

Donzelot, J. (1991). Le social du troisieme type. In J. Donzelot (Ed.), *Face l'exclusion: Le modèle français* (pp. 15-40). Paris, France: Editions Esprit.

Dugdale, P. (1998). The art of insider activism: Activism and the governance of health. In A. Yeatman (Ed.), *Activism and the policy process* (pp. 104-21). St. Leonards, New South Wales: Allen & Unwin.

Foucault, M. (1992). *The use of pleasures* (R. Hurley, Trans.). London: Penguin.

Goodin, R. (1986). Laundering preferences. In J. Elster & A. Hylland (Eds.), *Foundations of social choice theory* (pp. 75-101). Cambridge, UK: Cambridge University Press.

Holmes, S. (1995). *Passions and constraint: On the theory of liberal democracy*. Chicago: Chicago University Press.

Hunter, I. (in press). *Rival enlightenments: Civil and metaphysical philosophy in early modern Germany*. Cambridge, UK: Cambridge University Press.

Kingwell. M. (1998). *A civil tongue: Justice, dialogue, and the politics of pluralism*. University Park: Pennsylvania University Press.

Kymlicka, W., & Norman, W. (1995). Return of the citizen: A survey of recent work on citizenship theory. In R. Beiner (Ed.), *Theorizing citizenship* (pp. 283-322). New York: State University of New York Press.

Liberal and National Coalition. (1998). *For arts sake: A fair go*. Canberra, Australia: Author.

Lucas, J. (1974). *Democracy and participation*. London: Penguin.

Manin, B. (1997). *The principles of representative government*. Cambridge, UK: Cambridge University Press.

McNulty, R., with Page, C. (Eds.). (1994). *The state of the American community: Empowerment for local action*. Washington, DC: Partners for Livable Communities.

Miller, J. (1991). Direct democracy and the puritan theory of membership. *Journal of Politics, 55*(1), 56-74.

Miller, T. (2000). The National Endowment for the Arts in the 1990s: A black eye on the arts? *American Behavioral Scientist, 43*, 142-1445.

Minson, J. (1993). *Questions of conduct: Sexual harassment, citizenship, government*. London: Macmillan.

Minson, J. (1998). Ascetics and the demands of participation. *Political Theory Newsletter, 9*(1), 20-33.

Minson, J. (2000). *Civilizing democracy: Civility and "metacivics" in the ethics of citizenship*. Unpublished manuscript, University of Technology.

Office of Multicultural Affairs. (1994). *Consulting the multicultural way: Guidelines for Australian public service managers consulting and negotiating with non-English speaking background groups*. Canberra, Australia: Australian Government Publishing.

Osborne, D. (1994). Osborne Foreword. In R. McNulty with C. Page (Eds.), *The state of the American community: Empowerment for local action* (pp. xi-xiii). Washington, DC: Partners for Livable Communities.

Pateman, C. (1970). *Participation and democratic theory*. Cambridge, UK: Cambridge University Press.

Phillips, D. (1993). *Looking backwards: A critical appraisal of communitarian thought*. Princeton, NJ: Princeton University Press.

Rohr, J. (1978). *Ethics for bureaucrats*. New York: Dekker.

Rohr, J. (1994, Spring). The problem of professional ethics. *The Bureaucrat, the Journal for Public Managers*, pp. 9-12.

Rose, N. (1996). The death of the social: Refiguring the territory of government. *Economy and Society, 25*(3), 327-356.

Rose, N. (2000). Community, citizenship, and the Third Way. *American Behavioral Scientist, 43,* 1395-1411.

Sartori, G. (1987). *The theory of democracy revisited. Volume 1: The contemporary debate.* Chatham, NJ: Chatham House.

Shain, B. (1994). *The myth of American individualism: The Protestant origins of American political thought.* Princeton, NJ: Princeton University Press.

Shklar, J. (1984). *Ordinary vices.* Cambridge, MA: Belknap Press of Harvard University Press.

Skinner, Q. (1996). *Reason and rhetoric in the philosophy of Hobbes.* Cambridge, UK: Cambridge University Press.

Uhr, J. (1990). *Ethics in government: Public service issues* [Discussion Paper No. 19]. Australian National University Graduate Program in Public Policy. Canberra, Australia: Public Policy Program.

Uhr, J. (1994). Public service ethics in Australia. In T. Cooper (Ed.), *Handbook of administrative ethics* (pp. 551-569). New York: Dekker.

Weber, M. (1948). Politics as a vocation. In H. Gerth & C. Mills (Eds.), *From Max Weber: Essays in sociology* (pp. 77-128). London: Routledge Kegan Paul.

Yeatman, A. (Ed.). (1998). *Activism and the policy process.* St. Leonards, New South Wales: Allen & Unwin.

# 5. Popular Sovereignty and Civic Education

IAN HUNTER
*Griffith University*
DENISE MEREDYTH
*Swinburne University of Technology*

> *This article addresses some of the problems inherent in attempts to understand citizenship education through the concept of popular sovereignty and the formation of self-governing citizens. It does so via a historical investigation of the processes responsible for the separation of sovereignty and government and sovereignty and moral truth in the early modern state. It is argued that in losing sight of the importance of these separations for the formation of liberal pluralist states, current philosophical liberalism risks turning the school system into an instrument of moral coercion, jeopardizing its role as an instrument of social governance.*

**There is worldwide acceptance** of the need for national and international citizenship education. Yet time and again, initiatives to meet this need run into seemingly insoluble controversies. Rehearsals and attempted resolutions of these controversies in political theory appear only to compound them. This article identifies some neglected conceptual and historical sources of these recurrent problems. It argues that the cultural controversies in which citizenship initiatives are embroiled stem from the prevailing assumption, on all sides of debate, that the moral consensus that citizenship education seeks to build can only be understood and legitimated in terms of a concept of popular sovereignty. To underscore the insidious implications of exclusive reliance on this concept by the main rival theoretical contenders, this article digs up some telling historical antecedents of this way of addressing cultural antagonism. To this end, it draws out the parallels between postmodern cultural particularist approaches and the coercive Calvinist communitarianism of Althusius and between liberal universalists and the intensely religiose political metaphysics of Kant. The capstone of the argument is a brief epitome of the alternative early modern conception of state sovereignty developed by Pufendorf and Thomasius, an alternative that has been crucial to the formation of liberal pluralist states. This article explores the contemporary relevance of this supplementary way of legitimating the exercise of state authority, applying it to recent debates on schooling, cultural dissensus, and critical reason. These contemporary examples suggest that, in losing sight of this historically important conception of state sovereignty, modern political and

---

**Authors' Note:** *The authors thank Jeffrey Minson for editorial suggestions and the Australian Research Council for research support.*

educational theorists also ignore the hard-won separations between sovereignty, government, and higher moral truth on which it rests. Consequently, the theory and practice of contemporary citizenship risk turning the school system into an instrument of moral coercion, jeopardizing its role as an instrument of social governance.

## INTERNATIONAL AND NATIONAL CITIZENSHIP EDUCATION INITIATIVES

We are in the midst of a new enthusiasm for active citizenship and civic education. Recently, there has been extensive international discussion of the common problems of civic renewal facing both established and new democracies (Archibugi & Held, 1995; Dauenhauer, 1996; Oliveira, Tandon, & CIVICUS, 1994). The activity has been generated at an international level through bodies such as United Nations Educational, Scientific, and Cultural Organizations (UNESCO) (Augier, 1994; Meyer-Bish, 1995). It has also been addressed in regional and national policy debates in Britain, Canada, and Australia and in the context of the European Union (see, e.g., Bell, 1995). In the United States, national standards for civic education have been introduced through the Goals 2000: Educate America Act (1994). Also, in Australia, concerns about low standards of political literacy have generated a national civics curriculum program (Kemp, 1997). Much of the activity, especially in the United States, has been generated by private foundations and voluntary associations such as the Center for Civic Education (Quigley & Bahmueller, 1991). These have been supported by online forums, many of which emphasize the need for free and private association between the civic-minded as an answer to the problems of poor moral standards impossible to address through government action. These networks now extend internationally throughout Eastern and Central Europe, South America, Africa, and Asia. Although some hope to rebuild national identity, others aim to transcend and undermine it. If education for democracy is true to democratic principles, it is argued, then it must involve an organic connection to authentic local and global communities (e.g., Dufty, 1995; Jensen, 1995; Kreisberg, 1993).

It is important not to underestimate differences in the terms of these national debates on civic education, especially the historical differences between the American civics tradition and other "settler societies" such as Canada, Australia, and New Zealand (Merriam, 1931), but there are common elements, too. These include the invocation of an apocalyptic language of crisis. The rise of new democracies, it seems, has brought us to the threshold of a new age: "something is on the way out and something else is painfully being born. It is as if something were crumbling, decaying and exhausting itself, while something else, still indistinct, were arising from the rubble" (Havel, 1994, cited in Hughes, 1994, p. 175). The centrifugal forces of change have provided national and international agencies of government some unease, given the fear that the enthusiasm for civic participation could escalate into civic discord and violence. Bodies such as the International Commission on Education for the Twenty-First Century regard international movements for civic education as a remedy.

> In the future education would unquestionably have a greater role to play in the promotion of values: values related to all the attitudes, capacities and competencies required to live in harmony with one's own society and with other societies. Education could, and must, make the difference between an inexorable slide into degeneration and decline of human civilization and the discovery of new patterns of progress and tolerance. The eternal dialectics in education are between teaching of values and the neutrality of education . . . between the simultaneous needs to prepare for both individual freedom and solidarity, both autonomy and responsibility. (International Commission on Education, 1993, cited in Hughes, 1994, pp. 175-176)

The eternal dialectics alluded to in this passage point to a second point of commonality in these citizenship education initiatives, a particular way of framing the problem that all national education systems have to confront: namely, that of achieving consensus about the substance of civic education. The overwhelming tendency is to pose this problem in terms of a tension between the competing claims of cultural particularism and a liberal universalism that, even where it favors some values over others, justifies its choice in terms of a critical form of reasoning that allegedly transcends cultural limits. One expression of this tension is the often reiterated statement that consensus depends on striking a balance "between developing commitment to certain norms and values, whilst also offering opportunities for critical and reflective thinking" (Moon, 1994, cited in Hughes, 1994, p. 176). The eternal dialectics that recur include the following: Should schools teach core civic values, however contentious the issues raised, or does this breach the neutrality of state schooling? How is the balance between *solidarity* and *freedom* to be struck, given the current oscillation between optimism and unease about how much consensus can be expected in new democracies forged from multiethnic and multifaith communities?

The problem faces established democracies as much as new ones. Given the culture wars waged in the United States over political correctness, curriculum frameworks there have to be conspicuously pluralist and ecumenical in their philosophical emphasis (Quigley & Bahmueller, 1991). They must anticipate arguments for representative inclusion of indigenous or minority cultures while avoiding charges of either cultural appropriation or indoctrination. Civic educators have argued that, with appropriate concern for pluralism, it is possible to identify a minimal level of knowledges, skills, and values that all future citizens should possess (e.g., Bellah, 1985; Civics Expert Group, 1994; Pratte, 1988). But teachers continue to face the issue of how they are to promote a moral commitment to democratic values while fostering a liberal pluralistic acceptance of minority cultures (Butts, 1988; Callan, 1994).

For many, the answer lies in critical dialogue. Not only should students be asked to exercise their critical reason, but schools should encourage debate in both the classroom and the community to generate an articulate consensus on the values that should be taught (Levitt & Longstreet, 1993). Nevertheless, the objection remains that there is no single community and that to insist on unanimity, or even on participation in certain debates, is morally coercive. These objections to the bureaucratic monopoly on public morality are usually made in the name of individual liberal freedoms—conscience, self-determination, and choice (e.g., Donnelly, 1997)—as well as by those speaking in the name of excluded cultural identities, including women, indigenous communities, and ethnic groups (Kaltsounis, 1997; Torres, 1998).

The problem is how to reconcile centralist bureaucratic objectives focused on national problems of apathy, ignorance, and civic estrangement with the rhetorical appeal to popular sovereignty and to the core values of the moral community. There is little dispute that the school system has a responsibility to assist all citizens to understand key electoral, political, legal, and constitutional facts; that it should require them to develop historical understanding of important national debates; and that it should develop a core of values and ethical capacities. The central problem remains: Even as it is supposed to be expressing the moral consensus of the political community, civic education is in fact designed to construct such a consensus in the interests of social health, national security, and civil peace.

These debates on civic education replay a classic problem of liberal-democratic governance (Hindess, 1997). In democratically organized polities, the legitimacy of sovereign governance is widely held to depend on the free choice of the governed, which presumes the widespread existence of a capacity to exercise such choice, but there are routine doubts about the extent to which actual citizenries are capable of informed choice and of exercising freedoms. The question thus arises as to how the state can secure the conditions of freedom—the forms of civic conduct and capacities on which legitimate government depends—without impinging on freedom or transforming it into a mere artefact of government. As long as the popular democratic legitimacy of the state is taken to be the decisive factor, then the discussion of liberal-democratic government oscillates helplessly between the insistence on free choice and anxiety about the role of government in forming the capacity for it. The central reason for this cul-de-sac, we suggest, is lack of attention to the other, nondemocratic justification for the existence of sovereign power, the state's role in maintaining security. Failure to recognize the decisive nature of this second justification means that the liberal state's role in ensuring security through building the civil capacities of its citizens is routinely misunderstood. Under these circumstances, it is confused with the popular democratic justification of state sovereignty, leading to a situation in which the building of capacities is dogged by the appeal to a preexisting moral-political community, and the education of reasonable citizens is haunted by the appeal to preexisting "rational beings."

These issues have been articulately discussed at the level of international cultural policy initiatives. One such instance is the still developing UNESCO International Bureau of Education's What Education for What Citizenship? project, launched in 1994, which aims to establish international benchmarks for civic education in 34 nations, most of them new democracies (Albala-Bertrand, 1997a). Through a process of research, consultation, and shared expertise, new democracies will find their own way to teach the international liberal values of peace, toleration, pluralism, and democratic process. The program is construed as a humanitarian intervention by the international community, designed to redress the social costs of economic internationalization and the transition to liberal-democratic rule while maintaining stability in tension-riven territories.

The working documents for the program differ, as we shall see, from philosophical rehearsals of these problems, exhibiting a telling mixture of statist concern for security and moral-philosophical concerns about the prerequisites of a just society. Drawing on a Rawlsian philosophical-liberal version of *modus vivendi*, global civic education is seen as a social means to build a universal cosmopolitan moral culture. The entry point for this common action is the similarity between cultures discovered through international dialogue and expert empirical research. The working rationales stress the systematic, comparative, and representative approach to the study of civic and political socialization, building on studies initially conducted in Western industrialized countries. The goal of international dialogue and expert intervention is

> to favour the expression of differences—sources of enrichment and creativity—and the emergence of . . . Everywhere that democracy is sought, some specific functional and ethical conditions should exist. It is clear, however that similar functions may be accomplished by different cultural elements; what is important here is not that different societies must share the same sets of values, knowledges and institutions to become democratic, but rather that their values and institutions lead to a distinct democratic ethos. (Albala-Bertrand, 1997b)

"World events are there to remind us," the working papers remark, "that democracy and the rule of law are not historical necessities, are not ineluctable, but a victory of human moral sense that needs constantly to be reinforced and renewed in the minds of all individuals." (Albala-Bertrand, 1997c).

These bureaucratically organized philanthropic enterprises can be seen as instances of international governance in a liberal mode (Hindess, 2000 [this issue]). They are related to a variety of factors, including the increasing role of international NGOs in cultural policy and the extension of international legal agreements between sovereign nations in part through the agency of human rights advocates (Yeatman, 2000 [this issue]). Less sanguinely, these programs can also be described as forms of Western political and cultural imperialism, imposing liberal-democratic forms of governance on alien political cultures while disavowing the enabling condition of their success: the hegemony of the West—the United States in particular—in the post-Westphalian system of states (Falk, 1981, pp. 33-62).

A more complex criticism might identify dangers in assuming that dialogue, consultation, and expertise could perform the work of civil settlement required to secure peace in regions torn by civil war and ethnic and religious strife, making self-governing community capable of containing cultural conflict and violence (cf. Khilnani, 1991). Ideals of cosmopolitanism pale beside the concrete difficulties of pacifying a diverse and divided citizenry, and then equipping it for peaceful civil coexistence. Asserting membership and belonging as norms is all very well, but it is harder to work out criteria for membership, much less how to incorporate new members, build a community of interests, and construct some congruence between membership and the ability to exercise political-legal rights and duties. Nor will an educated consensus on the core values of democratic equality and self-determination remove the explosive potential of economic disparities, caste, ethnic or religious faction, or sexual oppression.

Nevertheless, such international cultural policy programs cannot be dismissed as merely theoretical or aspirational, any more than we would dismiss the impact of the liberal philosophical formulations driving the international efforts to establish an international legal recognition of human rights (Yeatman, 2000). As in that case, liberal moral philosophical discourse has concrete effects in structuring problems and options both for international cultural policy programs and for national civic education efforts. However, the problem lies in gaining a clear insight into the kind of effect such discourse has and, in particular, disentangling its role in forming enlightened public opinion from its less salubrious function as the moral face of Western political hegemony, should such a separation prove possible. There is little point in chiding these initiatives for their eclectic resort to both philosophical-liberal concerns about just consensus and statist concerns with stability. As we shall see in the next section, the application of purist theoretical solutions cannot solve the tension between common civic formation and the invocation of cultural difference and cultural rights: On the contrary, such efforts only succeed in deepening the moral-philosophical traps and circularities encountered in the cultural policy initiatives.

## THEORIZING CIVIC EDUCATION

When discussing the education of citizens, moral and political philosophers focus on the problem of forming the virtues—mutual respect, equality, rational deliberation—required for individuals to participate in liberal democratic government. Their discussion of this problem is shaped by a specific question: the question of how the state can form the political will of its citizens while remaining the expression of this will. In using this question to frame their discussion of the education of citizens, the philosophers display their prior commitment to a specifically democratic conception of sovereignty; for this problem only appears where it is assumed that the state only legitimately exercises supreme political power as the representative of a common will.

This problem, we have suggested, is endemic to discussions of liberal democratic government, arising perhaps from intractable difficulties in formulating the relation between the liberal and the democratic in this form of governance. But the factor that has given recent discussion of this problem its peculiar intensity is the appearance of arguments stressing the cultural difference of specific ethnic or religious communities and advocating the recognition of differentiated cultural and political rights on this basis. On the surface at least, the ensuing debate has been quite polarized. Advocates of cultural difference and community-specific rights have typically accused liberalism of abstracting individuals from their cultural identities and imposing an alien culture (White, male, Eurocentric) in the name of universal political virtues (cf. Baykan, 1997; Parekh, 1997; see, e.g., Young, 1987). For their part, liberal moral and political philosophers have been seeking means for harmonizing minority cultures within a general conception of democratic sovereignty grounded in rational choice (see, e.g., Feinberg, 1998; Kymlicka, 1995; Taylor & Gutmann, 1992).

The defenders of democratic liberalism have developed their response to cultural particularism in a variety of ways (see Kymlicka & Norman, 1994). Some have argued that the degree of cultural consensus (commonality of will) required for democratic sovereignty can be acquired through the exercise of rationality; for example, by making debates over different versions of the "good life" central to schooling (Gutmann, 1987). Others have resorted to variants on liberal philosophical theories of justice "to distinguish between those [incendiary] questions that can be reasonably removed from the political agenda and those that cannot" (Rawls, 1996, p. 151; cf. Callan, 1997; Kingwell, 1995). Still others, although remaining committed to the notion of a universal rational choice among cultures, have nonetheless attempted to make membership of a particular culture into a condition of such choice (Kymlicka, 1989). Then there are those, skeptical that public-spirited education can defeat the culture of economic self-interest, who hold out less hope for a common education in the democratic virtues, falling back on Kant's belief that cultural conflict will itself see to the education of mankind (Rorty, 1995).

From our viewpoint, however, the commonalities between the two sides of the debate are no less striking than the differences. The opposing positions both assume a democratic conception of sovereignty, holding that the supreme power should express the communal will and differing only over the question of how the communal will should be delimited and represented. The advocates of cultural difference and cultural rights argue that communal will is formed in the customs, rituals, and beliefs of a particular culture or way of life, typically that of a distinct religious or ethnic community. On this basis, they argue that the state should recognize a variety of community-specific cultural and political rights. For their part, the defenders of democratic liberalism continue to argue that some sort of common political culture—negotiated, overlapping—can be formed through rational deliberation or dialogue, thereby allowing the state to govern on the basis of a single general will and giving recognition to a single set of citizen rights. The conflict between the cultural particularists and the liberal universalists is thus not over the validity of popular sovereignty but over how it should be configured: as the representation of several culturally distinct communal wills or as the representation of a single communal will formed through rational negotiation of the competing cultures or versions of the good life.

In what follows, we argue that this debate is irresolvable in its current terms. The fact that both sides conceive the functions and legitimacy of the sovereign power in terms of its representation of a communal will mortgages the debate to an indecisive contest between rival schools of political metaphysics and imbues it with an undesirable moral absolutism. Only when this notion of sovereignty has been cleared away do the cultural and political functions of education become visible in a clearer and calmer light.

## THE POLITICAL COMMUNITY AND THE MORAL COMMUNITY

Lucky punch or not, in targeting the problem of the cultural formation of the political common will, the advocates of cultural difference have found philosophical liberalism's glass jaw. In doing so they have highlighted a problem with which post-Kantian political philosophy is ill-equipped to deal: the problem of the gap between an ideal communal will based on the universal community of rational or moral beings, and historically existing communal wills based on pedagogical discipline or political coercion. Seen historically, this problem first emerged for European polities during the 16th century when, with the emergence of rival Christian confessions, civil and religious government could no longer rely on the de facto social unity provided by the existence of a single religious culture. The construction of popular sovereignty doctrines provided one way of meeting this problem.

In fact, there are disconcerting parallels between some of these early modern solutions and those suggested by adherents of the politics of difference school. An exemplary illustration of these parallels is the recent attempt by an advocate of cultural difference, Daniel Elazar, to resurrect the early modern popular sovereignty doctrine of Althusius as a precursor for the cause. For Joahannes Althusius, whose *Politica* appeared in 1603, some 15 years prior to the outbreak of the Thirty Years War, the gap between the ideal and the real community presented no insurmountable problem. For Althusius, the twin functions of sovereignty (the achievement of man's physical welfare and spiritual salvation through the unified exercise of supreme power) are jointly grounded in the communio or "universal symbiotic communication" of the community, whose common will is thus the source of both the supremacy and the legitimacy of political power

(Althusius, 1603/1995, pp. 6-7, 69-78). The commonality of the general will is in turn grounded in the culture of a unified religious community (in this case, the ecclesiastical culture of Calvinism), which means that the common will responsible for the functions and legitimacy of democratic sovereignty is formed in an actually existing communal culture.

Althusius, argues Elazar, was "eclipsed for three centuries by the major thrust of the modern epoch toward the homogeneous nation-state built around the individual citizen, standing naked before the state machinery." Now, however,

> Althusian ideas seem much more in place in the postmodern epoch, with its more modern political networks, its renewed recognition of primordial groups and political associations as part and parcel of contemporary political life, and its federalistic striving for both universalism and particularism, ecumene and community. (Elazar, 1995, p. xlvi)

In his desire to provide a pedigree for a postmodern theory of difference, Elazar passes too lightly over the costs of grounding sovereignty in a political will whose commonality derives from the culture of a real moral community. For given that the state is legitimate only to the extent that it represents this common will, the state must act to maintain and enforce the (religious) culture in which this will is formed. Althusius thus declares that popular sovereignty includes the "sacerdotal" right to provide public schools "for the conserving of true religion and the passing of it on to later generations," commenting that "whatever the quality of the rulers and citizens the school produces, of such is the commonwealth and church constituted." This sovereignty also includes

> the right and power of restoring the uncorrupted worship of God, or expelling from the territory those alien to uncorrupted religion, and of compelling the citizens and inhabitants of the realm, by public ordinances and even by force, to worship God (Althusius, 1603/1995, p. 76).

The problem with deriving popular sovereignty's common will from an actual moral culture is that it requires the sovereign power to impose this culture as a condition of citizenship, by educational discipline if possible, through civil coercion and religious cleansing if necessary. Hence, although Althusius's (1603/1995) version of popular sovereignty and popular education provides the exercise of the sovereign power with moral legitimacy, it does so only at the cost of unifying the political and moral communities—the duties of the citizen and the Christian—with the result that civil rights are attached to participation in a particular moral culture. This is the recipe for cultural intolerance and religious civil war. The appeal to Althusian ideas in order to give recognition to primordial groups and political associations is perhaps less a sign of the transition to postmodernity than of the fact that we have not yet left the premodern epoch of confessional politics and religious war.

Elaborated nearly two centuries after Althusius's, Kant's construction of democratic sovereignty attempts to avoid the problems confronting its predecessor by incorporating two strategies that not only anticipate the modern liberal universalist recipes for coping with cultural conflict but also expose their religiose dogmatic streak. First, Kant attempts to avoid mortgaging the common will to an historical moral culture by deriving it instead from an ideal metaphysical conception of man as a rational being (*vernunftige Wesen*). For Kant, man's *humanität* or essential virtues (freedom, equality, and autonomy) arise from his immaterial intellectual substance, which is spontaneously self-determining and self-acting in accordance with a self-imposed moral law (Kant, 1948). In the moral domain, when men slough off their sensory attachments and inclinations and conduct themselves as pure intelligences, their communion of will is spontaneous, transparent, and immediate as they form a single spiritual community or "kingdom of ends."

> Now since laws determine ends as regards their universal validity, we shall be able—if we abstract from the personal differences between rational beings, and also from all the content of their private ends—to conceive a whole of all ends in systematic conjunction. (Kant, 1948, pp. 100-101).

In the juridical domain, formed when the immaterial intelligences exercise their freedom in order to possess material things, the commercium of wills is mediated through the principle of justice (*recht*) rather than the moral law. Here, the general will emerges via the universal reciprocal coercion that renders my rights (of possession) compatible with everyone else's.

> For a right against every possessor of a thing means only an authorization on the part of someone's particular choice to use an object, insofar as this authorization can be thought as contained in a synthetic general will and as in accord with the law of this will. (Kant, 1996, p. 420)

The Kantian moral law and principle of justice would thus appear to be based on a community of wills owing nothing to any particular empirical moral culture, arising instead from the rational being of the intelligences themselves, which permits them transparent intersubjectivity in the moral realm and mutual recognition of rights in the political-juridical realm.

Second, Kant attempts to avoid the problem of religious civil war by confining coercion to the external legal-political domain (civil society) and insisting that the actions of intelligences in the internal moral domain (spiritual community) are intrinsically free (Kant, 1996). Thus, Kant restricts the use of legal-political coercion to the preservation of external civil security, but he continues to make the legitimate exercise of sovereign power dependent on its expressing the common will. He does this by restricting the exercise of coercion to those acts infringing the principle of reciprocal freedom of choice (rights of possession) exercised by the totality of intelligences; that is, the principle of justice

(Kant, 1996). Kant's conception of a state acting in accordance with the principle of justice (the rule of law) is thus equivalent to the idea of a state acting in accordance with the common will. Kant's principle of justice is dependent on the notion of a general will both to determine this ideal reciprocal distribution of rights and to enforce it through the exercise of supreme power (Kant, 1996). Summarily then, Kant attempts to close the gap between the ideal and the real community—thereby solving the problem of cultural particularism—by grounding the common will in a universal metaphysical anthropology of man as a rational being. He attempts to solve the problem of cultural or religious civil war by restricting civil coercion to conduct infringing the reciprocal exercise of external freedom by the members of a "just" community.

To the extent, though, that Kant's solutions inform the work of today's philosophical liberals, they fall short of their goal in both regards. First, the attempt to abstract the formation of a common will from any empirical moral culture (to "abstract from the personal differences between rational beings, and also from all the content of their private ends") seems to produce a dilemma for modern defenders of the rational universal basis of democratic sovereignty. On one hand, it leads back to the assumption that humans are intrinsically rational by virtue of their intellectual substance and hence capable of arriving at political consensus (common will), independently of any particular moral culture or citizenship education, simply through exercising a quasi-ontological capacity for rational deliberation. This solves the debate over the cultural conditions of citizenship, but only by ignoring it and at the cost of introducing a concept of reason ungrounded in either pedagogy or history. On the other hand, however, it leads to the de facto adoption of some particular moral culture or discipline of rational deliberation that, because it is thought to be grounded in man's rational being, is not recognized for what it is: one instituted moral culture among others. This is the problem with the solution Kant (1996) proposes in the *Metaphysics of Morals*, where he discusses the cultivation of the virtues required to act on the basis of the moral law in terms of adopting certain "objectively necessary" ends (Kant, 1996, p. 513). Such a solution threatens to resolve cultural conflicts through the pedagogical imposition of a particular culture—one powerful enough to determine which ends count as "objectively necessary"—in accordance with the democratic sovereign's need for a common will in order to remain legitimate.

The insidious effects of this dilemma can be seen in Gutmann's (1995) discussion of the French controversy about whether Muslim girls should be permitted to wear *chadors* (head coverings associated with Muslim orthodoxy and the subordination of women) in schools dedicated to the education of civil equals. According to Gutmann, it is possible to solve this problem—and, indicatively, the more general problem of reconciling cultural particularism and liberal-democratic universalism—by making the wearing of chadors into a topic of school debate. She treats this as an instance of the more general process through which democratic education teaches future citizens to choose between different cultures or versions of the good life. This solution, though, shows the full force of the above-mentioned dilemma. On one hand, Gutmann's (1995) assumption that converting the problem into a topic for classroom debate will automatically resolve it—rather than, for example, exacerbate cultural tensions—is indicative of a deeper metaphysical assumption. This is the Kantian assumption that the students are already rational beings, capable of "mutual respect and rational deliberation" independent of all educational enculturation and thereby able to choose between different cultures on the basis of a transcendent rationality. On the other hand, it is clear that the classroom debate is itself conceived of as an exercise in enculturation of the virtues: an exercise designed to transform prior cultural dispositions through the imposition of a culture of rational deliberation in the name of forming the common will required for democratic sovereignty.

> Democratic education would not force the girls to give up wearing chadors in class, but it would expose them to a public culture of gender equality in public school. This exposure gives them reasons why women should view themselves as the civic equals of men, and it opens up opportunities (to pursue a career or hold public office, for example) that are not offered by their families and religious communities. By opening up such opportunities, democratic education may lessen the likelihood that certain kinds of cultural practices will perpetuate themselves. A democratic government should not go out of its way to perpetuate cultural practices that conflict with its constitutive principles. (Gutmann, 1995, p. 8)

More generally, we can suggest that the attempt to reconcile cultural particularism and democratic universalism, by turning cultural membership into both the condition and the object of rational deliberation, involves an intellectual sleight of hand. The practice of rational deliberation and free choice, as understood in Kantian political metaphysics, is itself highly culturally specific and must be imposed without prior rational deliberation. Here, the intellectualist culture of European metaphysics creates a blindspot with regard to practices of non-European religious cultures. Fully committed to the idea of its own grounding in free rational being, and completely oblivious to the religious inheritance and ascetic role of this intellectualist anthropology, the culture of rationalist metaphysics can only view other comportment educations—here the complex mix of religious ideas and body techniques associated with the wearing of the chador—as failures in relation to the intellectualist ethos.

Second, in this context, Kant's restriction of coercion to actions infringing the reciprocal harmonization of free choices (rights) gives rise to an unexpected outcome: namely, the use of coercion to achieve this harmonization. This is because, for Kant, the harmonization of wills, brought about through entrance into civil society, is constitutive of the "just condition." Hence, it is just for the democratic state to compel this harmonization of wills in order to fashion an empirical approximation of the ideal community of intelligences on which its legitimacy is based. This is what leads Gutmann to insist that the Muslim girls must be exposed to public deliberation on the civic rationality of their religious dress and deportment, which may lead to the abandonment of this cultural practice if it is one that conflicts with the constitutive principles of democratic government.

The intolerance harbored in Gutmann's preparedness to force the girls to be free becomes clear when we consider her reasons for rejecting the alternative solution to the problem advanced by the French Conseil d'Etat. The council had proposed that the wearing of religious symbols be permissible if it does not entail "pressure on others, provocation, propaganda, or proselytism" (Gutmann, 1995, p. 7). Gutmann rejects this solution in part because it would be unjust to make the Muslim girls responsible were others to be provoked by their dress. More fundamentally, though, she regards the council's strategy of toleration, based on the state's religious neutrality, as incompatible with democratic education. For if popular sovereignty's common will is to have a rational basis, then democratic education must compel students to exercise rational choice among the (religious) cultures forming this will.

> Non-neutrality is a necessity because an educational program would be empty were it to rest upon neutrality among different conceptions of the good life. Non-neutrality, more interestingly, is a virtue because citizens should support an educational system only if it is not neutral between those ways of life that respect basic liberty, opportunity, and deliberation, and those that do not. A liberal democracy should take its own side in arguments about the teaching of the skills and virtues that are constitutive of its own flourishing. (Gutmann, 1995, p. 8)

In other words, her Kantian insistence that its exercise be rational and just means that Gutmann refuses to countenance the moral neutrality of the sovereign power. It leads her to insist instead that state schools expose future citizens to debate about their moral-religious cultures, compelling them to enter the forcing house of the common will to secure the moral legitimacy of political compulsion.

We may suggest, then, that the important feature of the arguments between cultural particularists and philosophical liberals is not their disagreement over the universality of the communal will, but their shared assumption that the functions and legitimacy of the sovereign power derive from its representation of this will. Those who, like the Calvinist Althusius's postmodern champion Elazar, are again seeking to tie popular sovereignty's common will to actually existing communal cultures will rightly be reminded by liberals of the link between cultural particularism and cultural violence, whose full force Europe experienced during the 17th century and which remains a problem that all secular states must deal with. Despite its commitment to rationality and justice, however, philosophical liberalism is in turn equally incapable of confronting this problem; for driven by its own commitment to popular sovereignty, it is forced to make the metaphysical culture underpinning its ideas of reason and justice compulsory.

In so doing, philosophical liberalism loses touch with a different rationale for the legitimacy of the sovereign power: its capacity to maintain social peace and security. The parting of the ways is marked in Gutmann's refusal of the strategy proposed by the Conseil d'Etat. In arguing the state's right to compel its citizens to debate their religious cultures, Gutmann is driven by the idea that the functions and legitimacy of the state derive from the common will. This idea is held without consideration of any threats to social peace arising from such a policy, presumably on the grounds that social violence will be precluded through the process of rational deliberation and reciprocal harmonization of wills. In advocating a policy of toleration and indifference toward religious cultures (unless these involve pressure on others, provocation, propaganda, or proselytism), the council is locating a different source for the functions and legitimacy of the sovereign power: the maintenance of civil peace. Here, it is not the people's will that authorizes the exercise of irresistible coercive power, but their safety as determined by a superior political agency: *saluus populi est supreme lex*.

Despite its insouciant dismissal by the political metaphysicians, the policy of the Conseil d'Etat puts us in touch with a powerful nondemocratic form of liberalism whose conception of sovereignty goes a long way to solving the problems of cultural particularism versus the moral coercion required by liberal universalism in the debate over citizenship education. This form of liberalism emerged in the aftermath of the Thirty Years War, finding its most powerful German articulation in the political and natural jurisprudence of Samuel Pufendorf and Christian Thomasius, only to be forgotten, or rather politically ousted again (at least, in philosophical circles), with the rise of Kantianism (Tuck, 1987). It was Pufendorf in particular who showed how the early modern state could govern religiously divided communities, and he did so by introducing two fundamental divisions into moral and political philosophy: the separation of sovereignty from the form of government and the separation of sovereignty from moral will.

## SOVEREIGNTY AND GOVERNMENT, SOVEREIGNTY AND TRUTH

Pufendorf's reconstruction of sovereignty was based on a profound departure from existing moral- and political-philosophical conceptions. In the first three books of his massive *De Jure Naturae et Gentium in Libri Octo* (The Law of Nature and of Nations in Eight Books) (1672/1934) he used a powerful mix of theological voluntarism, Ciceronian duty theory, and German *staatsrecht* (political jurisprudence) to create a moral anthropology that he hoped would provide the basis for a civil ethics and secular politics. The outcome of this reworking is an image of man cut off from divine reason and metaphysical insight by a nature imposed on him for no fathomable reason, but giving rise to absolute duties. Man, for Pufendorf, is a being whose weakness means that he must be sociable to survive, but whose fractious mind and vicious passions stand in the way of sociability. This means that the natural ethical law is no longer derived from man's rational and social nature or from the higher rational being that he shares with God or reason. Rather, it is derived from his actual historical nature, whose need for sociality and capacity for mutual violence means that natural law reaches no higher than the end of this-worldly security. In the *De Officio Hominis et Civis* (On the Duty of Man and Citizen) (the student epitome of the *De Jure* published in the following year) Pufendorf (1673/1991) summarized the broad results of his secularisation of ethics.

> But by far the greatest difference [from moral theology] is that the scope of the discipline of natural law is confined within the orbit of this life, and so it forms man on the assumption that he is to lead this life in society with others. Moral theology, however, forms a Christian man, who, beyond his duty to pass this life in goodness, has an expectation of reward for piety in the life to come and who therefore has his citizenship [politeuma] in the heavens while here he lives as a pilgrim or stranger. (Pufendorf, 1673/1991, pp. 8-9)

Through this secularisation of ethics, Pufendorf not only expelled holiness and rational autonomy from the domain of civil ethics, consigning them to the sphere of moral theology, he also laid the basis for a secularisation of politics. Now he could reject the traditional Aristotelian doctrine that man enters civil state to perfect his moral nature as well as confessional-democratic improvisations on this theme of the Althusian kind, arguing instead that men enter the civil state solely to attain security by finding protection from each other. This conception of sovereignty is reflected in Pufendorf's version of the social contract or political pact, which men enter into not as a means of communio and self-realization, but in order to overcome the problems posed to sociability and security by their congenitally divided minds and staggeringly destructive passions. Hence, in Pufendorf's political pact, individuals achieve the unified political will and the supreme political force of sovereignty not by achieving actual or rational commonality of will—which Pufendorf regards as fantasmatic—but by giving up their wills to a single person or assembly in all matters pertaining to common security (Pufendorf, 1673/1991, pp. 135-138). The outcome of this pact is not the realization of man's prior moral personality, but the creation of two reciprocally related moral personae or offices: those of the political subject, characterized by the duty of obedience to the ruler in all matters pertaining to social peace, and the sovereign, whose duty is to maintain the security of his subjects through his governance of civil society.

For Pufendorf, then, the functions and legitimacy of the sovereign power come not from a higher religious or moral right, but from its being an artificial arrangement entered into by men solely for the purpose of achieving security from each other. If the functions and legitimacy of supreme civil power come from the achievement of social peace—through the deployment of this power as a unified and irresistible capacity for political decision and action—then it stands in no need of any higher right or justification, whether this is supposed to flow from the will of God, the will of a particular moral community, or an abstracted universal rational will.

This, then, was the basis on which Pufendorf divided sovereignty from government. Sovereignty is the function of exercising supreme political decision and power for the end of social peace. This function, though, can be exercised in several ways or by several forms of government: specifically, through monarchical, aristocratic, or democratic forms, depending on whether the office of sovereign is occupied by a single person, an assembly of nobles, or an assembly of the people. Despite his occasional expressions in favour of monarchy on technical grounds, Pufendorf's conception of the sovereign power is neutral with regard to the forms of government through which it may be exercised (Pufendorf, 1673/1991). Even democratic government is a suitable vehicle for the exercise of sovereign power as long as the election of parliament is treated as the selection of a body to occupy the office of sovereign and not as an attempt to represent the people's moral will. Pufendorf's separation of sovereignty and form of government is thus the direct result of his secularization of ethics and politics, as the secular reconstruction of political legitimacy in terms of the maintenance of security means that the three different forms of government are equally legitimate. Conversely, what ties sovereignty to form of government in popular sovereignty theories is the doctrine that as the functions of sovereignty—the perfection of man's moral nature, the execution of his rational judgment—arise from the communal will, the only legitimate form of government is the one that represents that will: democratic government. But, we recall, in requiring the sovereign power to represent the moral community, this doctrine risks having to enforce a moral culture capable of forming such a community (just as Althusius insisted that the sovereign power should represent and enforce Calvinist religious culture), which is precisely the catastrophe that Pufendorf's separation of sovereignty and government was designed to avoid.

Pufendorf completed his secularization of politics by supplementing his initial partitioning of sovereignty and government with a second separation, between sovereignty and moral truth. Drawing on the antimetaphysical, Ciceronian doctrine of differentiated civil personae or offices outlined in his *De Jure*, Pufendorf's (1698) *De Habitu Religionis Christianae ad Vitam Civilem* (On the Nature of Religion in Relation to Civil Life) proceeds to reconstruct the relations between politics and religion, state and church. He does so by supplementing the personae of sovereign and subject belonging to civil life with a second pair of offices, those of teacher and auditor, constituting the religious or ecclesiastical domain. Whereas the personae of sovereign and subject are related through the reciprocal duties of protection and obedience, mediated through the exercise of irresistible coercive power, the personae of teacher and auditor are related through the reciprocal duties of love and emulation, mediating the pursuit of spiritual truth, in which coercion can play no role. In this way, by combining his secularized conception of politics with a spiritualized conception of religion, Pufendorf was able to effect a profound separation of civil and religious authority, or what he called the "civil kingdom" and the "kingdom of truth." On one hand, he was able to justify the exclusion of the church from all participation in the exercise of civil authority. The church must give up the laws of blasphemy and heresy, forgo the power of ex-communication, and be restricted to the civil status of a college or voluntary association of teachers and auditors. In this way, the rights associated with participation in civil life would be separated from those associated with participation in a particular religious or moral community. On the other hand, Pufendorf could argue that the office of civil sovereign was neither dependent on nor capable of governing the pursuit of moral and religious truth, thereby affecting the religious neutralization (desacralisation) of the state. This allowed him to argue for systematic toleration of the three main German religions: Lutheranism, Calvinism, and Catholicism. The religious neutrality of the state, so insouciantly dismissed by Gutmann in her desire to make the pursuit of moral truth into a compulsory condition of democratic sovereignty, may thus be regarded as a cornerstone of political liberalism.

Taken together, Pufendorf's twin separations, of sovereignty and government and sovereignty and moral truth, offer important solutions to the problems of cultural particularism and moral coercion besetting the debate about the education of citizens. Summarily, they show how the legitimacy of sovereignty may be formulated independently of representing the communal will, and hence how the exercise of sovereignty can be freed from the necessity of forming this will. On one hand, by restricting the exercise of sovereign power to the end of civil security, Pufendorf is able to uncouple it from the higher (and more incendiary) moral end of representing a real common will. In a Pufendorfian democracy, parliament governs to maintain security and is deemed to stand for general will when it succeeds, regardless of whether it has actually or rationally represented this will. On the other hand, by insisting on the state's religious neutrality, Pufendorf allows it to withdraw from the sphere of argument over religious and moral truth, remaining indifferent to such questions unless their pursuit threatens social peace. Should this threshold be crossed, the state may exercise coercive force to settle religious arguments, but only in a manner suited to its complete indifference to the moral issues involved. This withdrawal from the policing of moral truth—the expulsion of the church from the state apparatus that gives rise to religious toleration—is what qualifies the Pufendorfian state as liberal.

What is striking about this complex of strategies is that it was used by Pufendorf and his younger colleague Thomasius to solve problems quite like the ones at stake in the debate between modern cultural particularists and philosophical liberals. By building on Pufendorf's work, Thomasius was able to develop a threshold for the state's intervention in religious education that is directly comparable with the one employed by Gutmann. In fact, Thomasius's marked an important advance on the threshold used in the *De Habitu*, for here Pufendorf had attempted to draw a firm line between the internal order of the church that should be left to the clergy (liturgy, sacraments) and the external order open to control by the prince (appointment of priests, funding and administration of church property) (Pufendorf, 1698). The problem with this solution,

Thomasius argued, was that it led to intractable argument about whether a certain matter should be regarded as internal or external, thereby paralyzing the sovereign's capacity for political action.

The two cases that Thomasius uses to exemplify this argument in the *Vom Recht Evangelischer Fürsten in Mitteldingen* (On the Right of Protestant Princes in "Middle Things"/adiaphora; coauthored with his student Enno Brenneysen) are directly comparable with the chador affair. Consider the case, says Thomasius, of a Catholic prince ruling over a territory inside whose Lutheran churches the congregations are singing hymns extolling the murder of the Pope. The question of whether the prince has the right to suppress this conduct cannot be solved via the distinction between the internal and external governance of the church, as the case can be argued passionately on both sides, depending on how hymn singing is classified. Using Thomasius's threshold, though, the prince can readily be assigned this right—regardless of whether hymns are normally seen as belonging to the internal liturgical order of the church—for this is conduct that foments hatred and thereby threatens civil peace (Thomasius & Brenneysen, 1705).

At the same time, though, the sovereign must not attempt to exercise this right on the basis of his own religion or in a manner that coerces the consciences of his citizens. This is the point of the second example, which concerns the question (disputed by the "doctors") of whether Protestant princes had the right to compel their Jewish subjects to attend Christian worship. Again, this case had proved irresolvable using the internal-external division due to the lack of agreement over how to classify church services. And again, Thomasius's floating threshold provides an unambiguous resolution, this time denying the right:

> The rule we have provided above decides the matter quite clearly. Because to attend the churches and participate in the worship of the Christians appears unjust and aggravating to the Jews. It is thus no assistance to the peace and calm of the country and so one should not compel their conscience. No matter how erroneous their conscience is, it will not be helped from error through compulsion, but only if one associates with them in a friendly manner, providing them with a good example so that they might better agree with reason and the teachings of Christ. (Thomasius & Brenneysen, 1705, pp. 112-113)

In short, like the French Conseil d'Etat, Thomasius argues that the state should maintain its neutrality in the domain of religious education, intervening only when those passionately engaged in convincing each other of the moral truth threaten the peace and calm of the country.

## THE LEGACY OF THE CIVIL DISCIPLINES

We have traveled some distance from the contemporary assertion that we are on the verge of a new realization of a neo-Kantian ideal of cosmopolitan citizenship, transcending the eternal dialectic in educational thought, between security and freedom, state neutrality, and moral values. On the contrary, we have argued that we continue to face problems similar to those that first arose during the period of deconfessionalization and state building. This suggests that intellectuals living under conditions of civil security—both philosophical liberals and cultural particularists—have forgotten some of the modes of political reasoning that were crucial to the establishment of the fragile social and secular settlements that underlie the achievements of modern political life. In particular, in confusing the ends of security and democratic representation—the concern with maintaining social peace and forming the moral community—philosophical liberals and cultural particularists have neglected the twin separations of sovereignty and government and sovereignty and moral truth, through which the early modern civil philosophers sought to secularize politics and privatize religion. These constructs remain alien to the prevailing post-Kantian moral philosophical framework, which stresses the higher rational or moral right to be found in a communal moral will.

Drawing on the legacy of civil philosophy, however, we have suggested that democratic sovereignty cannot and should not be confused with the pursuit of moral truth. Furthermore, there are real dangers in the prevailing insistence that sovereignty can only legitimately be exercised as an expression of a communal moral will transparent to critical rationality. Our examples include various efforts to use the moral disciplines of mass schooling to achieve global consensus across divided political, ethnic, and religious cultures. Such efforts, we have argued, are driven by moral and philosophical rationales that fail to recognize their origins in a particular (metaphysical) moral culture. The main historical change is that, where once the confessional imperative was that each individual should be their own priest, now each is to be their own philosopher (Minson, 1998).

By contrast, the settlement that Pufendorf proposed demonstrates the capacity to retain commitment to piety (including Pufendorf's brand of piety), separating this off from commitment to civil peace through state neutrality. This is not a matter of removing moral autonomy, but of developing a cultivation of the soul that can set limits to itself. Key to this are the distinctions between government and sovereignty, between sovereignty and the pursuit of truth, and between civic training and spiritual preparation. Pufendorf did in fact propose a form of general ethical training based on the model of promoting sociability as a means to security. He proposed some core values: setting thresholds and ensuring that citizens are taught everything required to live in a state. In his time, this worked as an alternative to the extensive theological training in metaphysics provided through confessional disciplines. The model requires those responsible for state decisions to be prepared to withdraw from the sphere of argument over religious and moral truth, unless and until the pursuit of such questions threatens social peace. On such occasions, the state can apply coercion through legal mechanisms, in a manner entirely neutral about the truth of the dispute on moral or religious principle.

As we have noted, such rationales are not so foreign to the reasoning that contemporary international and national governmental agencies now use in planning mass education systems. States today concern themselves with future citizens' abilities, including the capacity to understand and debate core issues of national citizenship and national history and the ability to carry out various roles of citizenship as householder, worker, voter, private individual, public official, and so on. But they rarely intervene directly into semiautonomous zones of social governance, such as school systems, except on the infrequent occasions when states are faced with the option of acting to neutralize cultural conflict, even in spaces that we now expect to be domains of liberal freedoms. The state, as a state, does not and must not care about the substance of such conflicts, nor is it concerned with their rationality or lack of it. Such concerns have been transferred to the mechanisms of social governance (see Donzelot, 1979). These mechanisms include the processes of consultation, liaison, and participation within schools and school systems, through which educational bureaucrats, school principals, and other pastoral-bureaucratic experts negotiate with parents, employers, unions, school boards, and councils to elicit voluntary cooperation with more or less common norms (Hunter, 1994; Meredyth, 1997; Rose, 1990, 1996; Smith, 1993). Such means have made it possible to treat schooling as part of the processes of social governance, making conflicts manipulable and manageable.[1]

Despite these achievements of social settlement, however, we have lost sight of the distinction between civil disciplines and the pursuit of truth. Many social studies educators urge that civic education *is* education in values. The classroom is a microcosm of political community: Therefore, citizens can learn all they need to know about democratic political life if they reflect critically on school rules and arrangements, referring back in class discussion to *justice*, *rule of law*, or *rights* as principles. Conflict can be managed as part of classroom dialogue, modeling collective decision making as part of the secularized techniques of self-revelation and self-examination. From within the classroom and the seminar, it seems possible to project these successes outward, remaking the community—and the international community—in the mold of moral education. The combination of moral philosophical reflection and pedagogic technique then becomes the correlate for the political-philosophical assertion that education for democracy can only be fully democratic if it represents a communal will. We have put the case, however, that such moral-political reflections on and in education should be seen as the product of a particular kind of ethical formation, with a heavy historical debt to confessional spiritual technique. They are not necessarily capable of providing a transcendent perspective on the complex problems of how to calm ethnic and cultural conflict in new democracies or how to treat as civic equals those with very different religions and cultural backgrounds within a mass school system.

## CONCLUSION

We have argued that many of the moral-philosophical appeals to the emergence of a new cosmopolitan democratic consciousness emerging from the rubble of political change actually indicate how close we remain to the epoch of civil war and confessional politics. Despite the seriousness with which national and international agencies of government have treated the link between security, solidarity, and the project of equipping citizens with the capacity to exercise rights with some moderation—and despite their recurrent emphasis on the need for state agencies to remain neutral about contentious issues of morality and values—the association between civil peace, state neutrality, and civic disciplines remains poorly understood. The problems of civic education are constantly deferred to the higher authority of popular sovereignty, rational consensus, and moral community.

What if popular sovereignty is not the key issue for cultural policy on citizenship education and cultural formation? What if we were to set the horizon for civic education at the point where citizens are given the minimal equipment needed to live in a secular state? This might include equipping them with the ability to restrain their own critical autonomy and confessional enthusiasm. Rather than giving undue say to moral autonomy as a civil religion, we can and should think of other, less purist, ways to organize ourselves.

## NOTE

1. From a longer historical perspective, these negotiations appear as part of the separation between state sovereignty and social governance, achieved in the process of the political neutralization of civil society. In the wake of deconfessionalization, radical statism found ways to adapt the pastoral pedagogy of post-Reformation Christianity into a deconfessionalized civil-moral pedagogy, providing a model of "pastoral bureaucratic" mass schooling since adapted within the mass education systems of the Western liberal democracies (for arguments to this effect, see Hunter, 1988, 1994; Melton, 1988).

## REFERENCES

Albala-Bertrand, L. (1997a). *International project: What education for what citizenship?* [Online]. International Bureau of Education, UNESCO. Available: http://www3.itu.int:8002/ibe-citied/the_project.html

Albala-Bertrand, L. (1997b). *The specific purpose of the study* [Online]. International Bureau of Education, UNESCO. Available: http://www3.itu.int:8002/ibe-citied/purpose.html

Albala-Bertrand, L. (1997c). *What is citizenship education?* [Online]. International Bureau of Education, UNESCO. Available: http://www3.itu.int:8002/ibe-citied/what_citizenship.html

Althusius, J. (1995). *Politica: An abridged translation of politics methodically set forth and illustrated with sacred and profane examples* (F. S. Carney, Trans.; 3rd ed.). Indianapolis, IN: Liberty Press. (Original published 1603)

Archibugi, D., & Held, D. (Eds.). (1995). *Cosmopolitan democracy: An agenda for a new world order.* Cambridge, MA: Polity.
Augier, P. (1994). *The sovereign citizen: Education for democracy.* Paris, France: United Nations Educational, Scientific, and Cultural Organization.
Baykan, A. (1997). Issues of difference and citizenship for "new identities": A theoretical view. *Innovation: The European Journal of Social Sciences, 10*(1), 61-67.
Bell, G. (Ed.). (1995). *Educating European citizens: Citizenship values and the European dimension.* London: David Fulton.
Bellah, R. N. (1985). *Habits of the heart: Individualism and commitment in American life.* Berkeley: University of California Press.
Butts, F. R. (1988). *The morality of democratic citizenship: Goals for civic education in the Republic's third century.* Calabasas, CA: Center for Civic Education.
Callan, E. (1994). Beyond sentimental civic education. *American Journal of Education, 102*(2), 190-222.
Callan, E. (1997). *Creating citizens. Political education and liberal democracy.* Oxford, UK: Clarendon.
Civics Expert Group. (1994). *Whereas the people: Civics and citizenship education.* Canberra, Australia: Australian Government Printing Service.
Dauenhauer, B. (1996). *Citizenship in a fragile world.* Lanham, MD: Rowman and Littlefied.
Donnelly, K. (1997). Civics and citizenship education. The dangers of centralised civics education. *Policy, 12*(4), 21-24.
Donzelot, J. (1979). *The policing of families.* New York: Random House.
Dreitzel, H. (1970). *Protestantischer Aristotelismus und absoluter Staat: Die "Politica" des Henning Arnisaeus (ca.1575-1636).* Wiesbaden, Germany: Franz Steiner.
Dufty, D. (1995). Civic consciousness, concern and commitment: Holistic and global perspectives on civics and citizenship education. *The Social Educator, 14*(3), 20-30.
Elazar, D. (1995). Althusius' grand design for a federal commonwealth. In J. Althusius, *Politica: An abridged translation of politics methodically set forth and illustrated with sacred and profane examples* (pp. xxxv-xlvi). Indianapolis, IN: Liberty Press.
Falk, R. (1981). *Human rights and state sovereignty.* New York: Holmes and Meier.
Feinberg, W. (1998). *Common schools, uncommon identities: National unity and cultural difference.* New Haven, CT: Yale University Press.
Goals 2000: Educate America Act (1994) [Online]. Available: http/www.ed.gov/legislation/Goals2000/TheAct
Gutmann, A. (1987). *Democratic education.* Princeton, NJ: Princeton University Press.
Gutmann, A. (1995). Challenges of multiculturalism in democractic education. *Philosophy of Education Society yearbook* [Online]. Available: http://www.ed.uiuc.edu/EPS/PES-Yearbook/95_docs/gutmann.html
Hindess, B. (1997). Democracy and disenchantment. *Australian Journal of Political Science, 32*(1), 79-92.
Hindess, B. (2000). Citizenship in the international management of populations. *American Behavioral Scientist, 43,* 1489-1497.
Hughes, P. (1994). International best practice in civics education. In Civics Expert Group (Ed.), *Whereas the people: Civics and citizenship education* (pp. 73-184). Canberra, Australia: Australian Government Printing Service.
Hunter, I. (1988). *Culture and government: The emergence of literary education.* Houndsmills, UK: Macmillan.
Hunter, I. (1994). *Rethinking the school: Subjectivity, bureaucracy, criticism.* Sydney, Australia: Allen & Unwin.
Jensen, K. (Ed.). (1995). *Democracy, citizenship and global concern.* Copenhagen, Denmark: Royal Danish School of Educational Studies.

Kaltsounis, T. (1997). Multicultural education and citizenship education at a crossroads: Searching for common ground. *The Social Studies, 88*(1), 18-24.

Kant, I. (1948). *Groundwork of the metaphysic of morals* (H. J. Paton, Trans; 3rd ed.). New York: Harper and Row.

Kant, I. (1996). The metaphysics of morals. In M. Gregor (Ed. and Trans.) *Immanuel Kant: Practical philosophy* (pp. 353-604). Cambridge, UK: Cambridge University Press.

Kemp, D. (1997, May). *Realising the promise of democracy.* Paper presented at the 1997 Curriculum Corporation National Conference, Sydney, Australia.

Khilnani, S. (1991). Democracy and modern political community: Limits and possibilities. *Economy and Society, 20*(2), 196-204.

Kingwell, M. (1995). *A civil tongue: Justice, dialogue, and the politics of pluralism.* University Park: Pennsylvania State University Press.

Kreisberg, S. (1993). Educating for democracy and community: Towards the transformation of power in our schools. In S. G. Berman & P. La Farge (Eds.), *Promising practices in teaching responsibility* (pp. 207-217). Albany: State University of New York Press.

Kymlicka, W. (1989). *Liberalism, community and culture.* Oxford, UK: Clarendon.

Kymlicka, W. (1995). *Multicultural citizenship.* Oxford, UK: Clarendon.

Kymlicka, W., & Norman, W. (1994). Return of the citizen: A survey of recent work on citizenship theory. *Ethics,* (104), 257-289.

Levitt, G. A., & Longstreet, W. S. (1993). Controversy and the teaching of authentic civic values. *The Social Studies, 84*(4), 142-148.

Melton, J. van Horn. (1988). *Absolutism and the eighteenth century origins of compulsory schooling in Prussia and Austria.* Cambridge, UK: Cambridge University Press.

Meredyth, D. (1997). Invoking citizenship: Education, competence and social rights. *Economy and Society, 19*(1), 1-29.

Merriam, C. E. (1931). *The making of citizens: A comparative study of methods of civics training.* Chicago: University of Chicago Press.

Meyer-Bish, P. (1995). *Culture of democracy: A challenge for schools.* Paris, France: United Nations Educational, Scientific, and Cultural Organization.

Minson, J. (1998). Ethics in the service of the state. In M. Dean & B. Hindess (Eds.), *Governing Australia: Studies in contemporary rationalities of government* (pp.47-69). Cambridge, UK: Cambridge University Press.

Oliveira, M. D., Tandon, R., & CIVICUS. (1994). *Citizens: Strengthening global civil society.* Washington, DC: CIVICUS. World Alliance for Citizen Participation.

Parekh, B. (1997). Dilemmas of a multicultural theory of citizenship. *Constellations, 4*(1), 54-62.

Pratte, R. (1988). *The civic imperative: Examining the need for civic education.* New York: Teachers College Press.

Pufendorf, S. (1698). *De habitu religionis Christianae ad vitam civilem* [Of the nature and qualification of religion in reference to civil society]. London: Roper and Bosvile.

Pufendorf, S. (1934). *De jure naturae et gentium libri octo* [The law of nature and of nations in eight books] (C. H. Oldfather & W. A. Oldfather, Trans.). Oxford, UK: Clarendon. (Original published 1672)

Pufendorf, S. (1991). *On the duty of man and citizen according to natural law* (M. Silverthorne, Trans.). Cambridge, UK: Cambridge University Press. (Original published 1673)

Quigley, C. N., & Bahmueller, C. F. (1991). *Civitas: A framework for civic education.* Calabasas, CA: Center for Civic Education.

Rawls, J. (1996). *Political liberalism* (2nd ed.). New York: Columbia University Press.

Rorty, A. (1995). The moral duty of promoting political conflict. *Philosophy of Education Society yearbook* [Online]. Available: http://www.ed.uiuc.edu/EPS/PES-Yearbook/95_docs/rorty.html

Rose, N. (1990). *Governing the soul: The shaping of the private self.* London: Routledge.

Rose, N. (1996). Governing "advanced" liberal democracies. In A. Barry, T. Osborne, & N. Rose (Eds.), *Foucault and political reason: Liberalism, neo-liberalism and rationalities of government*. London: UCL Press.

Smith, B. (1993). Educational consumerism: Family values of the meanest of motives? In D. Meredyth & D. Tyler (Eds.), *Child and citizen: Genealogies of schooling and subjectivity* (pp. 181-206). Brisbane, Australia: Institute for Cultural Policy Studies.

Taylor, C., & Gutmann, A. (1992). *Multiculturalism and "the politics of recognition": An essay*. Princeton, NJ: Princeton University Press.

Thomasius, C., & Brenneysen, E. R. (1705). Vom Recht evangelischer Fürsten in Mitteldingen oder Kirchenzeremonien (De jure principis circa adiaphora, 1695). In C. Thomasius (Ed.), *Auserlesene deutsche Schriften Erster Teil*, (Vol. 1; pp. 76-209). Halle, Germany: Renger.

Torres, C. A. (1998). *Democracy, education, and multiculturalism: Dilemmas of citizenship in a global world*. Lanham, MD: Rowman and Littlefield.

Tuck, R. (1987). The "modern" theory of natural law. In A. Pagden (Ed.), *The languages of political theory in early-modern Europe* (pp. 99-122). Cambridge, UK: Cambridge University Press.

Yeatman, A. (2000). Who is the subject of human rights? *American Behavioral Scientist, 43*, 1498-1513.

Young, I. M. (1987). Impartiality and the civic public: Some implications of feminist critiques of moral and political theory. In S. Benhabib & D. Cornell (Eds.), *Feminism as critique: Essays on the politics of gender in late-capitalist societies* (pp. 56-76). Cambridge, MA: Polity.

# 6. Citizenship in the International Management of Populations

**BARRY HINDESS**
*Australian National University*

> *Academic discussion of citizenship focuses primarily on the citizen in relation to the particular state of which he or she is a member. From this perspective, the modern spread of citizenship is usually regarded as a definite advance in human well-being, turning what had once been the privileges of the few into the rights of the many. This article argues that an understanding of the impact of citizenship in the modern world must consider not just its role in bringing together members of particular subpopulations and promoting some of their interests but also the effects of rendering the global population governable by dividing it into subpopulations consisting of the citizens of discrete, politically independent and competing states.*

**Modern democratic regimes** commonly express a commitment to the idea of universal human rights. They also discriminate against foreigners in their midst and at their borders, often subjecting them to arbitrary action by immigration officials, restricting their access to the courts and to the welfare protections accorded other residents, and incarcerating many would-be refugees and illegal immigrants. Consideration of the relationship between these two aspects of governmental conduct offers a revealing perspective on the role of citizenship in the modern world. On one hand, discrimination against noncitizens can be seen as reflecting an internalist view of citizenship, a view that focuses on relationships between an individual and the state in whose territory he or she happens to reside. This is the view of citizenship advanced in Marshall's (1950) account of the civil, political, and social aspects of citizenship in the societies of the modern West and adopted, with minor variations, in most academic discussions of what it is to be a citizen.[1] It suggests that states should be accountable to their citizens and responsible for the protection of their common interests. Although with this view there may be a sense in which certain rights are regarded as universal, primary responsibility for the implementation of those rights is seen as lying with the states to which the relevant individuals belong.

---

**Author's Note:** *An earlier version of this article appeared in* European Journal of Social Theory, *and the author is grateful to the editor and Sage Publications, Ltd for permission to adapt it for this volume. Earlier versions of this article were presented at the Culture and Citizenship inaugural conference of the Australian Key Centre for Cultural and Media Policy, Brisbane, Australia, 1996, and the 1997 conference of the Australian Political Science Association*

On the other hand, discrimination between citizens and others can be seen as belonging to that broader set of practices whereby states attempt, with greater or lesser degrees of success, to govern the populations under their nominal control. In a world of politically independent and competing territorial states, citizenship plays a fundamental role in rendering governable a global population of thousands of millions by dividing it into the smaller subpopulations of particular states.

There are, in effect, two conceptions of citizenship at work in the modern world. One sees it as a complex package of rights and responsibilities accruing to individuals by virtue of their membership of an appropriate polity. The other sees it as a marker of identification, advising state and nonstate agencies of the particular state to which an individual belongs. These conceptions of citizenship are not necessarily incompatible, but they are certainly distinct: There are many citizens in the world today, for example, who have few of the rights invoked in Marshall's (1950) classic account of citizenship. It is nevertheless tempting to bring these conceptions together, presenting the following as parts of the one developmental process: first, the secular extension of citizenship within a few Western states and to some degree elsewhere; second, the division of most of the world's population into citizens of a plurality of nominally independent territorial states; and third, the emergence of what seem to be supranational elements of citizenship (European citizenship, the growing emphasis on universal human rights in the international community, etc.).

Here, the story of citizenship in the modern period is commonly presented as a historical teleology of the kind set out with exemplary clarity in Kant's political writings. Kant's (1970) "Idea for a Universal History with a Cosmopolitan Purpose" unveils the "purpose in nature" that, in Kant's view, underlies the "senseless course of human events" (p. 42). Kant's argument here rests on an assumption that still commands considerable academic support: Namely, that the natural capacities of human individuals roughly correspond to the capacities of rationality and moral autonomy that modern constitutional republics promote in their citizens. Nature's plan, it seems, is to use conflict between individuals and between states to realize these *natural* capacities. Kant argues that conflict between individuals has led them to form states for their own protection, whereas at least in the more fortunate states, conflict within them has resulted in the formation of constitutional regimes. Finally, and in part because they are seen to foster the natural abilities of their individual citizens, he suggests that constitutional republics will turn out to be more powerful than other states with similar natural endowments. For this reason, we are told, competition between states will eventually lead to the spread of constitutional regimes throughout the world.

Although explicit invocation of nature's hidden plan has long passed out of fashion, it is clear that some such teleology underlies many contemporary discussions of citizenship and human rights.[2] Thus, the citizenship that results from the allocation of populations to states can also be seen as an early stage in the development within these states of the "citizenship" set out by Marshall (1950) and other sociological commentators. I argue on the contrary that the partitioning of populations has a significant systemic character and systemic effects that are thoroughly obscured by the failure to distinguish these two senses of citizenship. Despite its apparent universalism, the teleological understanding of citizenship focuses primarily on the citizen in relation to the particular state of which he or she is a member. In contrast to this internalist perspective, I suggest that an understanding of the impact of citizenship in the modern world must focus on its role in dividing a global population of thousands of millions into the smaller subpopulations of territorial states; just as, to understand citizenship among the Greeks of classical antiquity, we should focus not only on the citizens of, say, Athens or Sparta but also on the Greek population as a whole and that of the larger Mediterranean region.

This article brings out the significance of this broader perspective on citizenship in two stages. First, I consider a sense in which citizenship can be seen as a conspiracy against the rest of the world. In fact, we shall see that this perception is entirely compatible with the teleological understanding noted earlier and that it misrepresents the political character of the boundaries that divide the populations and territories of states from one another. Accordingly, I move on to locate the particularistic conspiracies to which citizenship gives rise within the modern division of the world into nations and societies. This involves consideration not just of the role of citizenship in bringing together members of particular subpopulations and promoting some of their interests, but also of the effects of rendering the larger population governable by dividing it into subpopulations consisting of the citizens of discrete, politically independent and competing states. Because these states are not self-contained, their existence as discrete political unities depends both on the maintenance of boundaries between them and on the continuing movement of people, ideas, goods, and services across those boundaries.

## CITIZENSHIP AS CONSPIRACY

The perception of citizenship as a kind of conspiracy is a simple corollary of the classical Greek understanding of citizenship according to which, as Aristotle puts it,

> He who has the power to take part in the deliberative or judicial administration of any state is said by us to be a citizen of the state; and, speaking generally, a state is a body of citizens sufficing for the purposes of life. (1988, pp. 19-22)

Citizens take part in the administration of the state, which encompasses a particular delimited territory and its population, and they are expected to do so in the general interest, that is, in the general interest of the citizens themselves. From the point of view of its own citizens, the state is a body of citizens like themselves working together, directly or indirectly, in pursuit of their common interests and treating much of the remaining population as means to their ends. However, from the point of view of the rest of the state's population (women, slaves, free resident aliens), the state appears as an exclusive body of adult males that shows little concern for their interests or desires. Moreover, of those Greeks in the classical period who did enjoy the status of citizen, only a minority were citizens of Athens or other powerful states. The majority were the actual or potential victims of those states. To be a citizen was to be involved to some degree in the collective government of one's own state, but it was also to be at the mercy of decisions made by or on behalf of one's fellow citizens or the citizens of other states. One could make related points today about the meaning of citizenship for citizen minorities within and citizens of states other than Japan, the United States, the leading states of the European union, or of the slightly larger group of states that dominates the World Trade Organisation, the International Monetary Fund, and the World Bank.

In fact, because contemporary states are hardly "bodies of citizens" in Aristotle's sense, this view of citizenship as conspiracy is one that should be substantially qualified. Although most states have now taken up some version of the idea of citizenship, they have usually extended it to cover a clear majority of the adult population. Thus, modern citizenship is no longer, as it was for the Greeks, the privilege of an exclusive minority within the overall population of the state. However, this extension of modern citizenship has developed alongside a significant attenuation of its meaning. Even in the democratic societies of the modern West, where the internalist ideal of citizenship has been most fully developed, the view that citizens directly rule the states in which they live has been displaced by the view that their governments should be answerable to the citizens through periodic elections.[3] It is doubtful whether such limited accountability of governments to their citizens amounts to quite the citizen responsibility for government action that the notion of conspiracy would seem to require. Indeed, it is not difficult to find cases in which citizens of modern states have been tempted to regard their own governments as conspiring against them.

I will add a substantial qualification of a different kind in the following section. Despite these points, however, to the extent that national governments respond to the demands of their citizens or of influential minorities among them, it remains tempting to describe citizenship as a conspiracy against the rest of the world. In practice, of course, much of what governments do to further the interests of their citizens need involve no damage to the interests of others (public health and education provide some obvious examples). Even so, it is clear that many governmental programs do discriminate in favour of their citizens and against others. Where, as in most contemporary states, an overwhelming majority of residents are also citizens, such conspiracies might seem to have little impact on the lives of noncitizens, although the treatment of refugees and other immigrants is often a cause for concern. But, as many commentators have noted, the effects of state action are not necessarily confined to either its specific territory or its own nationals.[4] Even the peaceful and openly acknowledged actions of powerful states (regarding, for example, tariffs, interest rates, or trade subsidies and sanctions) can have a substantial impact on people living outside their borders. Decisions taken by the governments of Japan and the United States or collectively by the European community may well affect much of the world, those of the South African government affect much of sub-Saharan Africa, those of Australian and New Zealand governments affect many Pacific island nations, and so on.

I began by noting that modern democratic regimes commonly express a commitment to the idea of universal human rights and that they frequently deny those rights to noncitizens in their midst and at their borders. Although such practices can be understood in terms of the conception of modern citizenship as involving a conspiracy against the foreigner, they are not inconsistent with the Kantian view noted earlier of progress toward a world of constitutional republics and universal human rights. Kant does not expect progress toward a world federation of republics to be brought about by either popular or elite endorsement of his historical ideal. On the contrary, he argues that this development will be forced on states by the effects of conflict and competition between them. It might be argued, then, that the often brutal and inhumane practices of contemporary democratic states show how far we still have to go before the Kantian vision can be realized, not that the vision itself is misleading. On this view, lack of elementary hospitality toward migrants would be seen as a feature of the modern world that will be overcome as states that are now poor, weak, or undemocratic become progressively wealthier, stronger, and more democratic; that is, as their own citizens have less reason to flee and other states have more reason to treat these citizens with respect.

However, if the Kantian story can readily accommodate the effects of citizenship as conspiracy, the political character of the division of humanity into citizens of discrete sovereign states presents it with a far more serious problem. This brings us to my second issue, the division of the world into nations and societies.

## NATIONS AND SOCIETIES

In effect, both the classical and the modern discourses of citizenship suggest that it is normal and acceptable for states to discriminate between their own citizens and others. Where the classical view of citizenship was that noncitizens would always form a substantial part of the state's population, the predominant modern view is that residents will normally also be citizens. For the modern discourse of citizenship, then, the fundamental division is between those who are citizens of the state in question and those who belong elsewhere. Thus, although there is now a widely held belief in the existence of at least some universal human rights, the assumption is that these will normally be exercised in the state of which one is a citizen. In this respect, the modern commitment to the universality of citizenship rights nevertheless suggests that states can, and in many respects should, treat their citizens differently from foreigners.[5]

What concerns us here is how we should understand the pervasive modern division between the citizen and the foreigner. This is an extremely complex issue and I can hardly do more in this article than touch its surface. We can begin by noting that, because citizenship is restricted to states of a certain kind, at least some of its essential features must be seen as artefacts of politics. I argue that the modern partitioning of the global population into citizens of numerous discrete states should be seen as having a similarly artefactual character. The most common alternative view is simply that this partitioning reflects a natural, or at least an extrapolitical, division of humanity into peoples and, more particularly, into nations or societies. On this view, in keeping with the distinctive culture or way of life that (despite minor regional and other variations) is or should be shared by all members of the society in question, citizenship would also be expected to have a particularistic character. It is the impact of this presumption that is at issue in contemporary debates around multiculturalism, the politics of difference, and the position of indigenous minorities.[6]

Participants in these debates generally take the internalist perspective on citizenship as their starting point. In other words, they focus on the rights and responsibilities of citizens who are differently situated members of a single state. What concerns us here, however, is the impact of this presumption on discussion of the differential treatment of citizens and foreigners and of interactions that cross citizenship and other political boundaries. Movements of people or interactions between them that take place within the borders of a state are regarded as normal and as made possible precisely by the expectations, patterns of conduct, and liberties that members of the nation or society share by virtue of their common heritage. Movement or interaction across borders, on the other hand, is usually seen as a very different matter, as the image of the state as a body of citizens sufficing for the purposes of life would also lead us to expect. As a result, noncitizens arriving at national borders are all too easily seen as suspect. Moreover, because states commonly reserve a variety of (usually lesser) statuses for those who are not their nationals, noncitizens find themselves with only limited defences against the arbitrary actions of state officials. In this way, the modern development of citizenship in terms of particularistic national and societal differences has ensured that there are border regions within states in which the rights of many individuals are poorly protected (and sometimes nonexistent) and minorities within their borders whose rights are similarly fragile.

It would be a mistake, however, to treat such particularisms as reflecting a natural or prepolitical division of humanity into nations and societies. Most historians and social scientists now accept that nations are artefacts that have been put together out of collectivities of other kinds, a process that disrupts collectivities that happen not to fall within appropriate "national" boundaries. As a result, national traditions tend to be seen as invented or as substantially reworked established traditions. There are, of course, competing accounts of these developments, with modernists (e.g., Gellner, 1983) and their critics (e.g., Smith, 1986) tending to emphasize different aspects, the one side stressing the element of artifice in bringing together disparate elements to form a nation and the other stressing the pre-national materials with which such artifice has to work.[7] In neither account can the nation be seen as providing an extrapolitical foundation on which to base a politics of inclusion and exclusion.

If the nation can hardly be seen as providing such a foundation, what of the less obviously political idea of society? Perhaps the most disappointing feature of the academic literature on nations and nationalism is that many of those who insist on the invented or artefactual character of nations continue to treat societies as if they were altogether more substantial entities. Gellner (1983), for example, presents nations and nationalism as if they were characteristic phenomena of certain kinds of society, appearing only in those endowed with some version of the modern state. He also observes that "not all societies are endowed with states. It immediately follows that the problem of nationalism does not arise for stateless societies" (Gellner, 1983, p. 4).

Thus, whereas nations are regarded as fabrications, the societies in which they appear or fail to appear are seen as having a more enduring status. Similarly, Hobsbawm and Ranger's (1983) analysis of the invention of tradition, in which the nation and national tradition are seen as being of central importance, presents such invention as occurring "more frequently when a rapid transformation of *society* weakens or destroys the social patterns for which 'old' traditions had been designed" (p. 4, emphasis added). Greenfeld's (1992) account of the emergence of the modern idea of the nation treats the modern idea of society as relatively unproblematic. Greenfeld examines the emergence of nationalism in England, France, Russia, Germany, and the United States but, she tells us, the fundamental questions addressed by her book have a more general character. They include,

> why and how nationalism emerged, why and how it was transformed in the process of transfer from one *society* to another, and why and how different forms of national identity and consciousness became translated into institutional practices and patterns of culture, moulding the social and political structures of *societies* which defined themselves as nations. To answer these questions, I focus on five *major societies* which were the first to do so. (p. 3, emphasis added)

In this passage, societies are presented as substantial and enduring collectivities, exhibiting their own cultural patterns, possessing definite social and political structures, and, in some cases, developing a sense of national identity.

I noted above that a population of citizens subject to the laws of a particular state is now commonly perceived in terms of a culture or way of life in which its members all participate and often also in terms of a common descent, in short, as having many of the features of Greenfeld's "societies." This all too familiar image of society as a substantial and enduring entity operating, at least in some cases, on much the same scale as the modern state is a pervasive feature of 20th century social thought. It is also dangerously misleading. The fact that human individuals interact frequently with others and the belief that they form many of their habits of thought and behaviour in the course of such interaction suggest that we might expect rather different habits to develop between interacting groups in widely separated parts of the world. It does not follow that human populations must therefore be divided into discrete societies, each with their own territory, language, and distinctive patterns of thought and behaviour; still less, as Greenfeld's discussion clearly requires, that many such societies will operate on the scale of modern states. To the extent that humanity can now be divided into discrete societies of this kind, it is the product of factors other than human sociality and especially, in the modern period, of the efforts of states to nationalize the populations under their control.

In fact, the particular concept of society employed by Greenfeld and many others in their discussion of nations and nationalism is a more recent historical innovation than that of the nation itself.[8] Unfortunately, although historians and social scientists have paid considerable critical attention to the image of humanity as divided into numerous distinct nations, the same cannot be said of the related image of a world of societies. For the limited purposes of this article, let me suggest that it is far too easy to treat societies as enduring collectivities, within some of which a sense of national identity was able to develop. On the contrary, we might more profitably regard the image of a world of nations and that of a world of substantial *modern* or *modernizing* societies (and of many, far smaller, premodern societies) as intimately related products of the same historical developments. The period of the emergence of the modern idea of the nation also saw the development of modern ideas of the state and the citizen (both significantly different from the classical models from which they seem to be derived). It was followed not much later by the idea of society as a distinct, substantial, and enduring entity and by the moral psychology of reasons, interests, and passions: in short, by the modern view of the world as consisting of discrete but interacting societies, the more properly modern of which are also nations of citizens who collectively manage their own affairs.

What should be noted here is that the emergence of a world both of nations and of modern or modernizing societies has depended on the ability of a number of states to each impose a substantial degree of exclusive control over a territory and the population within it. This ability is the outcome of many factors including, in particular, agreement on the part of other states to respect that control. Of course, many commentators have noted that there are external as well as internal dimensions to the development of modern states.[9] My point is a different one, namely, that the emergence of such states is itself an artefact of a supranational regime of government. By restricting the rights of other states to intervene in matters of religion, the agreements that ended the Thirty Years War effectively assigned to each territorial state the government of the population within its territory, thereby bringing under control the most destructive effects of religious differences within the larger German population. The international state system, initiated with the Treaty of Westphalia and later imposed more or less effectively on the rest of the world's population and territory, can be seen not only as regulating the conduct of states and indeed as constituting them but also as a dispersed regime of governance covering the overall population of the states concerned.[10]

These considerations suggest that the particularity of citizenship as we know it should not be seen primarily as a product of naturally occurring differences between nations or societies, each with their distinctive way of life or culture. On the contrary, although there are many distinctive ways of life or cultures, their establishment at the level of the populations of modern states (or at least the belief that such things can be identified at that level) should itself be seen as an artefact of government. The division of humanity into distinct national populations, many of them with their own national territories and states, operates as a dispersed regime of governance of the larger human population.

This point suggests a further important qualification to the view outlined above of citizenship as conspiracy. What makes it possible and even, in many respects, necessary for the governments of contemporary states to discriminate in favour of their citizens is the broader system of governance in which they are located. Such discrimination, in other words, is not only the result of decisions made by or on behalf of their own citizens but also a structural requirement of the modern state system. A system of governance that partitions the world into discrete, territorially based national populations requires the regulation of movement from one national territory to another. Insofar as such partitioning of populations invokes the idea that the members of national populations will normally share a distinctive culture or way of life, it suggests that movement within national boundaries will have a radically different character from movement across those boundaries. The assumption here is that, even if they move around within it, people will normally be settled in the society to which they belong and if they depart it will only be for a relatively short period. In fact, the historical record suggests a different story; namely, that large-scale population movement is as normal a feature of the human condition as is long-term territorial settlement. Indeed, the era that saw the consolidation of the modern system of territorial states was also an era of unprecedented movement across national borders and resettlement in foreign parts.

Nevertheless, the system of territorial states and the techniques of population management developed within it have turned the movement of people around the world into an exceptional activity, something that can and should be regulated by the states whose borders they threaten to cross. Because it classifies people on the basis of their citizenship, this regulation provides another striking sense in which citizenship can be seen as a conspiracy against outsiders. It is a conspiracy that can be particularly cruel and destructive because, as I noted earlier, individuals arriving at national borders, and many foreigners within those borders, do not have even the rights of citizenship to protect them from arbitrary official action.

## CONCLUSION

The development of the international states system has promoted a view of politics as taking place either in the interactions between states or in the interactions of citizens (and possibly others) within a state.[11] Western discussion of citizenship has generally been conducted at the second of these levels, treating it primarily as an aspect of life within a state. I have argued that this view of citizenship is seriously incomplete and that to properly understand the modern, international culture of citizenship we have to look at the role of citizenship in the overall government of the population covered by the modern state system.

Once we adopt this perspective we can see that, alongside the benefits that it delivers to those who are citizens of the state in which they live, citizenship also has a variety of other, less obviously benign consequences. I have suggested, in effect, that citizenship is an important component of a dispersed system of governing a large, culturally diverse, and interdependent world population and that it operates by dividing that population into a series of discrete subpopulations and setting them against each other. Within that larger population, citizenship serves to facilitate or promote certain kinds of movement and interaction between its members and to inhibit or penalise others. The culture of citizenship, and especially the commonly held view that individuals will normally be citizens of the state in whose territory they reside, provides all modern states with good reasons for discriminating against noncitizens who cross or live within their borders.

Thus, the modern culture of citizenship provides a degree of social and economic security, at least in certain respects, for many of those who conform to its requirements. Nevertheless, because the overwhelming majority of those who are citizens at all are the citizens of poor states, the focus in much of the academic literature on the benefits that citizenship delivers to the citizens of the more prosperous modern societies gives a misleading and unduly favourable impression of its global impact. The benefits of citizenship are clearly greater for the minority who are citizens of the more prosperous states. One of the most important effects of discrimination by those states in favour of their own citizens is to limit the influx of poor foreigners (thereby creating the especially vulnerable category of illegal immigrant) and of the goods and services that they produce. Even for the rest of the world's citizens—the majority who live in poor states—it is usually better to be a citizen (or to be a prosperous foreigner protected by a powerful outside agency) than not, and here, too, the effect of the state's discrimination in favour of its own is both to facilitate certain kinds of population movement and inhibit others and, in many cases, to create a range of disadvantaged legal statuses in which to place residents who are not themselves nationals of the state in question.

For the rest, citizenship serves as a significant marker in the international system of population management. At that level, the discourse of citizenship provides states with an internationally acceptable rationale for regulating the movements of those who appear (or threaten to appear) on or within their borders as refugees from war and other forms of institutionalized violence or simply in search of what they believe will be a better life. It helps to keep the poor in their place and, by promoting discrimination against the foreigner, it appears to offer some benefits even to the poorest of citizens who remain at home.

But there is another, more insidious effect of the international discourse of citizenship that should be noted. I have contrasted an internalist view of citizenship, which focuses on the status of citizens in relation to the state of which they are members, and the view that comes to the fore when we focus on its role within the international regime of population management. The assignment of millions of individuals to states of their own serves in the first instance as a supranational form of population management, but the teleological discourse of citizenship presents it as something more. To be a citizen in the more substantial, internalist sense it is necessary first to have a state, and the international states regime appears to secure this formal condition of citizenship for the greater part of the world's inhabitants. To present a regime of population control in this way (as a matter of citizenship for the masses), is thus to suggest that they can now achieve the substance of citizenship through the modernization of their own states. The teleological discourse of citizenship promises the poorest of the world's citizens that, if only they would stay at home and learn to behave themselves, they too could be citizens like us.

## NOTES

1. For more recent academic literature, see Turner (1986, 1993) and Kymlicka (1995).

2. Held (1995) endorses a modified version of Kant's cosmopolitan ideal but is clearly uncertain about its ultimate victory.

3. See Dahl (1989) and the essays by Walzer and Wood in Ball, Farr, and Hanson (1989).

4. This is an important part of Held's (1995) argument for the reconstruction of democratic theory.

5. See Miller (1995) for a recent attempt to defend, on universalistic grounds, the view that "the duties we owe our fellow-nationals are different from, and more extensive than, the duties we owe to human beings as such" (p. 11).

6. See, for example, Benhabib (1996), Kymlicka (1995), Lister (1997), Sharp (1997), Tully (1995), Yeatman (1994), and Young (1990).

7. For a judicious discussion, see Hutchinson (1994).

8. See Frisby and Sayer (1986), Helliwell and Hindess (in press), Hindess (1999), Wolf (1988), and the entry of "society" in the *International Encyclopedia of the Social Sciences*.

9. There are useful discussions of this extensive literature in Hirst (1998), Spruyt (1994), and Walker (1993).
10. See the outline of the Westphalian system and its successors in Held (1995).
11. The consequences of this distinction are examined in Walker (1993).

# REFERENCES

Aristotle. (1988). *The politics*. Cambridge, UK: Cambridge University Press.
Ball, T., Farr, J., & Hanson, R. L. (Eds.). (1989). *Political innovation and conceptual change*. Cambridge, UK: Cambridge University Press.
Benhabib, S. (Ed.). (1996). *Democracy and difference: Contesting the boundaries of the political*. Princeton, NJ: Princeton University Press.
Dahl, R. A. (1989). *Democracy and its critics*. New Haven, CT: Yale University Press.
Frisby, D., & Sayer, D. (1986). *Society*. London: Tavistock.
Gellner, E. (1983). *Nations and nationalism*. Oxford, UK: Blackwell.
Greenfeld, L. (1992). *Nationalism: Five roads to modernity*. Cambridge, MA: Harvard University Press.
Held, D. (1995). *Democracy and the global order: From the modern state to cosmopolitan governance*. Cambridge, MA: Polity.
Helliwell, C. J., & Hindess, B. (in press). "Culture," "society" and the figure of man. *History of the Human Sciences*.
Hindess, B. (in press). Divide and govern. In R. Ericson & N. Stehr (Eds.), *Governing modern societies*. Toronto, Canada: University of Toronto Press.
Hirst, P. (1998). *From statism to pluralism*. London: University College London Press.
Hobsbawm, E., & Ranger, T. (Eds.). (1983). *The invention of tradition*. Cambridge, UK: Cambridge University Press.
Hutchinson, J. (1994). *Modern nationalism*. London: Fontana.
Kant, I. (1970). *Political writings* (Hans Reiss, Ed.). Cambridge, UK: Cambridge University Press.
Kymlicka, W. (1995). *Multicultural citizenship: A liberal theory of minority rights*. Oxford, UK: Oxford University Press.
Lister, R. (1997). *Citizenship: Feminist perspectives*. London: Macmillan.
Marshall, T. (1950). *Citizenship and social class*. Cambridge, UK: Cambridge University Press.
Miller, D. (1995). *On nationality*. Oxford, UK: Clarendon.
Sharp, A. (1997). *Justice and the Maori*. Auckland, New Zealand: Oxford University Press.
Smith, A. D. (1986). *The ethnic origins of nations*. Oxford, UK: Blackwell.
Spruyt, H. (1994). *The sovereign state and its competitors: An analysis of systems change*. Princeton, UK: Princeton University Press.
Tully, J. (1995). *Strange multiplicity: Constitutionalism in an age of diversity*. Cambridge, UK: Cambridge University Press.
Turner, B. S. (1986). *Citizenship and capitalism: The debate over reformism*. London: Allen & Unwin.
Turner, B. S. (Ed.). (1993). *Citizenship and social theory*. London: Sage.
Walker, R.B.J. (1993). *Inside/outside: International relations as political theory*. Cambridge, UK: Cambridge University Press.
Wolf, E. R. (1988). Inventing society. *American Ethnologist, 15*(4), 752-761.
Yeatman, A. (1994). *Postmodern revisionings of the political*. London: Routledge.
Young, I. M. (1990). *Justice and the politics of difference*. Princeton, NJ: Princeton University Press.

# 7. Who Is the Subject of Human Rights?

## ANNA YEATMAN
*Macquarie University*

*What is distinctive about human rights, when compared with the rights claims associated with modern citizenship, animals, or nonbiological units of conscious being (artificial intelligence)? It is suggested that each of these discourses constitutes the subject of rights differently. This article concentrates on both philosophical and psychological means of registering the unique individuality of the subject of human rights. Because human rights is predicated of all human beings, it is a universal discourse and one that Kant called "cosmopolitan right." The subject of human rights is also the subject in its existential integrity or wholeness. This article explores tensions between the subject of human rights and the jurisdictionally limited and exclusive subject of modern citizenship, tensions that pose new demands on states with respect to international law and standards.*

**The subject of human rights** is the individual human being. In terms of established traditions of rights and citizenship, this is an astonishing state of affairs. It can be said to represent the constitution of individuality. This is achieved, at least rhetorically, in the constitution of a fundamental and inalienable right of the individual to recognition of and respect for his or her dignity, integrity, and freedom by the governing authorities of states. States, because at the time of the foundational texts of human rights, they were the only units of government that could ensure recognition for such rights. This is still largely the case, with the partial exception of the European community. Where a state is a military dictatorship that routinely violates human rights, for example, its action invites a similar disregard for human rights from nongovernment organizations such as multinational corporations, as has been evident in the recent case of the Nigerian military dictatorship under General Obacha and the operation of the multinational oil company, Shell, in that country. Arguably, in the 21st century, transnational levels of governance will become increasingly involved in the implementation of human rights. This is likely to increase, rather than to resolve, the tension between state sovereignty and the metastate discourse of human rights.

It is a universal individuality that is constituted in human rights discourse because it is all human individuals to an equal degree, and regardless of differences between them, who become the bearers of human rights. Because individuality is universally bestowed in this way, human rights discourse can be seen as historically responsible for the constitution of individuality as such, at least to the extent that individuality depends on the positive institution in both rhetoric and practice of individual political, civil, economic, social, and cultural rights.[1]

If law, as Durkheim (1963) insisted, is an index of social solidarity and allows us to understand how society morally constitutes the subject, then human rights discourse may be seen as the juridical constitution of the human being in general and, thus, of a cosmopolitan conception of humanity. It is also the juridical constitution of the individual as the irreducible unit of humanity.

Many take human rights discourse to be an ineffectual ideal because it is so constantly contradicted by how actual states treat both those who are subjected to their jurisdictional authority and those with whom they are at war. However, the institutionalization of human rights after 1945 onward represents a new set of positive demands of the governing authorities of states; namely, that they accord respect to the principle of human dignity not because the human beings in question are their subjects, their citizens, or their enemies, but because they are human beings. The resulting tension between the claims of state sovereignty and the claims of human rights has led to a decisive shift in the politics of legitimacy or in what is generally accepted as the basis of rightful action. It has also opened up a space for a cosmopolitan public sphere (see Bohman, 1997) wherein the various supporters and exponents of human rights can discuss, debate, and specify them. If the focus is entirely on how human rights are so often violated, ignored, or denied by the governing authorities of states, the point is missed; namely, that the positive institutionalization of human rights in international law and standards represents a reconstitution of the subject as no longer only a dependent, subject, citizen, alien, or enemy but as an individual human being.

Here, I want to discuss some of the issues that pertain to the question of who is the subject of human rights without necessarily settling them, for they are difficult issues. One of the principal points I make is that the subject of citizenship is not the same thing as the subject of human rights, and, for this reason, we cannot expect the former to be an appropriate advocate for the latter. Nor can we expect there to be a resolution of the tensions between citizenship discourse and human rights discourse. They implicate phenomenologically different territories of right and being. Before we proceed to this discussion, we need to be reminded of just how historically recent and revolutionary is the conception of human rights.

## THE HISTORICITY OF HUMAN RIGHTS DISCOURSE

Human rights is a historically recent positive discourse of legitimacy and law, established only with the United Nations Charter in 1945 and what many see as the foundational text that enabled the charter to be specified in terms of rights, the Universal Declaration of Human Rights in 1948.[2] The Universal Declaration was not a binding treaty in international law, and thus effort was made by the United Nations to translate it into detailed treaty law (Sieghart, 1991). This occurred in 1966 with the adoption of two United Nations covenants, the International Covenant on Civil and Political Rights (ICCPR) and the International Covenant on Economic, Social and Cultural Rights (ICESR), which took force

10 years later in 1976 (Sieghart, 1991). More human rights treaties followed, and "five of the six major human rights treaties are ratified by three quarters or more of the UN member states, 50 per cent in the case of the Torture Convention" (Bayefsky, 1997, p. 77).[3]

The implementation of human rights law is not only beset by difficulties arising from the existence of regimes that systemically contravene human rights, but, more fundamentally, by a radical tension that the cosmopolitan conception of right has introduced into all legitimacy and law, a tension between human rights on one hand and national sovereignty on the other (see Bayefsky, 1997). Notwithstanding the empirical triumph of state sovereignty over the claims of human rights more often than not, the existence of international human rights law and standards represents a new conception of legitimacy for all national or domestic law. In national jurisdictions where the rule of law operates and where the national governments have signed human rights treaties, how established domestic law and policy jibe with these new international standards of human rights becomes a matter of ongoing practical concern and, sometimes, positive reconciliation between the two. As Kirby (1997) puts it for the common law jurisdictions of England and Australia, "courts of high authority are beginning to accept the view that international statements of human rights may be used by judicial officers in resolving ambiguities of legislation and in filling the gaps in the common law" (p. 20). For example, the Australian High Court's Mabo (1992) decision, which recognized prior occupancy of Australia and the Torres Strait by aboriginal and Torres Strait islander peoples and thus established the new legal doctrine in Australia of native title, was profoundly shaped by contemporary human rights discourse that now includes the idea of a right of self-determination for indigenous peoples (for discussion of this idea, see Scott, 1996). Kirby (1997) aptly remarks, "A more dramatic impact of the standards of basic human rights would be hard to imagine in the Australian context" (p. 21). This is true regardless of the fact that this decision has provoked a counterrevolution on the part of most of the state governments in Australia and of the commonwealth government since the accession of the Howard government in early 1997. These governments have invoked the principle of parliamentary sovereignty against what is construed as the inappropriate "judicial activism" of the Australian High Court in this as in other instances bearing on human rights (for discussion of the general tension between parliamentary sovereignty and international human rights treaties, see Tenbensel, 1996).

Human rights discourse, then, is not simply an ideal discourse without any purchase in the real world of states, peoples, and individuals. Like all discourses of legitimacy, it commands the high ground when the standards of legitimacy involved command wide acceptance. Contemporary human rights discourse articulates the normative historicity of a postcolonial and post-Holocaust era at a time when globalism has intensified the dynamics of international migration and diasporas. Globalism has also extended the reach and scale of the market economy so that there is probably no human society at this point that is not caught up in the global economy, to more or less extent. What Kant (1970) called the idea of cosmopolitan right depends on individuals, peoples, and states regarding themselves as belonging to a "universal state of mankind (*ius cosmopoliticum*)" (pp. 98-99). Kant (1970) distinguished between (a) "the civil right of individuals within a nation (*ius civitatis*)", (b) "the international right of states in their relationships with one another" (*ius gentium*)", and (c) "cosmopolitan right, in so far as individuals and states, coexisting in an external relationship of mutual influences, may be regarded as citizens of a universal state of mankind (*ius cosmopoliticum*)" (pp. 98-99). Ours is an era when the idea of cosmopolitan right can be resisted, twisted, suppressed, and repressed, but its moral force and practical salience remain unassailable.

Human rights as a conception of legitimacy trumps all other alternative conceptions of legitimacy. This is true even of the nationalist traditions of human rights, which represent a domestic human rights law. Where nationalist traditions of human rights represent these universals in terms of the distinctive civic virtue of a particular nation or people (consider, for example, the American doctrine of *Manifest Destiny*), it is a civic nationalism we have to hand. It is to be distinguished from universalistic nationalism where "the nation is simply a particular jurisdiction which particularizes while at the same time it participates in and is accountable to universal standards of justice" (Yeatman, 1994, p. 253; and for the distinction between ethnocratic, civic, and universalistic nationalisms, see Yeatman, 1994). Because civic nationalism makes an attachment to human rights appear to be a distinctive virtue of a particular people, it is a rhetorical investment that can lead to gross violations of the human rights of other peoples as in, for example, the massacre of hundreds of Vietnamese villagers by American troops at My Lai in 1968.

It is increasingly the case that legitimacy accrues to a particular national sovereign state only to the degree that it instantiates universal standards of justice and right as these are articulated in the current international discourse of human rights. This discourse is inevitably and properly contested by states that are quick to discern bias in how the most powerful national actors can influence international agencies such as the United Nations Security Council against them (for some discussion of bias in the application of human rights standards by the governmental human rights bodies of the United Nations, see Bayefsky, 1997, pp. 81-83). In particular, non-Western newly independent sovereign states have pointed out the triumphalist and self-interested versions of human rights discourse that the United States of America and its allies have imposed, often with the use of force, on other states.

The subjection of human rights discourse to self-interested interpretation is also inevitable, but does not as such cancel the ethical force of cosmopolitan right especially at this time. As neo-Kantian/Lacanian theorists such as Copjec (1996a) and Salecl (1994, 1996) argue, there is an inherent emptiness in the universals of human rights. They become specified only in how they are violated (Copjec, 1996a) and in how they are contested (Salecl, 1996). Salecl (1996) argues that the historical origins of the universal ideas of human rights may lead to traces of racism and male domination in human rights discourse, "but since universals are in themselves empty, we have to engage constantly in the struggle for their meaning and for their expansion, so that they do not exclude groups of people" (p. 164).

## THE SIGNIFICANCE AND RHETORIC OF HUMAN RIGHTS LAW WITH REFERENCE TO THE CONSTITUTION OF THE SUBJECT OF HUMAN RIGHTS

The adoption of human rights as the master discourse of international law in 1945 signaled a historically unprecedented choice on the part of the victors of the previous world war. Sieghart (1991), the eminent legal theorist of human rights, puts it thus:

> This time, the victorious Allies chose a different path from the one they had trodden in 1919: instead of imposing peace treaties on the vanquished, they sought to establish a new international legal order, founded on the three main principles declared in Article 1 of the Charter: the peaceful settlement of international disputes "in conformity with the principles of justice and international law," and accordingly the outlawing of aggressive wars; friendly relations among nations "based on respect for the principle of equal rights and self-determination of peoples"; and "respect for human rights and for fundamental freedoms for all without distinction as to race, sex, language, or religion." (p. 27)

The choice for the kind of cosmopolitanism Kant (1970) recommended in "Perpetual Peace" was surely governed by the full exposure at this time of the scale and depth of the Nazi Holocaust, a case of such sustained "radical evil" (Kant's phrase; and see Copjec, 1996b) that has provoked ongoing enquiry into the conditions of its possibility. Evidently, the Allies realized, belatedly, the contribution of the Versailles Treaty after World War I to the rise of Nazism as a social movement in Germany. The Allies had also to cope with the demands for independent statehood from the peoples they had colonized at a time when it would be difficult to reassert the legitimacy of colonialism given a post-Holocaust awareness of the nature of racism and of its potential for human destruction.

Sieghart (1991) brings out clearly the significance of the change in international law that the adoption of human rights represented. Prior to 1945, international law was determined by the right of sovereignty as expressed in the obligation of states to recognize each other's sovereignty.

> Sovereignty, in this context, meant—and still means—the unfettered exercise of power within the prince's [or state's] "domain"; that is, the territory over which he [or it] ruled, and the individuals within that territory who owed him [or it]

allegiance, originally called his "subjects" but now more usually described as the state's "citizens." (Sieghart, 1991, p. 25)

Citizens they may be called now, but from the standpoint of the international law of sovereignty, they are subjects. Sieghart (1991) remarks,

> the notions of "civil rights" and "civil liberties" which began to be developed in the domestic law of England in the seventeenth century and found their full flowering almost simultaneously in the French *Déclaration des droits de l'homme et du citoyen* in 1789 and the US Bill of Rights in 1791, for a long time found no echo in international law. Private individuals could not be the subjects of that law: they were the subjects of their princes, having only those rights which they were allowed on the level of "national" or "domestic" law. (p. 25)

Pre-1945 international law (what Kant called *ius gentium*) permitted a prince or state to do as he or it pleased with those who came under his or its sovereignty. This being the case, international law could "have no concern for the rights and obligations of princes and their subjects towards each other" (Sieghart, 1991, p. 25). International law of this kind turns citizen rights, even rights that are framed in terms of a universalistic discourse of human rights, into privileges granted by the sovereign. The only exception to the right of the sovereign state over those who were its subjects was the case of resident and nonresident aliens, namely those who belonged to another prince's or state's jurisdiction. Maltreatment of them by the state "could constitute a violation of the 'personal' sovereignty of the state to which they belonged" (Sieghart, 1983, p. 11). Sieghart (1983) comments, "Accordingly, international law from early times imposed (and still imposes) an obligation on states to make their territories safe for the nationals of other States, even while there was no such obligation for their own nationals" (p. 11). The following passage from Sieghart (1983) is worth reproducing in full:

> In the result, international laws for a long time demanded substantial protection for the aliens within a State, while demanding none for the State's own citizens. But even that demand flowed from the doctrine of national sovereignty itself—so that, even if a State fell short of the requirement to protect another State's nationals, for example by expropriating their property, the compensation was due to the other State whose "personal" sovereignty had been violated, not to the individual whose property had been taken.
> And for centuries, one proposition remained without challenge: by reason of the doctrine of national sovereignty, the Law of Nations could not recognize any rights vested in any individual against any sovereign State—his own or another. (p. 12)

By 1945, the indifference of international law to the fate of national-domestic subjects was no longer sustainable: "The atrocities perpetrated on their own citizens by the regimes of Hitler and Stalin were not only moral outrages . . . they were a very real threat to international peace and stability" (Sieghart, 1991,

p. 25). And, so Sieghart (1991) proposes, "there was carried through a veritable revolution in international law,"

> within a single generation it developed a new code of law, enumerating and closely defining certain "human rights" and "fundamental freedoms" for all human beings, anywhere in the world, which were thenceforth no longer to lie in the gift of the sovereign states whose citizens these human beings were, but were said to inhere in them "inalienably," and so could not be abridged, denied, or forfeited— even by their sovereign rulers—for whatever cause. (pp. 25-26)

Rights are rights as distinct from privileges only if they are viewed as inherent in the human being and as inalienable in this way. This was the first time that such rights were attributed to all human beings, as distinct from those who were interpellated as rights-bearing subjects within the domestic law of a particular nation state. It was the first time that "cosmopolitan right" in the Kantian sense was accorded a positive existence. From thence forward, from the standpoint of international law and standards of legitimacy, the sovereignty of the state could not be used as justification for the violation of the human rights of nationals. As Sieghart (1983) puts it, the "strict doctrine of national sovereignty has been cut down in two crucial respects":

> First, how a State treats its own subjects is now the legitimate concern of international law. Secondly, there is now a superior international standard, established by common consent, which may be used for judging the domestic laws and the actual conduct of sovereign States within their own territories and in the exercise of their internal jurisdictions, and may therefore be regarded as ranking in the hierarchy of laws even above national constitutions. (p. 15)

A further consequence of this revolution in international law is that it is no longer necessary to appeal to either a divine or natural law as a basis for human rights, for they now have a positive existence in law.[4] Their positive reality produces a politics of human rights. Not only does human rights become an openly contestable discourse (Connolly, 1993), but the positive institutionalization of human rights discourse invites a critique from all those who have been marginalized or excluded by the historical terms of its specification.

Let us return to the significance of the point that, if in post-1945 international law it is not the first time that human rights constitute the discourse of legitimacy, nonetheless it is the first time this discourse acquires cosmopolitan salience and force. For the first time, all human beings are constituted as the subjects of right in a way that is not already qualified by nationality (or gender). What does this mean with regard to the unit of this universal humanity? Who or what is that unit? All thirty articles of the Universal Declaration of Human Rights are predicated on the individual as the subject of human rights. Article 1 states, "All human beings are born free and equal in dignity and rights," whereas Article 2 states what Sieghart (1983) calls the concept of nondiscrimination, namely, that no differentiation between persons or classes of persons is permitted in respect of human rights. Article 2 states the principle of nondiscrimination, or equality, thus: "Everyone is entitled to all the rights and freedoms set forth in this Declaration, without distinction of any kind, such as race, colour, sex, language, religion, political or other opinion, national or social origin, property, birth or other status."

If, in the adoption of human rights as international law, there is the first positive specification of cosmopolitan right, this is also the first time that the individual qua unit of humanity emerges as the subject of right: "In the words of the great British international lawyer, Sir Hersch Lauterpacht, in 1950: 'The individual has acquired a status and a stature which have transformed him [sic] from an object of international compassion into a subject of international right' " (Sieghart, 1991, p. 26).

To put it differently, this is the first time that individuality is specifiable in terms of what it means to be a unit of humanity. The principle of nondiscrimination ensures that this is the case. All individuals without distinction of any kind are to be counted as subjects of human rights and as sharing an equality of status because they are each individual units of humanity. This is not, as Sieghart (1983) emphasizes, a "simplistic philosophy of egalitarianism" (p. 18). When all human beings are in view as bearers of human rights, then this is a conception of individual rights that has to take into account the manifold differences between individuals. No such reduction of difference as modern liberalism effects, where all individuals come to instantiate a market-oriented possessive individual, is possible when all human beings have to be encompassed in a conception of individualized rights. Sieghart's (1991) formulation is useful.

> It does not of course follow that modern international human rights law adopts a simple philosophy of egalitarianism. On the contrary, it is the recognition that all human beings differ from each other, and that each individual is unique, which underlies the concept of the integrity and dignity of the individual person which human rights law is primarily concerned to protect. (p. 18)

It is because all differences between human beings have to be encompassed within the universality of human rights that the universals of human rights are empty until they are specified through their violation or contestation. At the same time there is offered in the discourse of human rights a substantive idea of the integrity and dignity of the human being, an idea that remains an empty universal in respect of differences between individuals (and groups), to be sure, but that nonetheless stands for a substantive conception of what it means to be human.

A people can be the collective subject of rights, and one of the fundamental rights contained in the United Nations Charter was the right of peoples to self-determination (Scott, 1996; and for discussion of this collective right that he argues is not a human right, see Sieghart, 1991, pp. 40-41; but see also the more nuanced and extended discussion of Jones, 1999, who argues that there can be collective human rights if they are based in a shared and universalizable interest of individuals, in this case, a shared interest in living in a self-determining political community or state). Given the historical assumption that a people is a nation, and a nation is a state with sovereign territorial jurisdiction, member states of the United Nations have resisted the extension of this right to indigenous peoples. Advocacy of the collective right of self-determination for indigenous peoples is argued with reference to the principle of nondiscrimination as is evidenced in this statement of Scott (1996) offered as an intervention at the first session of the working group charged by the United Nations Commission on Human Rights with working on a draft declaration of the Rights of Indigenous Peoples:

> The exclusion of an indigenous people from the status of being a "people" has at least the effect of creating discriminatory access to the special kind of freedom that other peoples enjoy, namely that of the human right to self-determination. (pp. 817-818)

Yet, recognition of a people's right to self-determination cannot be at the expense of individual human rights without undermining the nature of human rights, namely, their existence as inalienable rights that are not the privilege of any collectivity to grant or to withhold. It is for this reason that Sieghart (1991) argues that collective rights should not be regarded as human rights: "On grounds of fundamental principle as well as grammar, therefore, human rights are individual rights and not collective rights" (p. 38).[5]

This is not to say that the individual as the unit of human rights does not have a right to the kind of collective existence that fosters his or her rights. The Universal Declaration makes it clear that this is the case, and, in this way, also makes it clear that human rights depend on the social character and collective existence of human beings. For instance, the Universal Declaration (Article 15) states that "Everyone has the right to a nationality" that (Article 16) "the family is the natural and fundamental group unit of society," and (Article 22) that

> everyone, as a member of society, has the right to social security and is entitled to realization, through national effort and international co-operation, and in accordance with the organization and resources of each State, of the economic, social and cultural rights indispensable for his dignity and the free development of his personality.

Sampford (1997) formulates the general point here as a conception that "sees collective rights as individual rights to the benefits of group life" (p. 63). This includes the "right of all human beings to belong to a culture and to be able to engage in cultural activity to which they feel a personal affinity." Sampford draws out the logic of this conception; namely, that the individual has the right to choose which kind and extent of group life he or she wishes to belong to or participate in. Although his is a liberal-individualist emphasis on individual choice and is thus a contestable representation of human rights, it remains nevertheless that the unit of human rights discourse is the individual human being.[6]

## THE CONCEPT OF THE INTEGRITY AND DIGNITY OF THE INDIVIDUAL SUBJECT OF HUMAN RIGHTS

There are several things to be said of this concept. The first point to make is that the individual subject of human rights is not the same thing as the individual citizen. This is so even when the citizenship in question is conceived in terms of human rights as is true of the French *Déclaration des droits de l'homme et du citoyen*. Indeed, it is reasonable to argue with Balibar (1994), following Kant, that the idea of the citizen presupposes the abolition of subjection and the assumption of a subjectivity that gives itself its own law: "Citizenship is not one among the attributes of subjectivity, on the contrary: it is subjectivity, that form of subjectivity that would no longer be identical with subjection for anyone" (Balibar, 1994, p. 12). For Balibar (1994), it is the status of the citizen that is the necessary mediation of the Kantian categories of the subject on one hand and the "essence of man" on the other (pp. 7-8). This is because Balibar, rightly in relation to citizenship, insists on the political specification of the subject. If the citizen is the subject free from subjection—the subject who gives itself its own law, a rule of law to which it becomes subjected—then this legislative specification of the subject requires there to be a bounded state jurisdiction to which its citizenship attaches. In this context, one where the institution of citizenship actualizes the universality of the subject in the form of a jurisdictionally specified rights of man, it makes sense to view citizenship as this mediating third term in relation to the subject and the essence of man.

Thus, citizenship, at least in this modern republican sense, has a relationship to human rights, and, to this degree, there is common ground shared by the citizen and the subject of human rights. However, the subject of human rights is not the same as the subject of citizenship for two related reasons. First, citizenship, as already pointed out, is always citizenship of a particular state or legislative jurisdiction. Being this jurisdiction, and not that one, it has to work on the principle of exclusion of those who do not belong to this jurisdiction from the rights that inhere in citizenship (see Hindess, 2000 [this issue]). This is the case even if the criteria for belonging are positively accountable to standards of human rights; that is, for example, they are nondiscriminatory. Citizenship is inherently particularistic even when its principles are universal, and a plurality of particular jurisdictions of citizenship is needed to guarantee that an international order will be one that upholds human rights (an argument that Kant makes in "Perpetual Peace"). Thus, although the subject of human rights and the modern citizen are both constituted in terms of the universality of human rights, they are constituted as distinct kinds of subject. The individual as the subject of human rights belongs nowhere as far as any particular jurisdiction goes, but represents the substantive claim in relation to which any jurisdiction may be judged. The citizen, on the other hand, requires a particular jurisdiction in order to be a citizen. This is why the Universal Declaration of Human Rights (Article 15) states that everyone has the right to a nationality. At the same time, United Nations human rights treaties recognize the empirical existence of "stateless persons," that is, "persons who are not considered as a national by any State under the operation of its Law" (from the United Nations convention relating to the Status of Stateless Persons), and their function is to extend human rights to this class of noncitizen subjects.

Second, the individual as the subject of human rights is something more and less than his or her political capacity. It is all aspects of individuality that are implicated in what can be called the existential security (Künneman, 1995), the integrity and the dignity of the individual. *Existential security* is a term intended to capture the common ideal of the two international covenants on human rights, the "ideal of a human being free from fear and want" (a phrase taken from the common preamble to the two covenants on Civil and Political Rights and Economic, Social and Cultural Rights, respectively, as cited by Künneman, 1995, p. 326). Künneman (1995) usefully classifies what he calls "fundamental human rights principles" as falling into either (a) existential security, (b) participation in the life of the community, or (c) cultural and spiritual identity. These dimensions of individuality apply as much to those who do not have the political capacity to be citizens as they do to those who have this capacity. Young children and profoundly intellectually disabled adults are subjects whose cognitive incapacity or immaturity forces them to be dependent on others for assistance in becoming, being, and acting as an individual, an assistance that may or may not be given. Thus, they are not citizens, but they can be subjects who enjoy the human right to individuality. In jurisdictions where the rule of law obtains, there may be an argument for prioritizing the implementation and monitoring of their human rights over and above those of effective citizens. Certainly, if effective advocacy of human rights depends on subjects who identify and act as citizens, human rights are likely to be improperly reduced to citizen rights. Under these circumstances, it is unlikely that those who are not citizens in the political sense of the word will do very well in terms of recognition of their human rights. As Gibson (1998) may be taken to suggest, it is a category mistake to require the implementation of human rights to be contingent on the political participation of those who possess them. More forcefully, we cannot expect citizen subjects to be good or effective advocates of human rights. Only subjects who identify as the subjects of human rights can be such advocates.

The second point to make about who is the subject of human rights is this: If all human beings, because they are human, are to be accorded human rights, this is a conception of the dignity and freedom of the human being very different from that offered in patrimonial constructions of human society where some categories of human being are placed in a natural relationship of subjection to and dependency on those who are positioned as the kings, fathers, and masters of the former. For a start, human rights presuppose that all human beings are equal even if they are very different in their respective capacities and degree of wealth. That is, the idea of human rights is fundamentally at odds with any notion that one human being because of their characteristics is naturally subjected to another. Furthermore, the notion that those who are stronger, wealthier, and freer as kings, fathers, and masters are the effective protectors of those who are required to be dependent on them is a notion that the discourse of human rights came into being to discredit. Dependency, as far as human rights go, is not understood to qualify the humanity of individuals in ways that force them to be subjected to those who enjoy a freedom of independent wealth and embodied selfhood.

The subject of human rights, then, is a postpatrimonial individual. This is not the individuality of the patrimonial and masculine household head responsible for the welfare of those who come under his protection as his household dependents. It is a different kind of individuality. What kind of individuality is it, then, that is implicated in the idea that existential security, participation in the life of the community, and cultural and spiritual identity are all involved in the human rights of the individual? This is surely an individuality present in all its spheres of existence and all its modes of expression. Moreover, for existential security, participation, and cultural-spiritual identity to have reference to individuality, they have to refer to the uniqueness of the individual. They thus refer in turn to whatever it is that conduces to a sense on the part of this individual that he or she is alive and free to live his or her own life as distinct from living the life of another (these thoughts are stimulated by Winnicott, 1971, 1986), and that being so, this individual is able to participate as his or her own person in the social world(s) he or she inhabits, as well as being free to make his or her own interpretation of the cultural and spiritual dimensions of his or her existence. This is an individual who does not have to be independent in the sense of economically self-sufficient, militarily able to defend him- or herself, or socially mature such that he or she can be held fully responsible in a legal sense for the consequences of his or her choices, decisions, and actions. Rather, it is an individual free to be his or her own person, to achieve what Winnicott (1971) calls "unit status" (p. 70).

This fundamental idea of the own-ness, the integrity, the uniqueness, the dignity of the human person is the bedrock on which the conception of human rights stands. It carries with it unstated assumptions as to the integrity of an embodied self, assumptions that are more elaborated in post-Freudian psychoanalytic theory than anywhere else. These assumptions may be teased out by asking such questions as the following: First, can a nonhuman subject have human rights? Second, can a nonbiological unit of consciousness such as a self-reflective unit of artificial intelligence have human rights?

These questions seem to simply exaggerate the tautology involved in the proposition that it is the human being that is the subject of human rights. However, they require us to think more about what may be at stake in this conception of human and in this way require us to go beyond this tautology. For instance, it is reasonable to argue as animal rights activists do that animals as units of sentient being have integrity and that this integrity should be respected in the idea of animal rights. This is not, I think, what Winnicott (1971) had in mind when he used the phrase "unit status" in the context of writing an essay on "Creativity and its Origins." Winnicott was making a number of assumptions that have to do with a human claim to individuality; specifically, that it is a remarkable intersubjective as well as intrapsychic struggle for a human being to achieve a sense of its own embodied individuality that distinguishes it as a self in relation to its others, and furthermore, that the creativity of the human individual arises out of its attempt to master this struggle in ways that sustain its infantile fantasies of omnipotence in an environment that resists these fantasies. Winnicott, in short, associates the freedom to live one's own life as distinct from having to live the life of another with the freedom to be creative. In this regard, his conception of individuality is not unlike Arendt's (1958). Arendt (1958) makes action or the freedom to initiate a new beginning the distinctive attribute of human individuality. Winnicott's and Arendt's accounts of individuality show it to be entirely imbued with an intersubjective relationship of the self to its others, and, in this way, they do not offer an individualistic conception of individuality that is nonrelational in character. Winnicott's account is a useful supplement to Arendt's because Winnicott does not privilege action over being in respect of individuality. On the contrary, for Winnicott (1986), creativity arises only out of the experience of being one's own person: "To be creative a person must exist and have a feeling of existing, not in conscious awareness, but as a basic place to operate from" (Winnicott, 1986, p. 39).[7]

As to nonbiological units of consciousness, we can grant their prospective existence and even allow, in the future, that they may go beyond the reiteration of rule (their programming) and enter into some kind of meta-reflective relationship to rule. This might be what Arendt called "thinking," but it is certainly not what she called "action." Nor will such nonbiological units of consciousness achieve what Winnicott calls "unit status." By their nature, they are not their own subjects. On the contrary, they are thoroughly symbiotic subjects extending and mimicking as they do the consciousness of their human creators. Thus, if nonbiological units of consciousness are granted rights, these will not be human rights, but the rights of such entities.

## CONCLUDING REMARKS

Human rights, I am arguing then, is a conception of rights driven by the idea of the integrity of the human individual. Put differently, for human beings to be accorded human rights means that they are accorded the right to unit status or the right to individuality. This is a remarkable right to universalize and to make coextensive with the reach of humanity. Yet, it is clear that it is impossible to get to the essence of individuality without this universal conception of human rights. This is why it makes sense to enquire into whom is the subject of human rights.

Such attempt at enquiry here is only a beginning, requiring more systematic development and elaboration. If I have made one point well, I think it is the point that the subject of human rights is not the same as the subject of citizenship. If this point is correct, we cannot expect the governmental institutions of citizenship to secure human rights, as by and large they do not. Just as there is a fundamental and irresolvable tension between national sovereignty and human rights discourse, there is also a fundamental tension between the institutions that function on behalf of citizenship and those that function on behalf of human rights. For this reason, it is highly problematic for national state governments to be the only agents responsible for the funding and support of agencies charged with the implementation and monitoring of human rights. It is also highly problematic to expect citizen-subjects to be good or careful advocates on behalf of the human rights of individuals.

## NOTES

1. In an unpublished paper on relational individualism, I distinguish between two orders of interpellation and constitution of individuality: the one institutional and juridical, the other intimate and intersubjective. It is the former level that is being referred to here.

2. Sieghart (1991) comments on the relationship between the charter and the declaration:

> By the time of the adoption of the UN Charter it had not proved possible to define what these 'human rights and fundamental freedoms' were. In order to repair this omission, the United Nations proceeded to draft the famous Universal Declaration of Human Rights. (p. 27)

3. Bayefksy (1997) goes on to point out that "these superficial figures conceal the fact that there are hundreds of reservations to these treaties which purport to limit the scope of the ratifying states' actual obligations" (p. 77). In a footnote, Bayefksy (1997) points out, for example, that "there are 119 reservations and declarations from 47 states to the Convention on the Elimination of Discrimination Against Women" (p. 77). Her point is clearly important and crucially so in relation to the implementation of human rights, but it does not address the significance of the adoption of human rights rhetoric by states.

4. Sieghart (1983) makes this important point:

> Accordingly, the need for standards founded on systems of divine or natural law has disappeared, and with it the need for the legal positivist to object to them. To judge whether a national law is good or bad, just or unjust, recourse is no longer to the Creator or to Nature, or to belief in either of them. Instead, one may refer to the rules of international human rights law, as defined in the relevant instruments which have been brought into existence since 1945. (p. 15)

5. The passage preceding this concluding sentence reads,

> We must first recall that the principal oppressors throughout history have themselves been collectivities in the form of states and their public authorities, as well as collectivities (including political parties and even churches) within the state. The single objective of human rights theory, and now of human rights law, has therefore always been to protect weak individuals from the oppression of powerful groups, by giving them "inalienable" rights which "inhere" in them as individuals. This explains why all the human rights and fundamental freedoms which the modern international legal code defines and protects are formulated as individual rights or freedoms, using such phrases as "everyone has the right to" or "everyone has the freedom of"... this is just as much the case for the "economic, social and cultural" rights in the code as it is for the "civil and political" ones. (Sieghart, 1991, p. 38)

Again, for a more considered philosophical case for why the unit of human rights is the individual, see Jones (1999).

6. Individuals must consent to their participation in collective life, but it is not obvious that choice has to be the vehicle of consent.

7. The next two sentences read: "Creativity is then the doing that arises out of being. It indicates that he who is, is alive." These cryptic allusions to Winnicott's theory of the development of individuality belie, of course, the richness of this theory.

## REFERENCES

Arendt, H. (1958). *The human condition*. Chicago: Chicago University Press.

Balibar, E. (1994). Subjection and subjectivation. In J. Copjec (Ed.), *Supposing the subject* (pp. 1-16). London: Verso.

Bayefsky, A. (1997). The UN and the international protection of human rights. In B. Galligan & S. Sampford (Eds.), *Rethinking human rights* (pp. 74-87). Sydney, Australia: Federation Press.

Bohman, J. (1997). The public spheres of the world citizen. In J. Bohman & M. Lutz-Bachmann (Eds.), *Perpetual peace: Essays on Kant's cosmopolitan ideal* (pp. 179-201). Cambridge, MA: MIT Press.

Connolly, W. (1993). *The terms of political discourse* (3rd ed.). Princeton, NJ: Princeton University Press.

Copjec, J. (1996a). Introduction: Evil in the time of the finite world. In J. Copjec (Ed.), *Radical evil* (pp. vii-xxviiii). London: Verso.

Copjec, J. (1996b). (Ed.). *Radical evil*. London: Verso.

Durkheim, E. (1963). *Emile Durkheim: Selections from his work with an introduction and commentaries by George Simpson*. New York: Cromwell.

Gibson, D. (1998). *Aged care: Old policies, new problems*. Cambridge, UK: Cambridge University Press.

Hindess, B. (2000). Citizenship in the international management of populations. *American Behavioral Scientist, 43*, 1486-1497.

Jones, P. (1999). Human rights, group rights, and people's rights. *Human Rights Quarterly, 21*, 80-107.

Kant, I. (1970). Perpetual peace: A philosophical sketch. In H. Reiss (Ed.), *Kant: Political writings* (pp. 93-131). Cambridge, UK: Cambridge University Press.

Kirby, M. (1997). Human rights: An agenda for the future. In B. Galligan & C. Sampford (Eds.), *Rethinking human rights* (pp. 2-23). Sydney, Australia: Federation Press.

Künneman, R. (1995). A coherent approach to human rights. *Human Rights Quarterly, 17*, 323-342.

Salecl, R. (1994). *The spoils of freedom: Psychoanalysis and feminism after the fall of socialism*. New York: Routledge.

Salecl, R. (1996). See no evil, speak no evil: Hate speech and human rights. In J. Copjec (Ed.), *Radical evil* (pp. 150-169). London: Verso.

Sampford, C. (1997). The four dimensions of rights. In B. Galligan & C. Sampford (Eds.), *Rethinking human rights* (pp. 50-74). Sydney, Australia: Federation Press.

Scott, C. (1996). Indigenous self-determination and decolonization of the international imagination: A plea. *Human Rights Quarterly, 18*, 814-820.

Sieghart, P. (1983). *The international law of human rights*. Oxford, UK: Clarendon.

Sieghart, P. (1991). International human rights law: Some current problems. In R. Blackburn & J. Taylor (Eds.), *Human rights for the 1990s: Legal, political and ethical issues* (pp. 24-43). London and New York: Mansell.

Tenbensel, T. (1996). International human rights conventions and Australian political debates: Issues raised by the Toonen case. *Australian Journal of Political Science, 31*, 7-25.

Winnicott, D. W. (1971). Creativity and its origins. In D. W. Winnicott (Ed.), *Playing and reality* (pp. 65-86). New York: Routledge.

Winnicott, D. W. (1986). Living creatively. In D. W. Winnicott (Ed.), *Home is where we start from* (pp. 35-55). Harmondsworth, UK: Penguin.

Yeatman, A. (1994). Multiculturalism, globalisation and rethinking the social. *The Australian and New Zealand Journal of Sociology, 30*, 247-254.

Yeatman, A. (1999) *Relational individualism*. Unpublished manuscript, Macquarie University.

# 8. Culturally Appropriate Indigenous Accountability

## TIM ROWSE
*Australian National University*

*Since they renounced the policy goal of assimilation in the 1970s, Australian governments have encouraged indigenous Australians to form corporations. Such bodies receive public money to deliver services, and they have become the sinews of a mobilized indigenous constituency. By reviewing the research and recommendations of a recent Australian government report, this article addresses the controversy about the indigenous corporation's multiple accountability: to the taxpayer, their employees, and their clients. In addition, drawing on recent international theoretical debates about the rationales of liberal tolerance for cultural minorities, this article qualifies the widely held assumption that accountability in this instance must be culturally appropriate.*

**Australia is a settler colonial** nation-state. In 1788, Britain proclaimed sovereignty over a continent inhabited by people who came to be known as aborigines and Torres Strait islanders. The colonists' laws, structures of government, and land-use policies made no concessions to indigenous sovereignty and customary law. The land was simply there for the taking, and indigenous Australians, region by region, became subjects of laws, public policies, and private philanthropic strategies that both succoured and regimented them.

Although there has long been an intellectual anthropological tradition of recognizing and studying indigenous Australian customs, from the point of view of colonial law, indigenous traditions of self-government were of no significance.[1] Until the middle of the 20th century, social policies were consistent with a scientific opinion that aborigines were a "doomed race." Over the following quarter century (that is, until the early 1970s) that prognosis persisted in modified form as a pronouncement not on biological persistence but on the viability of indigenous culture and society. The policy of assimilation (c. 1950-1972) rested on the view that indigenous social forms were so ruined by contact with the modern world of the colonists that the state's only humane option was to absorb the remnant families and individuals into the Australian way of life.

---

**Author's Note:** *The author would like to thank Christos Mantziaris for first drawing his attention to the importance of the Fingleton review and for discussing the argument in this article with him on several occasions. The author thanks the editors, who have been very helpful, offering most interesting suggestions, and he also thanks those who responded to an earlier draft read to the anthropology seminar, Australian National University, March 1998.*

The most beneficial aspect of assimilation, from an indigenous point of view, was that it required Australia's state and commonwealth governments to repeal all legislation discriminating against indigenous Australians, but that civil rights agenda was accompanied by governments' strenuous denial of the possibility of specifically indigenous rights—the most contentious of which was rights in land. As well, social policy continued, until the early 1970s, to treat the indigenous family as a pathological structure from which children were best liberated by forced removal. The pain this has caused "the stolen generations" has only recently been given popular exposure. Notwithstanding the civil rights benefits of assimilation, this policy era was interpreted, in the behaviour and discourse of indigenous Australians themselves, as a continuation of colonial aggression.

In the early 1970s, Australian governments began to repudiate the social analysis, philosophy, and programs of assimilation. Essentially, progressive government practice ceased to view indigenous collectives as unsustainable vestiges of the precolonial past and began to see persisting indigenous communality in a positive and optimistic light. Assimilation was renounced and self-determination became the new policy rubric.

One can depict this policy change as a shift in governmental rationality. Assimilation favoured a rationality of individuation of the indigenous population: Each indigenous person or household would be separated from the heritage that inhibited their joining in the Australian way of life. Assimilation sought to emancipate the individual—by education and by exhortation and inducements—from the cultural group so that he or she could be an equal member of the wider nation. Self-determination policy, although leaving intact many relationships of government/individual (such as the civil rights to vote, receive welfare benefits, hold property, sue and be sued, make contracts), has encouraged indigenous Australians' legal incorporation. Governmental rationality is now not only individuating but also communalizing and corporatizing.

One of the most influential critics of assimilation policy, C. D. Rowley (1972), came to a consideration of Australia's domestic colonial policies from a postwar career of training officials for Papua New Guinea.[2] There, the village, the group, and the clan had been accepted as necessary and viable units of an indigenous social order that included continuing indigenous rights to land. The society of Papua New Guinea was not viewed as the ruins of an older culture now handicapping the progress of individuals, but as a sociality to be valued and strengthened. Impressed, rather than dismayed, by the continuing vitality of group life among indigenous Australians in the 1960s, Rowley (1972) urged Australian governments to facilitate incorporation among aborigines and Torres Strait islanders.

> The aim of "assimilation" has been to winkle out the deviant individual from the group, to persuade him to cut the ties which bind him and his family to it, and to set him up as a householder in the street of the country town. But policies which aim to change social habit by educating individuals, while ignoring the social context

which has made him what he is, can have only limited success. A program involving social change must deal with the social group. (p. 417)

Through incorporated organizations, indigenous Australians could more effectively pursue their own advancement.

Other policy intellectuals endorsed and elaborated Rowley's vision. For example, H. C. Coombs, chair of the policy advisory Council for Aboriginal Affairs (1967-1976), believed that it was possible to design an incorporation statute that drew on the strengths of indigenous Australians' communal traditions. Community representatives would be

> chosen by the Aborigines themselves as far as possible by their own methods, and the legislation [would] operate in a way designed to minimize interference with the internal workings of the traditional social structure, sources of authority and mutual economic obligations. (Commonwealth of Australia, 1972, p. 49).[3]

As such hopes gained authority within Australia's commonwealth government, a defining phrase emerged: *culturally appropriate*. When the Fraser government passed the Aboriginal Councils and Associations Act (ACA) in 1976, the Minister for Aboriginal Affairs, Ian Viner, genuflected to cultural difference:

> What is so important about this measure is that it will recognize cultural differences between Aboriginal and non-Aboriginal societies and enable Aboriginal communities to develop legally recognizable bodies which reflect their own culture and do not require them to subjugate this culture to overriding Western legal concepts. (cited in Fingleton, 1996, p. 32)

During the past 22 years, more than 5,000 indigenous organizations have been formed under the ACA and other statutes.[4] They perform a variety of tasks, but nearly all of them either hold title to land or use government grants to provide services (housing, educational, health) to indigenous Australians. Service in such organizations has become one of the contexts in which indigenous leaders acquire political experience, mediating between the demands of their communities and the requirements of the government agencies whose programs they help to implement. These leaders are legitimized both by the effectiveness of their organizations' delivery of services and by the claim that they deliver services in ways more culturally appropriate than the methods of mainstream government agencies.

## THE POLITICS OF INDIGENOUS ACCOUNTABILITY

Yet, there are problems for these indigenous leaders. As a settler colonial society, Australia remains home to political interests who see a threat in indigenous aspirations. The indigenous demand to get back some of their land has only partly been requited, and natural resource industries find its persistence threatening. The indigenous demand for greater self-government also looms as a threat to officials in local and state governments; they could lose authority and resources to emergent regional structures of indigenous governance. Finally, the discourses of populist politics in Australia have linked the political elites' endorsement of policies of economic restructuring with their endorsement of social policies predicated on respect for cultural difference: Indigenous Australians and non-English-speaking migrants have thus been scapegoated as privileged by the policies of Australia's misguided political elite. Politicians who wish to maintain what they see as economically rational policies are therefore tempted to propitiate these policies' victims by playing up to populist notions of ethnic privilege. In this defensive maneuver, such privileges as indigenous land rights and budgetary provision for indigenous organizations have become especially vulnerable.

Since self-determination policies were introduced, there have been scandals about the accountability of indigenous organizations in their expenditures of public subsidies. With so many organizations publicly endowed, the possibility of such scandal is endless. *Accountability* has thus emerged as a powerfully charged term in the language with which Australians now discuss indigenous rights, never more so than at the time of writing. To give readers a sense of this atmosphere, I will quote from a letter to a newspaper written by the commonwealth public servant whose job, under the ACA, is to maintain a register of indigenous corporations and monitor their acquittal of government grants. The registrar, Nourredine Bouhafs, was responding to Gatjil Djerrkura (chairman of the Aboriginal and Torres Strait Islander Commission [ATSIC], a statutory authority of the commonwealth government whose commissioners are chosen by an indigenous electorate and that distributes program money to many local aboriginal organizations incorporated under the ACA). Djerrkura and his fellow commissioners, nettled by Bouhafs's invigilation of some aboriginal legal services, had called for the abolition of the registrar's office. Bouhafs responded that this was "an arrogant attempt to say that accountability requirements for the expenditure of public funds do not apply to members of the Aboriginal elite."

> It is no exaggeration to say that, in Aboriginal Australia, ATSIC is a most unpopular organization. Aboriginal discontent with ATSIC is so widespread and so persistent that it cannot be responsibly ignored. In these circumstances, I would have thought that ATSIC had higher priorities to address than to attack a small statutory office that tries to bring some accountability and order to a difficult Aboriginal corporate environment.[5]

There is some basis for the registrar's rhetorical strategy of aligning popular indigenous sentiment with his own critical demand for "accountability and order." In competitive politics among indigenous Australians, it is not uncommon to question the financial competence and even probity of one's opponents. As well, there have been well-publicized occasions to criticize the administration of some aboriginal legal services. It is thus plausible for the registrar to drive a rhetorical wedge between the aboriginal elite and the indigenous Australians whom it is allegedly failing to serve through its resistance to what the registrar promotes as accountability. But what is the registrar's notion of accountability? Is it really so aligned with the perspectives of the indigenous constituency he invokes?

These questions bring us back to the policy rhetorics of the early 1970s that brought forth the ACA: The aspiration that aboriginal communities would (in Viner's words) "develop legally recognizable bodies which reflect their own culture and do not require them to subjugate this culture to overriding Western legal concepts" (p. 32).

In 1994, the board of ATSIC recommended to the Minister for Aboriginal Affairs Robert Tickner that the government fund a review of the ACA, to consider its effectiveness "in providing culturally appropriate forms of incorporation for Aboriginal and Torres Strait Islander communities" (Fingleton, 1996, p. 1). By the end of 1995, a review team had been assembled led by Jim Fingleton, a lawyer who, incidentally, also had experience of postindependence Papua New Guinea. Fingleton took to heart the stated aim that the ACA should provide for culturally appropriate accountability and self-governance. His report's findings and recommendations—including and reflecting the work of 13 researchers and consultants—are the focus of this article.

I see the Fingleton report as an essay in applied liberalism. To discuss the official and indigenous perceptions of indigenous organizations and their cultural appropriateness is not only to engage a topic of Australian public policy. To formulate a legitimate doctrine of indigenous accountability for a settler colonial nation-state is also a practical test for a postcolonial liberalism, for in that context legitimacy must be bicultural, that is, satisfactory to both indigenous Australians and the settler-colonial electorate that mandates policies of self-determination. The problem of formulating or inventing a culturally appropriate form of accountability is a practical instance of a question animating such liberal philosophers as Kymlicka (1995), Galston (1995), and Kukathas (1992): To what extent can a liberal state that protects the rights of national minorities also monitor and intervene in those national minorities' affairs?

My discussion begins by outlining Fingleton's (1996) main findings and recommendations. I then use Kymlicka (1995), Galston (1995), and Kukathas (1992) to sketch the debate about the tension between *tolerance* and *autonomy* as the ethical basis of a postcolonial liberalism, treating Kukathas's promotion of freedom of association as the key to resolving that tension. The lesson of the Fingleton report, I argue, is that we can more fruitfully conceive the indigenous constituency as an ensemble of associations rather than as a culture. Finally, I suggest that our consideration of the problems of indigenous accountability requires us to be reflective and strategic in holding notions of *custom* and *corporation* simultaneously in play.

## FINGLETON'S FINDINGS

Fingleton (1996) used his consultants' 32 case studies of aboriginal organizations to discover the practical problems of the 2,600 bodies incorporated under the ACA. Two kinds of problem emerged: defects within the act itself and defects in the registrar's administration of the act.[6] Without exceeding his statutory powers, Fingleton concluded, the registrar has been more prescriptive and prohibitive than the ACA's architects and early apologists intended. Fingleton doubted the registrar's cultural sensitivity, finding a high level of frustration among indigenous organizations and a high percentage of corporations breaching their legal obligations to report their financial affairs. His conclusions included the following points:

1. The act was too rigid in forbidding nonindigenous people from being members of indigenous corporations. He conceded that not all the submissions and studies find fault with this restriction; because there is no indigenous consensus on this matter, he recommended that each organization should decide for itself whether to accept nonindigenous people as members.
2. In prescribing that an incorporated body must have a minimum of 25 members, the ACA inhibits much indigenous incorporation. Small groups are typical of the fragmented indigenous polity and should not be so discouraged.
3. Because a member must be a "natural person," the act fails to allow the incorporation of umbrella organizations whose members are a number of smaller corporations. The act thus inhibits the formal consolidation of coalitions and networks of organizations.
4. By requiring membership to be made explicit in the form of lists of names and addresses, the act does not permit eligibility for membership to be defined with reference to a specified class of person.
5. The act is too specific in its prescription of decision-making procedures. It accords too much importance to general meetings, both annual and special, and it gives the registrar power to call such meetings and determine their procedures and agendas. As well, the act looks to governing committees to run organizations, without conceding that such committees may not be legitimate according to aboriginal norms, which see senior men and women as figures of authority. Finally, the registrar's "Model Rules" require members of governing committees to stand for election every year.

According to Fingleton (1996), the registrar sees benefits flowing from the tribulations of this regime; the registrar is reluctant to accept organizations' requests to vary the procedural demands encoded in the Model Rules. The local circumstances justifying requested departures from the Model Rules do not interest him. The Model Rules, as the registrar sees them, enable and enforce compliance with financial reporting requirements.

One interpretation of data cited by Fingleton (1996) supports the case for strict financial invigilation. Of the aboriginal corporations, 48% "had not submitted financial statements as required for the previous financial year" (p. 21). It is also estimated that 67.5% of corporations are in breach of their funding requirements; that is, requirements imposed not only by the ACA but by the terms of agreement between aboriginal organizations and the variety of government agencies funding them. Delinquency enough to justify the registrar's strict regime, one might say. However, the significance of such statistics is debatable: These many failings are in a sense an artefact of a regulatory regime that is unreasonably strict and pedantic. Regulatory regimes, in policing delinquency, also produce it as a quantifiable phenomenon. Indigenous Australians, Fingleton complained, have been stigmatized by this regulatory regime.

Fingleton's (1996) recommendations sought to reduce this emphasis on financial accountability and procedural correctness. Indigenous accountability, he argued, is multidimensional: The taxpayer is only one interest. Organizations that provide community services are accountable to their members, clients, other bodies with whom they have contracts, and their employees (by virtue to industrial statutes) and they are expected as well to enhance the broader political goal of indigenous self-determination. These various lines of accountability may be in tension with one another. For the government to highlight one strand of accountability (through the ACA and the registrar's interpretation of it) is arbitrary. The ACA, argued Fingleton, is not sufficiently concerned with internal accountability: the representative appropriateness of a body's objectives, the equity of its delivery of services, and the practical adequacy of its staffing. At best, the registrar has adopted narrow ways to consider and measure these factors. With the fetishizing of the registrar's prescriptions, resources have been devoted to activities of doubtful utility. ATSIC, seeking to justify elected commissioners' control over public money, has tended to forget stakeholders who are more interested in program outcomes than in compliance with the ACA. Fingleton recommended that funded indigenous organisations be accountable to ATSIC and to other funding agencies through negotiated service agreements, specifying program goals and measures of their attainment. He set out the following two conditions of real accountability:

> internal accountability—the incorporation has been culturally appropriate, such that the group has legal mechanisms in place which it has approved, understands and can be expected to observe in a reliable way; and external accountability—the service agreement has been negotiated, so that again a reliable arrangement for delivery of the service is in place. (Fingleton, 1996, p. 90)

Cultural appropriateness is central to Fingleton's vocabulary for advocating his revised notions of accountability. To see what broader lessons can be drawn from this feature of Fingleton's advocacy of reform to the current regime of aboriginal accountability, let us now turn to the very different world of debate in political philosophy.

## LIBERALISM, CULTURE, AND ASSOCIATIONS

In contemporary liberal political philosophers' efforts to set out the ethical basis of multiculturalism, two contrasting accounts of liberalism have emerged. One influential view is Kymlicka's (1995): "liberals can only endorse minority rights insofar as they are consistent with respect for the freedom or autonomy of individuals" (p. 75). Any culture is valuable, he argues, insofar as it is the condition of individual autonomy, for it is "only through having access to a societal culture that people have access to a range of meaningful options" (p. 83). If liberal states fail to protect the minority societal cultures within their borders, they are undermining the conditions of some people's options. No liberal state worthy of the name should fail to uphold individual autonomy. This perspective gives Kymlicka a criterion of the worth of any culture's proclaiming its right to respect as a minority. Kymlicka would not uphold the rights of any culture that "inhibit[s] people from questioning their inherited social roles," for such cultures condemn their members "to unsatisfying, even oppressive lives." He continues: "The national culture [Kymlicka's term for those cultures which pass this test] provides a meaningful context of choice for people, without limiting their ability to question and revise particular values or beliefs" (Kymlicka, 1995, pp. 92-93).

An alternative view of liberalism has been stated by Galston (1995).

> Liberalism is about the protection of diversity, not the valorization of choice. To place an ideal of autonomous choice ... at the core of liberalism is in fact to narrow the range of possibilities available within liberal societies. In the guise of protecting the capacity for diversity, the autonomy principle in fact represents a kind of uniformity that exerts pressure on ways of life that do not embrace autonomy. (p. 523)

Later he adds,

> autonomy is one possible mode of existence in liberal societies - one among many others; its practice must be respected and safeguarded; but the devotees of autonomy must recognize the need for respectful coexistence with individuals and groups that do not give autonomy pride of place. (p. 525)

In describing what is essential to liberalism, Galston elevates tolerance of ethical diversity above the value—autonomy—that one ethical tradition (represented in Kymlicka's work) promotes as liberalism's essence.

The nature of accountability—not the relative values of autonomy and tolerance—is the central problem of this article. Yet, I find the tension between these two versions of liberalism relevant in the following way. If Fingleton (1996) is right to point out that accountability is multi-dimensional, then there is scope for diversity in the ways that accountability is institutionalized. It could be argued that one way differentially to respect indigenous citizenship is to devolve to indigenous political elites the responsibility for defining accountability in a way culturally appropriate for them. If, in some critics' eyes, that puts too little emphasis on financial accountability and hands too much discretion to indigenous elites, then the liberal value of tolerance of difference can be invoked to defend diversity in political traditions. I find it easier to make this argument within Galston's (1995) perspective than within Kymlicka's (1995). Just as Kymlicka wants to submit minority cultures to a cross-cultural test (How well do they facilitate individual autonomy?), so a financial rationalist might argue that indigenous organisations should preeminently oblige financial accountability. I imagine that the ACA's registrar would be, in this sense, in sympathy with Kymlicka's autonomy and at odds with Galston's tolerance.

If the reader finds my application of Galston (1995) and Kymlicka (1995) to this problem of public policy a little fanciful, then some consideration of Kukathas's (1992) position within this debate might bring relief. I find Kukathas's work useful because he addresses a sociological issue that Kymlicka finds difficult: What is a culture? Although Kukathas's answer to this question will dismay many anthropologists and sociologists, to me it has a kind of governmental merit. Kukathas is critical of a liberalism that advances a social ontology of cultures and groups. To him, it is neither possible nor necessary to give the concept of the ethnic group or the cultural minority special status within liberal political theory. It is not possible because such groups or minorities are made up of individual actors whose association, as a group, is comparatively fragile and artificial. It is not necessary because what defines liberalism as a tradition of political thought is its defence of individual liberty. To defend liberalism by jettisoning its central idea is no defence at all. Kukathas wishes to show us liberalism's individual-centred ability to theorize the minority and the ethnic group. From the point of view of liberal political theory, a minority cultural group or community is best conceived, he suggests, as an association.

In his critique of earlier work by Kymlicka, Kukathas (1992) introduced the term *association* in parentheses: "Groups or communities have no special moral primacy in virtue of some natural priority. They are mutable historical formations—associations of individuals—whose claims are open to ethical evaluation" (p. 112). An individual's interests, he goes on to argue, were best defined by liberal political theory as his or her liberty to exit from any given association. This proposition required Kukathas to say something about the internal constitution of minority cultures. Groups and communities should not be assumed to be internally homogeneous, he warns. Commonly, there are differences of interest among subgroups and, more important, between ethnic elites and their mass memberships. Liberals must take note of such internal differences because "liberal theory is generally concerned to avoid entrenching majorities or creating permanent minorities" (Kukathas, 1992, p. 114). In particular, individuals and minorities within ethnic groups should be assured of their ability to challenge conceptions of the ethnic groups' interests that are currently dominant within an ethnic group. "In the end," he summarizes, liberalism views cultural communities more like private associations or, to use a slightly different metaphor, electoral majorities. Both are the products of a multitude of factors, and neither need be especially enduring, although they can be. The possibility that they might be, however, does not justify entrenching the interests they manifest. (Kukathas, 1992, p. 115)

A social scientist, more than a philosopher, will want to ask at this point how literally Kukathas wants us to take the notion of association. My sense is that for Kukathas, *association* is a normative analog. That is, states imbued with liberal principle should, in Kukathas's view, treat minority cultures, groups, and communities as if they were associations. To the extent that this assumption is descriptively inadequate, the putative association must mend its ways if liberals are to respect and defend each minority's conduct of its affairs. The normative force of *associations* goes in two directions.

Kukathas (1992) argued that to recognize cultures as associations binds the state to respect their political autonomy, provided that such groups and communities impose no restrictions on their members' freedom of association. If an individual is free to exit the association, then the association can determine freely whatever conditions of membership are culturally appropriate. Kukathas's liberalism would bind the state to acknowledge and respect the authority of the leaders of cultural minorities. Liberalism is thus, in this view, not intrinsically a source of arguments or pressures for assimilation. Nor does liberalism make it legitimate for governments to intervene in the affairs of minority cultures. As for the minority cultures, Kukathas's (1992) liberalism "imposes no requirement on those communities to be communities of any particular kind," other than that they must preserve the "inalienable right to leave" (p. 117). Although there is a Kukathian test of minority groups' internal relations—"the acquiescence of individuals with its cultural norms"(p. 117)—Kukathas believes that minority elites will voluntarily comply with that criterion without governmental pressure because people will otherwise exit their imperium.

## CULTURES AND ASSOCIATIONS

Does it make any sense to conceive the ensemble of indigenous Australians to be an association or even to be like an association? At first this might seem a strange question, a result of trying to give literal grounding to what is essentially a liberal fable. It could be objected that to pursue the likeness between *indigenous Australia* and an *association* is no more than a grotesquely comic indulgence of a Western liberal imagination that is so impoverished that it can think about other cultures only by refusing their difference and deploying, as a substitute, inappropriate but comfortably familiar notions of sociality.

Although I find that answer tempting, I think it is useful to refuse it for now. Let us rather dwell on the points of correspondence between indigenous

Australia and association. First, the very fact of colonial encapsulation produces the option of exit. There are certain conditions, Kukathas (1992) points out, which render substantive the "freedom of an individual to dissociate from a community." A person enclosed within a minority culture based on kinship is more likely to be able to exercise his or her freedom to dissociate if that minority culture is surrounded by a society based on the market and governed by elites with a robust respect for freedom of association. Second, although indigenous Australia is not one single association, it is made up of a myriad of associations. To protest that these social forms are insufficiently traditional is nostalgic. One indigenous leader and a consultant to Fingleton, Helen Corbett (1996), declared that "Indigenous peoples in Australia have an inherent right to self-determination. A constituent part of this right are [sic] the rights to a group identity and choice of membership, aims and structures of their political institutions" (p. 7). In this perspective, formal associations are an adaptive continuation of indigenous traditions, not a symptom of their capitulation and decline. In the course of asserting themselves as peoples with rights, indigenous Australians have incorporated.

One way to reconcile, or at least link, culture with association is to employ the rhetoric of *culturally appropriate* incorporation. Although Fingleton adhered to such language (e.g., Fingleton, 1996, pp. 138, 141), his report gives grounds for reflecting critically on it.

One strategy for dealing with cultural appropriateness is to pluralize it by reference to local variation in indigenous custom. Fingleton (1996) uses the phrase "any custom which they nominate" to refer to the liberty that indigenous groups should have to devise their own version of accountability (p. 141). The content of *custom* and *culture* is therefore to be locally determined by indigenous people themselves. Yet, in taking local circumstances into account, why refer to them in the idiom of *custom* or *culture*? The first published critical comment on the Fingleton report was alive to the need for diversity in modes of incorporation, but made no use of the rhetoric of custom in advancing this view. Mantziaris (1997a, 1997b), noting diversity of type and purpose among the bodies incorporated under the ACA, suggested that the ACA encompass three regulatory options: for land-holding bodies, service providers, and "mixed function bodies." Through such internal diversification of the act's regime, "corporations would be subject to accountability mechanisms appropriate to their social, political and financial composition" (Mantziaris, 1997b, p. 12). Mantziaris's "spectrum of incorporation need" seems to me to allow for, but not depend on, a diversity of local constructions of the demands of custom.

A second strategy for recognizing cultural appropriateness also found in the Fingleton report is to evoke the similarities, across many regions and circumstances, in the ways that indigenous Australians do their political business. Neither Fingleton nor his consultants explicitly postulate a model of aboriginal politics, but there is some consistency in the ways in which each writer evokes the indigenous polity in his or her region of study. Some of the authors of the case studies see political conflict as endemic to the indigenous domain and imply that we should not be dismayed that indigenous people, like other humans, have their competitive politics of land and resources. According to one consultant, Patrick Sullivan (1996a), the ACA is

> predicated on a false assumption of the simplicity of Aboriginal culture. That is, of single cohesive groups with delimited areas of concern and a widely held community of interest. Groups of this kind are, in fact, extremely rare and, where found, very small scale. (p. 32)

In most of his case studies, Sullivan found "an ongoing dispute between Aboriginal groups, whether within an Aboriginal corporation or outside it, about rights to the land" (Sullivan, 1996a, p. 1). To Martin (1996), "the native title arena... is characterized by a high degree of mutual suspicion and conflict between various Indigenous interests" (p. 3). Crough and Cronin (1996) refer to "instances where Aboriginal people have used the rules of the association to further their own objectives... taking over as senior office-holder and then using this position to dominate the community" (p. 16). In the small towns of western New South Wales, Cunneen and Libesman (1996) found that

> representative democracy has not been a part of traditional or in most instances contemporary Aboriginal culture. Aboriginal culture is characterized by close kinship and family ties. These result in commitments and obligations which do not necessarily accord with responsibility to the community as a whole. (p. 16)

In short, these consultants seem to agree that aboriginal politics is characterized by what Martin and Finlayson (1996) call "localism." The paradox of this evocation is that, in the one move, it does two opposed things. On one hand, localism as a cultural description allows for the heterogeneity of circumstances that makes it impossible to formulate a transcending criterion of culturally appropriate; on the other hand, localism is itself a homogenizing image, an evocation of the recognizable similarities, across Australia, of indigenous political cultures.

Because the Fingleton report exemplifies these problems in using a notion of culturally appropriate, the objection that association is a poor model for culture is further weakened. That is, no cultural model emerges clearly from the Fingleton review to show association to be counterfactual.

Let me now turn to some further implications of Kukathas's (1992) argument. When Kukathas likens cultures to associations, he poses two linked questions to our understanding of the indigenous domain: the relationships between leaders and led and the availability of the "exit" option.

What makes an indigenous leader today? In a world in which the association is becoming an important social form, our answer must include certain forms of cultural capital: practical knowledge of how organizations work and a life structured around the time commitments typical of bureaucracies. The case studies in the Fingleton review frequently touch on the problem of the gap between those indigenous people who are culturally familiar with the processes of formal associations and those who are not. However, it is far from clear whether such specialization poses a threat to indigenous self-determination or whether it affords a kind of cultural autonomy for those who remain uninvolved in organizational matters.

It was reported that some organizations in the Kimberley had given little thought to their formal rules of association because there were more urgent problems to think about. Incorporation had been no more than an expedient step in getting funding or land title. Particularly in the case of land-holding corporations, "the rules of their incorporated association do not determine how they run their lives and how they relate to each other and to other groups in the region," report Crough and Cronin (1996, p. 15). Indigenous people of western New South Wales were heard to say that they knew little about the ACA and were unaware of any problems with its provisions, unless and until they set out deliberately to change their constitution. Cunneen and Libesman (1996) remark their "lack of understanding about accountability requirements and about office holder responsibilities" (p. 27). Incorporation, they report, "is seen as simply a practical necessity and is not seen as having any direct connection to the nature and purposes of the group." This struck them as a bad thing.

> If there is no connection between the process and nature of incorporation, and the nature and purposes of the organization, it is difficult to see how the form of incorporation can be culturally appropriate. Incorporation is an imposed necessity without organic links to the organization. (Cunneen & Libesman, 1996, p. 27)

It could be objected that this lack of knowledge about the rules and processes of the ACA is not necessarily a problem. Nonaboriginal people could be employed to take care of most of those processes. However, there is a possibility that such nonaboriginal staff, by virtue of their competence in the processes of organizational governance, will acquire a lot of informal power. Certain qualified aboriginal people could share that informal power. Together they could comprise an elite without mandate.

If such specialization in organizational matters is seen as a threat to accountability among indigenous people, then one solution is to train more people in organizational participation. Support for such training is evident in a number of consultants' reports, but who are the trainers to be? Some people told the consultants that this was the registrar's responsibility (Martin, 1996). Sullivan, however, disagreed: ATSIC and the registrar are physically and culturally remote—clumsy and, at best, ineffective. Training could best be effected, he argued, if there were a regional, two-tiered structure of incorporation. Small, internally cohesive, often land-based and family-based, corporations would make up the bottom tier, whereas the upper tier would be made up of regional associations of which the bottom tier associations would be members. The larger regional associations would employ professional staff, many if not most of them nonindigenous. The regional bodies' services would include monitoring and mentoring the smaller member corporations. Neither the registrar nor ATSIC should be entrusted with the delicate task of monitoring and mentoring indigenous organizations (although Sullivan conceded to ATSIC regional officers a role in advising organizations on financial acquittal). Note that Sullivan's two-tier model of incorporation would require an amendment to the ACA so that a member of an association need not be a natural person; one association could be a member of another association.

Sullivan (1996a) argued that incorporation is a slow process of cultural learning, not a legal status acquired over a few weeks through an exchange of letters with a bureaucrat in Canberra. A large, experienced, and professionally staffed indigenous regional association would have the skills to monitor the processes of its constituents' incorporation.

> With the benefit of local knowledge and consistency of contact over time, both the initial structure and the continuing performance of community groups could be better addressed. Local control would need to find a vital balance between the power to intervene and impose solutions and allowing the continuance of small group autonomy. . . . Local organisations are needed to provide specialist advice on appropriate forms of incorporation and to themselves determine what is appropriate in any particular case. They should provide a monitoring role to see that organisations are carrying out their functions and meeting the social purposes of grant conditions in an appropriate manner. They should have the power to intervene, and in some circumstances temporarily assume an organization's functions on a caretaker basis, if required. (Sullivan, 1996a, p. 33)

Sullivan's two-tier scheme would formalize regional indigenous leadership and recognize that *leadership* includes mentoring and guided acculturation. In this context, accountability points to an ongoing and irresolvable duality between a leadership that is sensitive to the external demands associated with formal organization and government funding, and a leadership detached from that world and sensitive to the demands of kin-based solidarity groups and of a temporal order determined more by season and ceremony than by budget cycles, annual reviews, and the like.

## EXIT

To conceive of leadership and accountability in these terms affects how we think about *exit*, another topic implicitly present in Fingleton's review. Before attending to Fingleton (1996) and his colleagues, however, I want to note that Kymlicka (1995), like Kukathas (1992), sees the importance of *exit*. He writes,

> The exact point at which intervention in the internal affairs of a national minority is warranted is unclear, just as it is in the international context. I think a number of factors are potentially relevant here, including the severity of rights violations within the minority community, the degree of consensus within the community on the legitimacy of restricting individual rights, *the ability of dissenting group*

*members to leave the community if they so desire,* and the existence of historical agreements with the national minority. (Kymlicka, 1995, pp. 169-170, emphasis added)

However, Kymlicka (1995) believes that to leave one's community is not easy. It is "best seen as renouncing something to which one is reasonably entitled," and it is "analogous to the choice to take a vow of perpetual poverty and enter a religious order" (p. 86). Responding explicitly to Kukathas in an endnote, Kymlicka (1995) writes that Kukathas has overstated, first, the helpfulness (to dissenters) of having a market-based society into which to exit, and second, the likelihood that members of a repressive national minority would be socialized to have "the preconditions for making a meaningful choice" and so possess "a substantial freedom to leave" (pp. 234-235).

Kymlicka (1995) thinks "choosing to leave one's culture is qualitatively different from choosing to move around within one's culture" (p. 121). Let us call this the "soft exit" option. Kymlicka wishes to defend the survival of national and societal cultures, which are sufficiently internally differentiated to facilitate soft exit.

If we consider indigenous Australian social life as an ensemble of formal associations, then Kymlicka's (1995) rather softer version of exit (moving around within) seems closer to what is likely to happen than Kukathas's all-or-nothing notion of exit. That is, indigenous Australians make up an internally differentiated sector of Australian society. The exit option is available in many forms and gradations: moving from one community to another (while remaining within an extended family network), visiting the city from the hinterland for a while, choosing forms of housing that enable one politely to refuse importuning relatives.

The Fingleton review can be read as dealing with softer exit options. The case studies give many instances of indigenous Australians seeking to resolve local tensions by exit and reincorporation. It was argued, by some informants, that the ACA made incorporation too easy and that, as one aboriginal organization was paraphrased, "in a situation of endemic conflict [easy incorporation] facilitates the formation of ever increasing numbers of organisations competing for funds and influence" (Martin, 1996, p. 4). Finlayson (1996) reported the view that easy incorporation "had become a de facto way to dispute resolution within Aboriginal communities" leading to "fragmentation of resources" and "duplication of services" and "undermining efforts to think regionally or strategically about issues of community concern" (p. 15). Crough and Cronin (1996, pp. 8-9) found that some Kimberley organizations "have set up incorporated bodies to foster their recognition as a culturally distinct group," especially if colonizing processes had been disruptive of their way of life. In western New South Wales, there was concern about the proliferation of aboriginal organisations. In that view, "the control of certain organisations by particular groups led to an ever-increasing number of Aboriginal organisations as an alternative means to access funds and develop services" (Cunneen & Libesman, 1996, p. 33).

These depictions of the fractious quality of indigenous politics stimulate further thought about what might be meant by culturally appropriate. Does culturally appropriate mean consistency with ancient tradition? From the ethnographic record (low population densities, an ecology of small—30 to 50 persons—groups) it is possible to generalize that aboriginal political differences have long been settled by separation. The splitting of large collectivities into small groups was and remains a normal and mutually beneficial response to political difference. If you do not get on, you can always get out. In this perspective, it is culturally appropriate that the incorporation threshold is set low (in terms of numbers of members and amount of paperwork) by the ACA. However, the tenor of most of the observations quoted above is more critical. Indigenous tendencies toward schism, it is argued, are wasteful and strategically unwise. If there is a notion of culturally appropriate at work in this view, it arises from a political judgment about how aboriginal people should now be grouping themselves for effective participation in Australian political life. Sullivan's two-tier proposal—a model of indigenous leadership, as I argued above—seems to me to address this issue: Within his confederations, the size and relative autonomy of constituent groups would be negotiable.

## THE CONTINGENCIES OF CUSTOM AND ASSOCIATION

The aspiration that emergent indigenous corporations should keep faith with custom and culture, rather than advance their dissolution, gives logical, historical, and evaluative primacy to custom and culture. To think in these terms for the past 30 years has been necessary in order to question the culturally arrogant and historically destructive assumptions of the assimilation policy era.

Joske's (1996) consultant report on politics within the Ngaanyatjarra Council is an example of an unhesitating use of *culture* to judge *association*. She discerned two social orders within that body and then made one the standard by which to judge the other. What she calls "conventions" were important in the Ngaanyatjarra Council: "The rules of the organization did not properly reflect the way things have been done (successfully) for a long time." However, when one faction made use of those rules in a takeover bid, they became unprecedentedly important and so threatened to displace the council's conventions of representation, accountability, and decision by consensus. Joske's (1996) point was that the possibility of such opportunistic invocation of formal rules in order to upset conventional practice is "in itself . . . reason to question the appropriateness of the ACA Act" (p. 6). She implied that indigenous conventions should have priority in determining the way the Ngaanyatjarra Council really works.

Sullivan (1996b), by contrast, seems to me to refrain from assigning priority to custom. "In practice," he writes, "in the functioning of Aboriginal corporations there are two social entities—the community and the corporation. The community operates according to customary laws. The corporation operates according to statute" (p. 13). Sullivan's proposed confederation would have the effect not of giving custom ascendancy over corporation, but of mediating relations between the two. Mediation could mean that there might be very little contact between the two: Their lack of organic connection may preserve both.

However, this mediated autonomy of political orders can be upset by two kinds of contact between them. Contact might be triggered by community processes somehow compromising the effective functioning of the corporation. The consequent failure of the corporation to satisfy statutory requirements can provoke the registrar's inspection. If custom clashes with corporation, as we have seen, the registrar's view (which influences funding) is that corporation must rule. The other mode of contact between the two parallel political orders is through someone's attempt to use the rules of the corporation to make political gains within the processes of the community. The registrar may see no irregularity but, as reported by Joske (1996) in her Ngaanyatjarra case study, some will see a willful and self-interested disruption of political relations governed by convention and custom.

It is often thought that indigenous Australians are particularly given to factional politics. Those disturbed by factionalism tend to divide into those who would deal with it by making corporation supreme, and those who think that indigenous political traditions—rich in conventions of balance, reciprocity, and complementarity of roles—will ultimately take care of factionalism if allowed. The more thoughtful of Fingleton's consultants were searching for new strategies of corporate accountability, through service agreements and evaluation studies, for example. If Fingleton's (1996) "two conditions for real accountability" were fulfilled, it would imply a voluntary rationalization of much indigenous political behaviour, as indigenous elites submitted themselves not only to membership votes but also to negotiated measures of their performance in the delivery of services. If Sullivan's (1996b) suggestions were taken up, regional indigenous organizations would be entrusted with the propagation of the association as a form of indigenous sociality recognizable to the liberalism of settler colonial states.

In seeking to ensure that indigenous corporations are accountable in culturally appropriate ways, we should avoid assigning evaluative priority to custom and culture as if they were realities preceding contemporary indigenous organizations. Any behaviours to which we refer as customary and traditional now coexist with indigenous social forms that are recently developed and consciously contrived. How these two orders of behavioural regularity and normative discourse will interact is not foreseeable because it is not possible to predict the degree to which indigenous Australians will find it useful to express and reconstruct their social lives according to the demands of formal associations.

Political leadership among indigenous Australians is a matter of experiment. Current discussions in political theory allow us to put such experiments in perspective. Indeed, the richness of the Fingleton report suggests that liberal political theorists might well study the institutional developments among indigenous peoples as avidly as they attend to jurisprudence. If liberalism has a postcolonial future, some of its developmental sites may be found in the remote territories of settler colonial nation-states.

## NOTES

1. This changed in 1992, when a High Court judgment deemed "native title" to be recognizable in Australian common law, where it had not been extinguished by the lawful actions of the Crown.
2. Australia accepted British New Guinea as a territory in 1901, and occupied German New Guinea in 1914. Under international mandate, Australia governed the territory known as Papua New Guinea until 1975, when the nation of Papua New Guinea became sovereign.
3. The Committee of Review was chaired by C. A. Gibb, and this document has commonly been referred to as the Gibb Report. However, Coombs can be credited with authorship of this passage.
4. The ACA is a Commonwealth statute. Each state and territory of the federation has the power to develop its own body of corporate law, giving indigenous people a choice of laws under which to incorporate.
5. From Bouhafs's (1998, July 11) letter, Brisbane.
6. I have summarized only that part of Fingleton's review that covers Part IV of the act. I have omitted his discussion of why Part III of the act—providing for the incorporation of indigenous local governments—has never been used, and how it could be used. Fingleton shows that the commonwealth has always deferred to the states' and territories' policies and laws for facilitating (or otherwise) indigenous local government. Portraying the nonimplementation of Part III as a lost opportunity to encourage the development of culturally specific organs of regional indigenous self-government, Fingleton (1996) entertains the idea that the commonwealth government repeal Part III.

> This may be the time for the Commonwealth to clarify its policy position by stating that it believes that assimilation into mainstream political structures is the only way forward for Aboriginal people. In practice, this has been the effect of the Commonwealth's policy framework in regard to Part III for the past twenty years. (p. 135)

However, his final recommendation is that the commonwealth rethink its financial and legal approaches to indigenous local government.

## REFERENCES

Commonwealth of Australia. (1972). *The situation of Aborigines on pastoral properties in the Northern Territory* (Parliamentary Paper 62/1972). Author.

Corbett, H. (1996). Indigenous Woman Aboriginal Corporation, Perth, Western Australia. In J. Fingleton (Ed.), *Final report: Review of the Aboriginal Councils and Associations Act 1976* (Vol. 2). Canberra, Australia: Australian Institute of Aboriginal and Torres Strait Islander Studies.

Crough, G., & Cronin, D. (1996). Aboriginal resource centres in the Kimberley region. In J. Fingleton (Ed.), *Final report: Review of the Aboriginal Councils and Associations Act 1976* (Vol. 2). Canberra, Australia: Australian Institute of Aboriginal and Torres Strait Islander Studies.

Cunneen, C., & Libesman, T. (1996). New South Wales case studies. In J. Fingleton (Ed.), *Final report: Review of the Aboriginal Councils and Associations Act 1976* (Vol. 2). Canberra, Australia: Australian Institute of Aboriginal and Torres Strait Islander Studies.

Fingleton, J. (1996). *Final report: Review of the Aboriginal Councils and Associations Act 1976* (Vol. 1). Canberra, Australia: Australian Institute of Aboriginal and Torres Strait Islander Studies.

Finlayson, J. (1996). North Queensland case studies. In J. Fingleton (Ed.), *Final report: Review of the Aboriginal Councils and Associations Act 1976* (Vol. 2). Canberra, Australia: Australian Institute of Aboriginal and Torres Strait Islander Studies.

Galston, W. (1995). Two concepts of liberalism. *Ethics, 105,* 516-534.

Joske, C. (1996). Case study: Ngaanyatjarra Council Aboriginal Corporation. In J. Fingleton (Ed.), *Final report: Review of the Aboriginal Councils and Associations Act 1976* (Vol. 2). Canberra, Australia: Australian Institute of Aboriginal and Torres Strait Islander Studies.

Kukathas, C. (1992). Are there any cultural rights? *Political Theory, 20,* 105-139.

Kymlicka, W. (1995). *Multicultural citizenship.* Oxford, UK: Clarendon.

Mantziaris, C. (1997a). Beyond the Aboriginal Councils and Associations Act? Part 1. *Indigenous Law Bulletin, 4*(5), 10-14.

Mantziaris, C. (1997b). Beyond the Aboriginal Councils and Associations Act? Part 2. *Indigenous Law Bulletin, 4*(6), 7-15.

Martin, D. (1996). Queensland case studies. In J. Fingleton (Ed.), *Final report: Review of the Aboriginal Councils and Associations Act 1976* (Vol. 2). Canberra, Australia: Australian Institute of Aboriginal and Torres Strait Islander Studies.

Martin, D., & Finlayson, J. (1996). *Linking accountability and self-determination in Aboriginal organisations* (Discussion Paper 116). Canberra: Center for Aboriginal Economic Policy Research, Australian National University.

Rowley, C. D. (1972). *Outcasts in White Australia.* Ringwood, Victoria: Penguin.

Sullivan, P. (1996a). Western Australian case studies. In J. Fingleton (Ed.), *Final report: Review of the Aboriginal Councils and Associations Act 1976* (Vol. 2). Canberra, Australia: Australian Institute of Aboriginal and Torres Strait Islander Studies.

Sullivan, P. (1996b). The needs of prescribed bodies corporate under the Native Title Act 1993 and regulations. In J. Fingleton (Ed.), *Final report: Review of the Aboriginal Councils and Associations Act 1976* (Vol. 2). Canberra, Australia: Australian Institute of Aboriginal and Torres Strait Islander Studies.

# 9. Multicultural Broadcasting and Diasporic Video as Public Sphericules

STUART CUNNINGHAM
*Queensland University of Technology*

GAY HAWKINS
*University of New South Wales*

AUDREY YUE
*Melbourne University*

TINA NGUYEN
*Queensland University of Technology*

JOHN SINCLAIR
*Victoria University of Technology*

> *Broadcasting constitutes a major platform on which contemporary public cultures may be built and managed. However, mainstream broadcasting, even when its charter responsibilities focus on service to and representation of a culturally pluralistic social field, has limits as it seeks to meet these responsibilities. Diasporic video, although marginal to most national media ecologies, is important at a global level in addressing cultural maintenance and renewal. This factor is neglected in existing accounts of the emergence of a genuinely multicultural and international public culture.*

**Broadcasting, or more broadly,** the "mediascape" (Appadurai, 1990) constitutes a major platform on which contemporary public spheres and public cultures may be built and managed.[1] There are those for whom the contemporary Western public sphere has been tarnished or even fatally compromised by the encroachment of media, particularly commercial media and communications (Schiller, 1989). For others, the media have become the main vehicle for sustaining what remains of the public sphere in such societies. Hartley (1999) provides the following suggestive formulation:

> The "mediasphere" is the whole universe of media... in all languages in all countries. It therefore completely encloses and contains as a differentiated part of itself the (Habermasian) public sphere (or the many public spheres), and it is itself contained by the much larger semiosphere... which is the whole universe of sense-making by whatever means, including speech.... It is clear that television is a crucial site of the mediasphere and a crucial mediator between general cultural sense-making systems (the semiosphere) and specialist components of social sense-making like the public sphere. Hence the public sphere can be rethought not as a

category binarily contrasted with its implied opposite, the private sphere, but as a "Russian doll" enclosed within a larger mediasphere, itself enclosed within the semiosphere. And within "the" public sphere, there may equally be found, Russian-doll style, further counter-cultural, oppositional or minoritarian public spheres. (pp. 217-218)

Provocatively media-centric though it may be, Hartley's (1999) topography has the virtue of clarity, scope, and heuristic utility, and we agree with his iconoclastic insistence that commercial and public/state-supported spheres of activity are closely related and interdependent.[2] Our aim here will be to complicate Hartley's topography by suggesting that minoritarian public spheres are seldom subsets of classic nationally bound public spheres, but are nonetheless vibrant spaces of self and community-making and identity.

Gitlin (1998) has also posed the question as to whether we can continue to speak of the ideal of a public sphere or culture in the singular as an increasingly complex, polyethnic, communications-saturated series of societies develop around the world. Rather, what might be emerging are numerous public *sphericules*: "Does it not look as though the public sphere, in falling, has shattered into a scatter of globules, like mercury?" (Gitlin, 1998, p. 173). Gitlin's answer is the deeply pessimistic one of seeing the future as the irretrievable loss of elements of a modernist public commonality.

In contrast, we argue that the emergence of ethnospecific global media–tized communities suggests that elements we would expect to find in the public sphere are to be found in microcosm in these public sphericules. Such activities constitute dynamic counterexamples to a discourse of decline and fragmentation while taking full account of contemporary vectors of communication in a globalizing, commercializing, and pluralizing world. We develop this position through a discussion of the strengths and limitations of Australian mainstream broadcasting as it seeks to meet its charter responsibilities to focus on service to and representation of a culturally pluralistic social field. To exemplify its limitations, we draw attention to the phenomenon of diasporic video. Marginal to most national media ecologies and largely missing in accounts of the emergence of a genuinely multicultural and international public culture, the production and uses of diasporic video are important at both national and global levels in addressing cultural maintenance and renewal.

## OFFICIAL MULTICULTURALISM AND CULTURAL PLURALISM

Australia is one of the most multicultural nations on earth, with 40% of its population born elsewhere or with at least one parent born elsewhere. In 1947, the Australian population was 7.6 million, of whom only 9.8% were overseas-born. Of these, 90% were from Great Britain and Ireland. By the mid-1980s, the proportion born overseas had grown to 21%, whereas another 20% had one or both parents born overseas. More than half of Australia's post–Second World War population growth was driven by immigration, with the proportions changing from overwhelmingly British and Irish to migrants from eastern and southern Europe and, since the 1970s, Asia, Africa, the Americas, and the Middle East. In response to this, from the late 1970s to the mid-1990s, Australian governments constructed an official policy of multiculturalism and organized an impressive array of state support for this policy, including the Special Broadcasting Service (SBS). This is both a television and radio broadcaster, one of the few major public broadcasters in the world dedicated to both the reflection and the propagation of multiculturalism.

However, although Australia is, in proportional terms, the world's second largest immigrant nation next to Israel, the relatively low numbers within any individual group have meant that a critical mass of a few dominant non–English-speaking background groupings has not made the impact that Hispanic peoples, for example, have made in the United States.[3] Other reasons for this relative lack of impact include the fact that historically, when compared with the variety of immigrant and refugee/humanitarian communities (at present, more than 150 ethnic groups speaking more than 100 different languages), the largest immigrant groups have been Anglo-Irish. Moreover, in Australia, immigration has occurred in several distinct waves during a period of 50 years. Some earlier groups successfully negotiated their resettlements more than a generation ago, but many Asian groupings have only begun the process. Also, Australians do not experience strong cultural diversity through policies of official multilingualism (such as in Canada) or through cultural intermixing caused by the sheer contiguity of the major imperial languages in Europe. Finally, non-indigenous Australians have not had to make the significant accommodation in daily life, in the polity and in public rhetorics, of their counterparts in societies with a critical mass of indigenous persons, such as New Zealand.

Direct subvention from Australian government arts bodies to multicultural cultural forms has focused on the folkloric and the literary rather than on the most popular cultural forms such as video and popular music. Typically, then, with the exception of zones of official contact, such as the SBS, community radio, and the like, most mainstream cultural institutions' embrace of cultural diversity tends not to go beyond mutual distance and monolingual incomprehension. As a recent study put it, the bulwarks of monocultural power in Australia have not yet been fundamentally challenged (Jamrozik, Boland, & Urquhart, 1995).

Nonetheless, in recognition of the political power and skills of the ethnic lobby reflected in elections during the 1970s, the Fraser Conservative government decided to set up a special multicultural television service in the late 1970s. In contrast to grassroots ethnic radio, what became SBS-TV was a creature of government initiative. Over time, this distinction has consolidated: SBS-TV differs markedly from multilingual radio services, which are found both within the

SBS and in the community-based sector. The model for television centres on the employment of broadcasting professionals rather than of community representatives and volunteers.[4] Furthermore, there is a policy that virtually all material is subtitled in English, the national *lingua franca*, which is assumed to be the common linguistic denominator uniting disparate ethnicities. There is also an expectation that the programming schedule should not be radically different from the norm, especially with broad appeal material being broadcast in prime time, and that the core programming of the service—news and current affairs— should be English-language based.

Although SBS radio allocates broadcast time to language groups largely on the basis of their numerical representation in the community, there has always been a (perhaps necessary) disparity between community languages and SBS-TV programming. Programming centres on that which is of conventional broadcast standard. The effect is to automatically preclude materials that communities actually watch, such as diasporic video. Instead, the SBS runs what programming its limited budget can afford from the major non–English language film and television industries. Indian films are often too expensive, whereas French, German, Brazilian, or Swedish films and television long-form drama are overrepresented (given the demographic proportion of these language groups in Australia) because these are the products of experienced export industries that can sell some of their material cheaply. Programs are chosen on the basis of their ability to address potentially all Australians generically within the discourse of multiculturalism rather than on the grounds of their capacity to address specific language groups. Added to this, as the service has mainstreamed in the last decade, the policy discourse of the SBS has effectively displaced the broadcaster's original charter of multiculturalism in favor of contemporary notions of cultural diversity. Sexual orientation, age, and physical disability have now become markers of cultural difference as valid as ethnicity (Jakubowicz et al., 1994; O'Regan, 1993).

It is therefore easy to see how the service could be perceived as a general interest station for cosmopolitan taste cultures rather than as a social change agent for those marginalized by language and (non–Anglo-Irish or broad European) culture. This has been the major criticism that the service has had to field in the 1990s, and it has come from high-ranking politicians and senior representatives of ethnic communities as well as from critics and journalists (see Lawe Davies, 1997). So it is refreshing to see that there can also be a spirited defense of the SBS in its catering to cosmopolitan taste cultures (see especially Hawkins, 1996).

Hartley (1992) argues that the SBS offers a distinct model of structural diversity in a broadcasting system. Despite the introduction of broadcast pay television in 1995 and its current penetration rate of approximately 18% of television households, the model is characterized by an overwhelmingly dominant free-to-air sector, with all the in-built issues of access and channel scarcity that terrestrial free-to-air television displays. Real diversity in Australian television,

Hartley argues, should be based not on geographic localism, but on serving "psychographic" lifestyle and cultural constituencies: "That means turning from space to time as the structuring principle, and from local communities to audience constituencies" (Hartley, 1992, p. 199).

Hartley's structuring principle is exemplified in the programming philosophy of the SBS. Both the commercial television sector and the major public broadcaster, the Australian Broadcasting Corporation (ABC), are yoked into geographically defined television service areas. These require them to mirror or even construct spatial difference that (although very marked in a thinly populated country such as Australia) is largely illusory from the point of view of cultural difference. The SBS, by contrast, is a time-based channel (offering a programming smorgasbord that no one viewer is expected to consume based on the old notion of flow and network or station loyalty). It sets as its benchmark for success audience or cumulative reach (the number of viewers who tune in at least once in any given week) rather than ratings points. This approach does not attempt to maximize the number of viewers for any and every program.

The SBS shows how a national network that cannot afford anything but centralized production and dissemination can still be the "TV of tomorrow": "lean, hungry, efficient," yet also committed to advancing social and cultural diversity (Hartley, 1992, p. 200). The service engages in very little local production apart from a relatively cheap news and current affairs portfolio supplemented by special programming such as indigenous talk shows and one-off production specials funded off-budget. It operates no regional production or broadcast facilities beyond retransmission facilities, and it is completely centralized in Sydney. Because of these two factors, it is able to run on a comparatively shoestring budget: about 12% of the budget of its larger public service broadcasting cousin, the ABC. This approach to shrinking public sector budgets is absolutely essential in the present climate.

As might be expected, assessing the role and functions of the SBS has engaged critics, broadcasters, and policy makers in large-scale issues of social and cultural power and representation precisely because of the SBS's enthusiastic uptake of its charter responsibility not only to reflect multiculturalism, but to proselytize for social change. In a concerted critique, Jakubowicz et al. (1994) argue that "multiculturalism as a policy has not achieved significant change in the commercial media, though its impact on the state sector has been crucial— SBS quite simply is the most outstanding expression of multiculturalism as policy" (p. 136). Nevertheless, the creation of a special multicultural service has "allowed the television industry in general to remain largely unaffected by the cultural changes wrought by migration" (p. 14).

Not surprisingly, in an era of postmodernist media literacy and the ambiguities of political correctness, such views do not go unchallenged. The problem is that the debate in its current form is largely insoluble within the structural constraints of channel scarcity in a terrestrial free-to-air environment. SBS programming cannot meet the diverse and incommensurate needs of its multifarious communities within the constraints of a single channel service. There are also the changing demographics of multicultural Australia to take into account, particularly the middle classing of a core SBS demographic, as a consequence of the post-1945 waves of immigration from southern and central Europe. The structural conflicts between the established European ethnic lobby and the emerging influence of the 1970s and 1980s waves of migrants and refugees (which have had increasing components of Asian origin) make the ground of debate a shifting one. It is also a debate about class overlaid on the combustible rhetorics of race and ethnicity, especially Asian ethnicity.

In this article, we take the question of the adequacy of multicultural social and broadcasting policy in Australia from two complementary angles. Both of these address Asian immigrant and refugee groupings, the Chinese and the Vietnamese. One is a case at the limits of public service broadcasting as it strives to serve polylingual and polyethnic audience fractions. The other is the use made of "global narrowcast" music videos by a community whose media diet is composed of significant amounts of nonbroadcast material because of their almost complete marginality in relation to established broadcast television. Each displays the dynamics of the construction of public sphericules in an era of globalization, ethnic pluralism, and commercialization.

To focus on diasporic media that serve global but ethnically specific narrowcast audiences is to question two assumptions: that media globalization necessarily spells homogenization and that the development of such often commercial media-based sphericules, linking widely dispersed peoples outside single nation states, entails a fatal loss of public culture. The Chinese case is one of narrowcasting within a broadcasting environment, whereas the Vietnamese case is the reverse, needing to maximize audiences within a narrowcast environment. This approach assumes a high level of global cosmopolitanism inherent in the reality of migrancy, whether the migrant is working class, middle class, or "middle classing." It is an argument for moving beyond the debate about whether the SBS exists basically for an internationalizing Australian middle class or cosmopolitan world citizen or whether it should exist for a marginalized lumpen proletariat defined by an essentialist ethnicity.

The question of local versus imported product is best addressed by assuming that the community of the migrant, refugee, cultural tourist, or long-term business resident is a globally or at least regionally dispersed community: imported product therefore best reflects that community. We explore this possibility drawing on a recently completed study of Asian immigrant communities and the way they use media for maintaining their home cultures and for negotiating with their host (Cunningham & Sinclair, 2000). This investigation of the diasporic imagination (Gillespie, 1994; Kolar-Panov, 1997; Naficy, 1993)[5] allows us to identify a key challenge facing Australian broadcasting: to provide genuine programming for cultural pluralism and social change by attending to "the daily negotiation by ethnic minorities for cultural and personal integrity and survival against elements of a culture which defines itself as 'mainstream' and 'established' " (Jakubowicz et al., 1994, p. 13).[6]

## "EPISTEPHILIC DESIRE": CHINESE NEWS AND THE SBS

Cultural products such as television services and programs attest to the formation of transnational networks of media circulation and (re)production between home and host sites, the technological means for cultural maintenance and negotiation. Within the diverse complex of media used by Chinese viewers in Australia, narrowcast television services have a special place. Whereas broadcasting generally denies difference, narrowcasting exploits it, often fetishizing a notion of a singular or special identity determined by a fundamental essence (ethnicity, race, sexuality, etc.). There are, of course, other forms of narrowcasting that service various taste markets or restricted localities, but for diasporic Chinese viewers in Australia it is those television services that speak directly to their Chineseness and that invite various forms of diasporic identification that are the most significant. As the marketing slogan for New World TV (a Chinese-language subscription channel) used to declare, "Intimacy is to speak your language."

For Naficy (1993), narrowcasting remains an underappreciated discourse. He argues that the processes at work in the specialization and fragmentation of television demand more thorough attention. This is not simply because these developments are important evidence that the media imperialist and global homogenization theorists are wrong, but also because ethnic narrowcasting is a manifestation of the emergence of new media sites that address the experience of hybridity, migration, and diaspora and that speak to the disruptive spaces of postcolonialism. Narrowcast media, then, are one example of a growing third or multiple cultural space where various "othered" populations are creating sites for representation and where all kinds of "resistive hybridities, syncretism, and mongrelizations are possible, valued" (Naficy & Gabriel, 1993, p. x). Implicit in this valuation is a fundamental opposition between broadcasting as the heartland of nation and family and narrowcasting as the space of the migrant, the exile, and the refugee.

At the simplest level, the SBS is a narrowcaster because it imagines the nation as a series of fragments, as a multiplicity of constituencies produced through various axes of difference—often those very differences that broadcasters are unable to see in their obsession with maximizing audiences. In fragmenting the nation, the SBS also recognizes its members' connections with other places and acknowledges identities constituted through relations of movement and longing across national boundaries. Programs in languages other than English and programs imported from outside the dominant Anglo-American nexus implicitly disrupt narratives of national cohesion. Most significant here is the example of

"WorldWatch," the SBS's morning news service, which broadcasts satellite-delivered national news bulletins from around the world.

WorldWatch began on SBS in 1993, with screenings from 6.30 a.m. onward of daily news services from CCTV (China Central Television) Beijing in Mandarin; France 2 Paris; Deutsche Welle Berlin; the Russian news "Vreyma"; and two current affairs programs from public broadcasting stations in the United States. These services were generally picked up the night before by various satellites to which the SBS had access, taped, and then broadcast unsubtitled the following morning. Access rights were free, and since its inception WorldWatch has steadily increased its representation of nightly news or weekly current affairs magazines to now include bulletins from Italy, Indonesia, Japan, Hong Kong, Lebanon, Spain, Hungary, Chile, Poland, Greece, and the Ukraine.

The significance of WorldWatch for the SBS is that it demonstrates its capacity to establish a particularist or minority stance within a broader multicultural framework. Whereas most non-English shows on the SBS are subtitled in the interests of national access, in not subtitling WorldWatch (a decision predicated on cost and time pressures) the SBS addresses migrant and diasporic audiences without symbolically assimilating them into the nation. However, the absence of subtitles also means that these bulletins are subtly marginalized within the overall institutional politics of the network, in that the SBS remains primarily a broadcaster, albeit of a very particular kind. Thus, prime time is the privilege of multicultural programming accessible to all rather than minority or narrowcast programming.

It is especially significant that WorldWatch provides one of the main sources of audiovisual news for Chinese audiences in Australia. As many studies of the migrant experience have shown, news from or about home has special status and value. It is a privileged form, watched avidly and intently and often in a state of what Naficy (1993) terms "epistephilic desire" (p. 107). News generates strong demand: All services programming Chinese news in Australia report intense viewer requests for more. In the maze of diverse cosmopolitan forms available to Chinese audiences, news is distinctive not just in terms of the way that it is watched but also in the symbolic value it holds as a source of direct access to information about homelands. News generates very specific relations in space between here and there because of the way it mediates the play of separation and connection in time, then and now. By contrast, in the absence of any referent in real space or time, purely fictional texts function quite differently in the kind of longing they work on.

This very distinctive use of news shows how crucial this genre is in mediating senses of liminality and in providing a space where the movements of separation and connection, of ambivalent and unstable points of personal and national identification, are negotiated. There are several reasons why news occupies this role, beyond the obvious fact that it is a major source of information and national imagining. Studies of the relationship between television and everyday life point to the central role of news bulletins in ordering the lived experience of time. For Scannell (1996), the structuring principle of broadcasting is *dailiness*: the processes through which radio and TV retemporalize time via institutional regimes such as the schedule and audience viewing rituals that are shaped in relation to this. News is crucial in this process because of its location in the schedule as a marker of each day passing and because of its textual principle of liveness, specifying what is going on and what marks the particularity of this day rather than what has been. Broadcast television news, then, is central to how senses of home and the everyday are both ritualized and temporalized.

What then of news bulletins on narrowcast media screened out of the context of a national television service and in a different time zone and frame? How do viewers experience these? Chinese audiences for SBS (and for subscription television channels such as New World TV) watch yesterday's news. They wake in the morning and switch on last night's bulletin from Hong Kong, Beijing, or Taipei. In research with these communities, Chinese viewers of the news services described how they delayed going to work in the morning in order to find out what happened at "home" yesterday. They needed this information, this sense of ritualized summation of the day over there, even if it was experienced in another place and temporal order. For these audiences, narrowcast news generates a double imaginary of time, a sense of being in two temporalities: here and there, then and now. Scannell's argument about dailiness applies more to the national rhetorics of broadcasting. In the cultural and economic logics of global narrowcasting, the schedule has a different function and generates correspondingly different audience rituals and temporalities.

The desire to live within at least two informational spaces simultaneously, as it were, with their necessary daily rituals, attests to the existence of a global cosmopolitan public sphericule based on the vast Chinese diaspora and made possible by communications networks. This public sphericule does not seek to supplant the national informational space, but supplements it so that the diaspora can function effectively as overlapping interconnected family, business, association, and political networks on a global scale.

## FROM CULTURAL MAINTENANCE TO HYBRIDITY: VIETNAMESE MUSIC VIDEO

The Vietnamese is by far the largest refugee community in Australia. For most, *home* is a denegated category while "the regime" continues in power, and so media networks, especially music video, operate to connect the dispersed exilic Vietnamese communities. Small business entrepreneurs produce low budget music videos mostly out of southern California (but also Paris), which are taken up within the fan circuits of America, Australia, Canada, France, and elsewhere. The internal cultural conflicts within the communities centre on the need to maintain prerevolutionary Vietnamese traditions as distinct from the formation of hybrid identities around the appropriation of dominant Western popular cultural forms by Vietnamese performers.

Although by no means exhausting the media diet of the Vietnamese diaspora, live variety shows and music video are undeniably unique to it as audiovisual media made specifically by and for the diaspora.[7] These media forms bear many similarities to the commercial and variety-based cultural production of Iranian television in Los Angles studied by Naficy (1993), not least because Vietnamese variety show and music video production is also centred on the Los Angeles conurbation. The Vietnamese grouped there are not as numerous or rich as Naficy's Iranians and so have not developed the extent of the business infrastructure to support the range and depth of media activity recounted in *The Making of Exile Cultures* (Naficy, 1993). The business infrastructure of Vietnamese audiovisual production is structured around a small number of small businesses operating on very low margins.

To be exilic means not, or at least not officially, being able to draw on the contemporary cultural production of the home country. Indeed, it means actively denying its existence in a dialectical process of mutual disauthentification (Carruthers, 1999). The Vietnam government proposes that the *Viet Kieu* (the appellation for Vietnamese overseas, which carries a pejorative connotation) are fatally Westernized. Ironically, the diasporic population makes a similar countercharge against the regime, proposing that the homeland population has lost its moral integrity through the wholesale compulsory adoption of an alien Western ideology: Marxism-Leninism.

Together, the dispersed geography and the demography of a small series of communities frame the conditions for global narrowcasting: that is, ethnically specific cultural production for widely dispersed population fragments centripetally organized around their disavowed state of origin. This makes the media, and media use, of the Vietnamese diaspora fundamentally different from that of the Indian or Chinese diasporas. The latter revolve around massive cinema and television production centres in the home countries that enjoy international cachet. By contrast, the fact that the media uses of the Vietnamese diaspora are globally oriented but commercially marginal ensures that they flourish outside the purview of state and major commercial vectors of subvention and trade.

These conditions also determine the small business character of the production companies (Thuy Nga, Asia/Dem Saigon, May/Hollywood Nights, Khanh Ha, Diem Xua, and others). These small enterprises run at low margins and are constantly undercut by piracy and copying of their video product. They have clustered around the only Vietnamese population base that offers critical mass and is geographically adjacent to the much larger ECI (entertainment-communications-information) complex in southern California. There is evidence of internal migration within the diaspora from the rest of the United States, Canada, and France to southern California to take advantage of the largest overseas Vietnamese population concentration and the world's major ECI complex.

During the course of the 25 or so years since the fall of Saigon and the establishment of the diaspora through flight and migration, a substantial amount of music video material has been produced. Thuy Nga Productions, by far the largest and most successful company, organizes major live shows in the United States and franchises appearance schedules for its high-profile performers at shows around the global diaspora. It has produced more than 60 2- to 3-hour videotapes since the early 1980s, as well as a constant flow of CD-ROMs, audiocassettes, and karaoke discs in addition to documentary specials and re-releases of classic Vietnamese movies. The other companies, between them, have also produced hundreds of hours of variety music videos.

Virtually every overseas Vietnamese household views this music video material, most regularly attend the live variety performances on which the video materials are based, and a significant proportion has developed comprehensive home libraries. The popularity of this material is exemplary, cutting across the several axes of difference in the community: ethnicity, age, gender, recentness of arrival, educational level, refugee or immigrant status, and home region. The material is also widely available in pirated form in Vietnam itself, as the economic and cultural thaw that has proceeded since Doi Moi policies of greater openness has resulted in extensive penetration of the homeland by this most international of Vietnamese forms of expression.[8] As the only popular culture produced by and specifically for the Vietnamese diaspora, these texts attract an emotive investment within the overseas communities that is as deep as it is varied. The social text that surrounds, indeed engulfs, these productions is intense, multilayered, and makes its address across differences of generation, gender, ethnicity, class, and education levels and recentness of arrival. Audiovisual images "become so important for young Vietnamese as a point of reference, as a tool for validation and as a vehicle towards self identity" (T. Nguyen, personal communication, June 1997).

The key point linking attention to the textual dynamics of the music videos and media use within the communities is that each style cannot exist without the others because of the marginal size of the audience base. Thus, at the level both of the individual show or video and company output as a whole, the organizational structure of the shows and the videos reflects the heterogeneity required to maximize audience within a strictly narrowcast range. This is a programming philosophy congruent with broadcasting to a globally spread, narrowcast demographic: "the variety show form has been a mainstay of overseas Vietnamese anti-communist culture from the mid seventies onwards" (Carruthers, 1999).

In any given live show or video production, the musical styles might range from precolonial traditionalism to French colonial era high-modernist classicism, to crooners adapting Vietnamese folksongs to the Sinatra era and to bilingual cover versions of *Grease* or Madonna. Stringing this concatenation of taste cultures together are comperes, typically well-known political and cultural figures in their own right who perform a rhetorical unifying function.

> Audience members are constantly recouped via the show's diegesis, and the anchoring role of the comperes and their commentaries, into an overarching conception of shared overseas Vietnamese identity. This is centred on the appeal to... core cultural values, common tradition, linguistic unity and an anti-communist homeland politics. (Carruthers, 1999)

Within this overall political trajectory, however, there are major differences to be managed. The stances evidenced in the video and live material range on a continuum from pure heritage maintenance and ideological monitoring to mainstream cultural negotiation, through to assertive hybridity. Most performers and productions seek to situate themselves within the mainstream of cultural negotiation between Vietnamese and Western traditions. However, at one end of the continuum there are strong attempts to keep the original folkloric music traditions alive and to keep the integrity of the originary anticommunist stance foundational to the diaspora through very public criticism of any lapse from that stance. At the other end, Vietnamese American youth culture is exploring the limits of hybrid identities through the radical intermixing of musical styles.

## POLICY IMPLICATIONS AND CONCLUSION

Most state-supported programs of multicultural production feature typically traditional high cultural forms such as literature and the visual and performing arts, or residual folklorics practiced firmly within the boundaries of the nation state, even as they draw on cultural traditions established elsewhere. Our focus on the public sphericules of diasporic communities goes below and beyond these norms and forms of public broadcasting. It goes *below* them in its concentration on vastly popular cultural practices such as Vietnamese music video, which public broadcast standards exclude. It goes *beyond* them in focusing on the dynamics of ethnospecific narrowcast mixed entertainment and information media, which may originate in specific locale, but which are also consumed globally.

Ironically, the official discourse of Australian multicultural policy, which aims to protect immigrants' rights to keep their cultural differences, not only obliges them to have a culture with which they come but also to maintain it. This rhetoric valorizes an essentialist concept of culture, largely manifest as language, food, and ritual. The peoples of the Southeast Asian and Indochinese countries are accustomed to living in societies that, although not necessarily tolerant and harmonious, at least give them some experience of cultural pluralism and sense of difference. This is not true for the Taiwanese or for the mainland Chinese who have come in increasing numbers to Australia. These groups have not been prepared by their culture of origin to know how to respond to the discovery of their own racial and cultural difference. To make matters worse, even the most benevolently promulticulturalist Australian officialdom seems to have a knack of making these groups acutely aware of their Chineseness.

Furthermore, since 1996, having to bear the role of Asian Australian subject ascribed by the official discourse of multiculturalism has acquired a more painful side given that all Asian ethnicities have been very publicly racialized by the notorious Pauline Hanson and the One Nation party. This, together with the current conservative government's thinly concealed desire to displace and defund multiculturalism, makes it imperative to defend policies of cultural and linguistic pluralism vociferously, even as their limits are explored.

Genuinely taking account of a cultural pluralist polity will always involve two essential elements of policy. The first is the need to track the often rapidly changing nature of a country or region's demographics given the heightened mobility of world populations in the modern period. The second is the need to structure television services for both majoritarian and minoritarian populations in the interests of equity, access, and social justice. The most important conclusion, with broad implications for mainstream television systems, is that mass market free-to-air and subscription services will rarely meet all the needs of culturally pluralistic societies. To meet the needs currently serviced mostly through diasporic video, it will be necessary to develop stronger community-based media, operated by minoritarian communities themselves but supported by the state to a greater and more creative degree than is currently the case almost anywhere in the world.

## NOTES

1. The concept of the public sphere has been used regularly within the disciplinary fields of media, cultural, and communications studies to theorize the media's articulation between the state/government and civil society. As classically conceived by Habermas (1974), the concept of public sphere designates a space of open debate between equals, a special subset of civil society. Subsequent work based on Foucault's concept of governmentality has questioned the binary opposition between state and civil society implied in Habermas's concept. Habermasian accounts of the erosion of the public sphere under neoliberalism, it is argued, underestimate the extent to which, in modern postindustrial societies, state and civil society interpenetrate and are interdependent.

2. We will also be stressing another neglected aspect of the public sphere debate developed by McGuigan (1998, p. 92): the "affective" as much as "effective" dimension of the public communication of information and debate, which allows an adequate grasp of the place of entertainment in this field.

3. This expression, usually found in the acronym form NESB, is a standard part of the lexicon of official Australian multicultural policy.

4. This feeds one source of consistent criticism of the SBS: Although it presents an adequately multicultural face to its audience through on-air personalities, its managers and production heads have tended to be largely Anglo and male because structural barriers to professional and managerial careers are very real for non–English-speaking citizens.

5. Naficy's (1993) study of what he calls the "exilic" television produced by Iranians in Los Angeles in the 1980s is a model for how communication media can be used to negotiate the cultural

politics of both *home* and *host*. Largely Shah-supporting exiles from the Islamic revolution of the late 1970s in Iran, this community was able to fashion a wholly advertising-supported cable television presence redolent with longing, nostalgia, and the fetishization of an irrecoverable homeland displayed in low-budget fiction, variety show, and information formats. Naficy, by incorporating the industrial as well as the narrative features of the television services and program genres developed by the Iranian exile community, explores the relationship between the transnational experiences of displacement and migration (enforced in this case) and strategies of cultural maintenance and negotiation within the liminal slipzone between home and host, as seen on TV produced by and for the Iranian American community. Gillespie's (1994, p. 205) study of "the microprocesses of the construction of a British Asian identity among young people in Southall [west London], against the backdrop of the emergence of 'new ethnicities' in the context of post-colonial migration and the globalization of communications," sets a benchmark for detailed audience ethnography. It also demonstrates the need for different methodologies to capture the consumption of diverse media formats (mainstream soaps, news, advertising, and community-specific or narrowcast media such as Hindi television and film). The same attention that Naficy (1993) pays to the liminal experiences of the exile from a broken national community is seen in Kolar-Panov's (1997) *Video, War and the Diasporic Imagination*. Like Naficy's, Kolar-Panov's work goes below the level of consumption of mainstream media in capturing the role played by video "letters" used as news media by overseas citizens of the former Yugoslavia as their country broke up during the early 1990s. The politics of intercommunal discord in the homelands as they are played out in the diasporas and the dramatic textual alterity of atrocity videos that perform the role of virtual palimpsests of the real-time destruction of the homelands are features of Kolar-Panov's work dramatically relevant for our purposes.

6. Jakubowicz et al. (1994) argue that focusing only on policy pronouncements and the intentions and practices of established broadcasting institutions fails to comprehend the hegemonic power of the established media to resist or, more passively, simply fails to embrace social change.

7. The study of Vietnamese uses of media can embrace the interpretative community at work negotiating dominant broadcast and print media, as well as language-specific print forms such as ethnic newspapers. It should also embrace the consumption of broadly generic Asian media such as Hong Kong video product, karaoke forms, and site-specific Internet use (Cunningham & Sinclair, 2000).

8. Carruthers (1999) points to data from 1996 that estimate 85% to 90% of stock in Saigon's unlicensed video stores was not locally made.

# REFERENCES

Appadurai, A. (1990). Disjuncture and difference in the global cultural economy. *Theory, Culture and Society, 7*(2-3), 295-310.
Carruthers, A. (1999). National identity, diasporic anxiety and music video culture in Vietnam. In Y. Souchou (Ed.), *House of glass: Culture, representation and the state in Southeast Asia*. Singapore: Institute of Southeast Asian Studies (ISEAS).
Cunningham, S., & Sinclair, J. (Eds.). (2000). *Floating lives: The media and Asian diasporas*. St. Lucia, Australia: University of Queensland Press.
Gillespie, M. (1994). *Television, ethnicity and social change*. London: Routledge.
Gitlin, T. (1998). Public sphere or public sphericules? In T. Liebes & J. Curran (Eds.), *Media, ritual and identity* (pp. 175-202). London: Routledge.
Habermas, J. (1974). The public sphere. *New German Critique, 1*(3), 49-55.
Hartley, J. (1992). *Tele-ology: Studies in television*. London: Routledge.
Hartley, J. (1999). *Uses of television*. London: Routledge.
Hawkins, G. (1996). SBS—Minority television. *Culture and Policy, 7*(1), 45-63.

Jakubowicz, A., Goodall, H., Martin, J., Mitchell, T., Seneviratne, K., & Randall, L. (Eds.). (1994). *Racism, ethnicity and the media.* Sydney, Australia: Allen & Unwin.

Jamrozik, A., Boland, C., & Urquhart, R. (1995). *Social change and cultural transformation in Australia.* Melbourne, Australia: Cambridge University Press.

Kolar-Panov, D. (1997). *Video, war and the diasporic imagination.* London: Routledge.

Lawe Davies, C. (1997). *Multicultural broadcasting in Australia: Policies, institutions and programming, 1975-1995.* Unpublished doctoral dissertation, University of Queensland, Brisbane, Australia.

McGuigan, J. (1998). What price the public sphere? In D. K. Thussu (Ed.), *Electronic empires: Global media and local resistance* (pp. 91-107). London: Arnold.

Naficy, H. (1993). *The making of exile cultures: Iranian television in Los Angeles.* Minneapolis: University of Minnesota Press.

Naficy, H., & Gabriel, T. (Eds.). (1993). *Otherness and the media.* New York: Harwood.

O'Regan, T. (1993). *Australian television culture.* Sydney, Australia: Allen & Unwin.

Scannell, P. (1996). *Radio, television and modern life.* Oxford, UK: Blackwell.

Schiller, H. (1989). *Culture Inc: The corporate takeover of public expression.* New York: Oxford University Press.

# 10. Liberal Machines

JULIAN THOMAS
*Griffith University*

> *This article considers the ways we may regard the new public computer networks as "liberal machines." Although libertarian expectations of the Internet's potential as a technology of freedom are likely to be disappointed, digital communications networks remain the source of powerful but unrealized aspirations on the part of governments, "netizens," and international agencies. The tasks we assign to liberal government may be more complex in the new media environment, but they have not disappeared. New technologies are perceived as creating new problems for governments and citizens, but through the prism of information policy these same technologies are also seen as offering unprecedented new capacities for redressing perceived deficiencies in Western cultural and political communities. This article discusses the role of governments and international bodies in two key fields of information policy: the management of illegal or harmful material and the adaptation of intellectual property rights to digital networks.*

**Global computer networks** promise to make the circulation of information easier, cheaper, and faster than ever before; new digital technologies are transforming the production and distribution of media of all kinds, but the social, political, and economic consequences of the emerging digital communications technologies are not clear. Although the commercial and legal systems designed to manage analogue communications and the movement of physical information products are slowly adapting to the new digital environment, the place of governments, citizens, and nation states in this process is still uncertain. Cultural policy, increasingly seen through the optic of information policy, has a no less uncertain place. National governments have historically exercised strong controls over communications and the distribution of books, films, and other packaged cultural materials across their borders. In most countries, the electronic media and telecommunications were directly owned by governments or subject to interventionist government regulation well into the 1980s. In key areas of the world information economy, such as telecommunications and intellectual property, national governments have long cooperated to enforce technical standards and legal rules.

National cultural and economic policies shaped the development of the world's communications for more than a century, but many theorists of the digital revolution believe that nation states will lose their relevance in a borderless future cyberspace, where transactions and communications will occur beyond the reach of government regulation or control. Libertarians see such a decline of national regulation as a positive step toward the exercise of greater individual freedom in communications and enhanced democratic participation; netizens would prefer the Internet to govern itself; techno-dystopians believe that the digital enfeeblement of government will strengthen unaccountable transnational commercial interests that are already dominant.

In the early 1980s, Pool (1983) brilliantly spelt out the ways in which the new electronic media might be realized as technologies of freedom. The freedom he had in mind was personal; the rights that concerned him most were privacy rights and the rights of freedom of expression. Pool's extraordinary analysis was a reconfiguration of United States media law, technology, and history. Although often uncited, his account of the changing technological contexts of legal rights remains a key source of the libertarianism now dominant in discussions of the law of the Internet. His case rested on the distinction between the regulation of print media and electronic media: between the ancient, albeit compromised, liberal ideal of the free press and the more recent history of government control over electronic media. Pool's argument that the new electronic media were more analogous to the print model (and should therefore be regulated lightly) has reverberated through the debate over the Internet, finding strikingly clear expression in the 1996 landmark decision of the United States District Court in *ACLU vs. Reno*. In the aftermath of that momentous defeat, are national governments now doing no more than persisting with what Castells called "a lost battle" (Castells, 1997, p. 259) against the liberalizing circuits of information technology?

On the face of it, their origins in military research would give public computer networks an unlikely provenance as technologies of freedom, but in this case the historical irony is facile. Computer networks may well be liberal machines if they are regarded as such, but beyond the somewhat specific First Amendment context of Pool's essay, the striking fact is that around the world their liberalism consists primarily in many different unrealized possibilities. Libertarian claims for the ungovernability of the Internet appear to be mainly false: The Internet has not proved to be the end of proprietary rights in information, and it seems unlikely to bring the long history of government regulation of communication to a close. Equally, the Internet's efforts to regulate itself are likely to prove far more limited in scope than was once imagined; governments, commercial bodies, and international organizations have become more rather than less closely involved in administration issues such as the assignment of Internet domain names. The policy focus is, as always, pragmatically and strategically trained on the economic, legal, and policy factors that influence the emergence and adoption of new services. At the international level, discourses of human rights and economic development play a major role in framing the programs of the United Nations Educational, Scientific and Cultural Organisation (UNESCO) and the Organisation for Economic Cooperation and Development (OECD). Recognizing the fact that few, if any, governments will have the capacity or inclination to control every aspect of increasingly sophisticated communications systems does not mean the end of long-standing policy responsibilities.

National governments constitutionally represent the individual citizen; they must always weigh the potential benefits of new technologies against perceived threats.

The theme of this article is that the program of liberal government persists in the digital age. The historical conglomerate of disparate civic and social expectations having to do with controlling crime, fostering economic growth, enabling participation in the political process, protecting children from harm, and enforcing property rights may be more difficult to formulate in the new media environment, but it has not disappeared. New technologies are perceived as creating new problems for governments and citizens, but through the prism of information policy these same technologies are also seen as offering unprecedented new capacities for redressing perceived deficiencies in Western cultural and political communities.

## NEW TECHNOLOGIES

Traditional mass media are going through a process of transformation. The transition to digital broadcasting transmission systems in developed societies and the proliferation of subscription television are likely to lead to much greater diversity in media services, including interactive data transmission, high-definition television, more targeted special interest programming, pay-per-view programming, and electronic commerce facilities. The technical key here is the expansion of bandwidth, the capacity of communications channels to convey information. This has had conspicuous ramifications for policy: In the context of a more market-oriented policy approach to media and telecommunications, spectrum scarcity can no longer function as a primary rationale for close government regulation of electronic media. At the same time, the diversification of electronic media challenges the traditional unifying, nation-building missions of public sector broadcasting services.

Revolutions in the computer industry have also had a major impact. Global computer networks have recently become mass communication systems in their own right. Computer networks developed rapidly from the late 1960s as a means of communication for highly specialized purposes. They were expensive to build and maintain, and they supported a limited variety of data transfer applications. They belonged to and served the needs of large institutions in wealthy countries (education, defence, business, and public administration). By the early 1980s, technological and economic shifts began to transform this rarefied medium into a singular form of mass communication. Smaller, cheaper, and easier to use desktop computers began to appear in small businesses, schools, and households. New telecommunications technology enabled the adaptation of the telephone system for data transmission. New kinds of software expanded enormously the variety and purpose of networked information: Beyond their traditional messaging and database functions, computer networks became systems for publishing and distributing information of all kinds. As their sophistication increased, networks ceased being strictly text based. High-resolution colour images, video, and sound documents have become commonplace network resources. At the same time, the world's computer networks have become more interconnected and therefore more readily accessible. The network of networks that has evolved into the Internet uses a decentralized, packet-switched architecture to link computers in more than 90 countries. Proprietary online services—the self-contained, subscription-based, market-oriented systems of the early 1990s—were, by the mid-1990s, forced to connect to the Internet; many failed to compete with the larger, freer, public system.

Although these technologies have developed quickly, and the technical and policy objective of an accessible, low-cost global information infrastructure has become attainable, the consequences of the diffusion of these new technologies will take much longer to recognize and act on. Actual applications and benefits remain hazy. It is not yet clear that greater diversity in services will deliver greater diversity in content. Critical issues yet to be resolved include the scope of the public domain in the digital environment and the ability of governments to adapt existing systems regulation.

## POLICY RESPONSES

Since the beginning of this decade at least, governments and international organizations around the world have devoted substantial resources to understanding the implications of the digital revolution in communications. Indeed, such is the volume of this material, and the enthusiasm with which it embraces technologically-driven change, that we can scarcely doubt that the very concept of an information revolution must be in part the product of official policy discourse, despite the advocates of a cyberspace without rulers. The phenomenon of governments embracing new communications technologies has several facets. In highly industrialized societies, the early and middle years of the 1990s were characterized by a visionary fascination with the promise of future interactive broadband delivery systems. National government documents such as Denmark's "Info-Society 2000" (Ministry for Research and Information Technology, 1994), the United States' *National Information Infrastructure and Global Information Infrastructure* reports (1993), and Singapore's "IT2000" (National Computer Board, 1992) policies fell into this category; at the international level, the European union's Bangemann Report and the G-7 summit's Information Society conference were comparable.

The communications scholar William H. Melody argues that these visionary information policies "tend to be more statements of aspiration than realistic policies aimed at achievable goals" (Melody, 1996). Yet, these grand if somewhat unfocused visions still shape information policies around the world. New technologies were seen as the key to improved delivery of key government services, especially in health and education. They were also seen as major drivers for economic growth, offering improved productivity and new demand for skilled labour. In general terms, governments accepted without critical scrutiny the putative benefits of information technology, focusing on the perceived need for a broadband infrastructure. At the same time, the absence of this infrastructure was uniformly seen as a significant disadvantage, from which other problems flowed: deficiencies in technological skills, uncompetitive industries, low growth rates. The analysis was circular. As Melody (1996) points out, a broadband infrastructure was not in fact necessary for many practical improvements in communications, either in the West or elsewhere. The success of the narrowband Internet, for example, rests on its accessibility through standard twisted-pair telephone lines and comparatively inexpensive modems. The rise of the Internet has made possible the proliferation of network computing earlier than the most ambitious prophets of the information revolution imagined, but it has done so without the expensive broadband infrastructure that was so widely considered a prerequisite for information societies.

Nevertheless, the best of these broad policy statements have had a number of important effects. First, information policy was inaugurated as a new administrative geography. It was not a territory on its own; instead, information policy was the recognition of a new set of connections between elements of industry, financial, media, and cultural policy and the conviction that these formerly unrelated objectives required coordination at national and international levels. Governments have begun to make strategic connections between problems that were hitherto fragmented across traditional administrative boundaries, addressing in a more coherent way issues such as data protection, intellectual property, electronic commerce, and the provision of computers in school education.

Second, some of these early government responses adopted a distinctive social policy perspective on the possibilities and consequences of the new communications environment. Denmark's Info-Society 2000 policy, for example, looked beyond the provision of infrastructure. It was concerned with how a future "info-society" might retain the distinctive Danish characteristics of equity, democratic participation, and openness. It was much more concerned with applications than with the supply of technology and addressed the ways in which the public sector could cooperate with business. It emphasized the need to consider questions of access to government information. These issues were developed alongside an agenda for microeconomic reform, which concentrated on the need to liberalize Danish telecommunications (Ris, 1997).

Third, the wide-ranging information policies developed in the mid-1990s have led to more concrete, if somewhat scaled-down, programs for change. The aspirational thinking of the mid-1990s may have diverted attention from such practical policy questions as access to the Internet, improvements in basic telecommunications, and the development of real services and industries, but these issues have recently become the focus of policy attention, especially since the emergence of the Internet as the most important and fastest-growing global computer network. Here, Singapore's IT2000 plan provides an example. Like so many other visions of the information age, IT2000 was aimed squarely at a universally accessible broadband network. The rise of the Internet changed this priority, forcing Singapore's National Computer Board to concentrate on the emergence of markets for interactive services rather than the development of the enabling technologies. This in turn meant an analysis of Singapore's particular strengths in fields such as logistics, transport, and government information provision.

The growing ubiquity of information technologies in the daily lives of citizens has spurred governments to develop policies aimed at fostering greater community participation. In *A Strategic Framework for the Information Economy* (Commonwealth of Australia, 1998), the Australian government states its commitment to provide all Australians with open and equitable access to information available online as a way of securing "a strong democratic, informed and inclusive society" and avoiding a social polarization between the so-called "information rich" and "information poor." The challenge highlighted by the Secretary-General of the United Nations is to use the technologies to make information available to all and harness its democratizing power (United Nations, 1998a). However, citizens in many countries do not have the opportunity to share in the benefits of the new technologies. The participation of developing countries in particular is being impeded by a lack of adequate communication infrastructure and relatively high computing costs. These issues were highlighted at a seminar sponsored by the United Nations Population Fund and the government of Turkey in December 1998. This seminar also discussed the need for policies to address social and gender inequality to prevent information and communication technologies from further marginalizing disadvantaged groups (United Nations, 1998b). Even so, available information and communication technologies are seen in developing countries as advocacy tools in promoting social change.

## FRAMEWORKS FOR GOVERNANCE

New communication technologies provide comparatively decentralized and open environments that appear to promote rights to freedom of expression, information, and communication. Networked environments such as the Internet allow individual users to create their own content and interact with a large community of other users around the world at relatively low cost. This in turn increases the diversity of information and views that are expressed by and accessible to users around the world. In particular, information and communication technologies are seen as promoting the democratic process by facilitating greater accountability and transparency of governments: Official documents are increasingly being made available online and opportunities for direct communication with elected representatives are being created (Rabb, 1997). A concomitant of this in pluralist states is that the medium is used to disseminate content that may itself be seen as antidemocratic or offensive.

The characteristics of the new media mean that (unlike traditional broadcast media) there are stronger expectations of individual freedom and autonomy. However, as more parts of the networked world and the real world overlap, the need for governance increases. Numerous commentators have highlighted the difficulties of governance in a computer-generated public domain that has no territorial boundaries or physical attributes and is in perpetual use. Furthermore, democratic governance requires public interests and values to be visible within the rule-making processes. In attempting to meet these challenges and retain the democratic characteristics of networked environments, there has been a tendency in Europe, North America, and Australia toward a governance model that involves the combination of industry self-regulation with legal sanctions.

International organizations, especially UNESCO, have played a major role in seeking to apply notions of universal rights to digital communications. UNESCO organized an Asia-Pacific Regional Experts meeting in Seoul in September 1998, followed by a full UNESCO forum in Monaco to develop a legal framework for cyberspace. These meetings reflect an aspiration to use the Internet to enhance democratic participation. The issues discussed included freedom of expression, universal access to digital information, language diversity, regulation of global information, intellectual property rights, a cyber community, and cultural diversity. The universal principles recommended for UNESCO's consideration are based on international and regional cooperation, national responsibility, industry and private sector responsibility through schemes of self-regulation, and user empowerment. It was intended that the proposals would be considered at the following general conference of UNESCO in November 1999.

The OECD has been a major contributor to emerging frameworks for global electronic commerce. In October 1998, the OECD and the government of Canada held a ministerial conference on electronic commerce in Ottawa, Canada. The OECD action plan reflects an intention to bring notions of physical-world governance into the networked world. The OECD is particularly interested in two aspects of commercial development: the establishment of trust, or confidence, among users and consumers in the digital environment, including the negotiation of ground rules that provide protection of the same level as that provided by legal and commercial frameworks in the physical world; and the enhancement of information infrastructures, especially through the liberalization of national telecommunications markets.

## CONTROLLING INFORMATION CRIME

One of the great attractions of the Internet remains its capacity for comparatively free global communication, including communication to and from countries where open discourse may be suppressed. It can collapse geographical space, apparently transcending boundaries, but as the United States scholars Brian Kahin and Charles Nesson (1997) have written, "with this empowerment comes enormous potential for unbalancing, even upending, social, business, political and legal arrangements" (p. vii). A recent Irish government report describes what it calls the "downside" of new technologies. A host of potentially illegal uses of the Internet have emerged as major issues for national policy and international coordination. These include the following:

> piracy: infringement of copyright in cultural property, the infringement of moral rights of authors, and the illegal distribution of copyrighted works such as books or videotapes;
> illegal gambling: emergence of unlicensed and unregulated Internet casinos;
> infringement of privacy: unsolicited electronic communications, misuse of personal information in databases, theft of personal information, or unauthorized interception of personal communications;
> commercial crimes: fraud, including credit card piracy;
> harmful communications: illegal material, including child pornography, violent material, and racial or religious vilification; defamatory publications; and
> hacking or cracking: illegal entry into private or government computers, theft of data or malicious damage to data.

Perhaps the most significant area of need for regulating new information services is in the field of illegal or harmful material. We know that whether information is considered harmful depends on the cultural, religious, and social context in which it is circulated. Within and between nations, these standards vary enormously. At local, regional, and national levels, governments have long sought to control the distribution of material deemed harmful. Clearly, the task has become much more complicated in the age of global digital networks. It is no longer possible for government censors to mandate the classification of all the material that may be available in any jurisdiction. It is no longer possible to physically police the information that crosses jurisdictional borders, and although screening or filtering technologies may be effective in some circumstances, data has the capacity to slip across a frontier in many forms and from many sources including international phone lines, Internet services, satellite transmissions, and broadcasting. In the face of this more open global system, how are local legal and cultural standards to be sustained?

Moreover, many countries have constructed classification or censorship systems that work by making distinctions between different kinds of analogue media based on assumptions about the different patterns of circulation and consumption of, for example, books and broadcast television. How are these carefully graduated systems of classification or censorship to be applied to digital media? It becomes too simplistic to merely insist that what is illegal off-line is illegal online.

A recent Human Rights Watch report demonstrates the range of methods employed to control content on the Internet (Human Rights Watch, 1998). Some countries, such as Ireland and Australia, are moving toward adoption of co-regulatory structures, sharing responsibility between national agencies and industry bodies for raising public awareness, responding appropriately to illegal material when necessary, and providing effective complaints procedures. Co-regulation is being facilitated by technologies that make the development of tools such as content labeling and complaint hotlines possible. Other national authorities, such as those in Saudi Arabia, Bahrain, and Malaysia, have sought to control the Internet more tightly, often by restricting access to the global network through a limited number of gateways, which may then be monitored and configured to block access to sites considered harmful or undesirable. The Human Rights Watch report notes the widespread international endorsement of technical tools to assist in the regulation of content on the World Wide Web. In particular, the labeling technology known as PICS (Platform for Internet Content Selection), first developed by the World Wide Web Consortium, has attracted great interest in Europe, Australia, Asia, and North America. PICS provides a means for the labeling, and subsequent filtering, of Web content that may be both more standardized and more powerful than simple site-blocking software. One of its features is that such labels may be generated, published, and used by anyone: It brings control of an effective classificatory apparatus within the reach of associations, schools, libraries, community groups, or any interested parties.

The PICS protocol supports a variety of ratings and labeling systems with the intention that these systems can be tailored to the needs of specific users or groups of users. PICS thereby allows content rating to reflect the vast range of cultural perspectives on what constitutes appropriate material. It belongs to that tendency of thought about the Internet that stands in opposition to the notion of a distinct and remote digital space separated from the daily circumstances and places of its use. Instead, PICS works from the assumption that the Internet is embedded in the real world. Supporters of PICS have pointed to its feature of enabling, and in fact encouraging, a multiplicity of classification standards as the means to retain local control and responsibility over content. PICS is seen, in the European union and elsewhere, as a pluralist tool preserving cultural and social diversity within a global system. Organizations in several countries have established labeling schemes designed for use by parents and schools that conform to the PICS standards. Many of these are based in North America, and they include the Recreational Software Advisory Council labeling scheme for the Internet (RSACi), SafeSurf, Cyber Patrol, and SurfWatch. The Internet Content Rating Alliance (ICRA), previously the International Working Group on Content Rating, is working "to develop an internationally acceptable rating system which provides Internet users world-wide with the choice to limit access to content they consider harmful, especially to children." ICRA is currently developing a consultation paper that is intended to garner responses from different countries and cultures about the range of matters that an international rating scheme could address.

Whether PICS achieves the promised results remains very uncertain. Software solutions have a tendency to be quickly hacked. One important limitation of PICS is its restriction to the Web: It is not designed for other Internet services, although work is under way to extend its application to newsgroups and e-mail. But PICS has been criticized mainly on other grounds. As a tool it can be used in many different ways, including the suppression of free speech. Although it is true that PICS enables specific communities and organizations to manage Web content, it can also be applied at the level of state control. In Singapore, the National Internet Advisory Committee has recently recommended that a PICS-based rating system be mandatory for all Internet users, with the effect that unrated sites would become inaccessible from Singapore-based internet service providers.

## PROTECTING PROPRIETARY RIGHTS IN INFORMATION

In the field of copyright, there is a long history of international coordination in managing the global circulation of information. The World Intellectual Property Organisation (WIPO) has recently played a crucial role with the adoption in late 1996 of two new international treaties designed to bring copyright into the era of digital networks. These treaties extend the older right of communication to the public to include an exclusive right over the wired transmission of text and images. In addition, they create a new exclusive right of "making available" to the public, which is plainly designed with public computer networks in mind. The treaties also aim to provide additional protection for copyright owners in the digital environment by sanctioning the abuse of technological copyright protection measures, such as hardware or software locks or other encryption mechanisms. Sanctions are also provided against any deliberate tampering with rights management information, the information concerning provenance and ownership that often forms part of digital works. Largely as a result of argument from African countries at the 1996 diplomatic conference, these measures do not limit existing fair use or fair dealing exceptions to owners' proprietary rights.

The new treaties are likely to be enacted in member countries in the near future. The challenge for policy makers in this field has been the preservation of an appropriate balance between the proprietary rights of copyright creators and owners and the public interest in the free circulation of information. There has been criticism, particularly from developing countries, that enhanced copyright protection inhibits equitable participation in the global information economy because it further increases the cost of accessing content and applications. The international politics of copyright also bring into play the more general principle of freedom of expression, especially where that right is guaranteed in the Universal Declaration of Human Rights, Article 8 of the European Convention on Human Rights and Fundamental Freedoms and other relevant conventions. A major achievement of the 1996 WIPO diplomatic conference in Geneva was the recognition in the preamble to the treaties of the importance of this balance. Copyright law is not merely a legal means to protect the rights of copyright owners: It is directly concerned with the wider goals of enhancing education, science, and culture (Mason, 1998).

Copyright laws around the world have been designed to protect original information, although what constitutes originality in this context varies considerably across jurisdictions. Beyond the problem of protecting creative work, however, there are also major policy issues concerning the circulation of factual information, that is, data (e.g., environmental information), which in itself is usually unprotected by copyright. The new international information economy means that what was once a recondite legal question is now a pressing policy issue at an international level. Information once freely exchanged between countries and organizations is now increasingly seen in a commercial light, with serious consequences for those smaller countries economically dependent on information such as meteorological data that has been gathered by others. This is particularly the case where countries have privatized or commercialized public sector organizations that collect and distribute such information.

Governments around the world are grappling with the question of who should own data and what rules should govern public access and use. The new global networks have made data more valuable than ever before. The market for information has increased enormously as expensive proprietary networks have been replaced by ubiquitous public systems, but these same public networks are also seen as a threat to the data that they carry. In Europe and the United States, database publishers claim that they are now at greater risk from pirates and hackers. They argue that tough new laws are required to protect existing databases and provide sufficient incentives for industry growth. They highlight the vulnerability of data, pointing to the ease with which large quantities of digital information can be copied and redistributed internationally. A database worth millions of dollars, they say, can now be pirated and resold at minimal cost over the Internet.

There are currently three closely related proposals from the European union, the United States, and WIPO to deal with this problem. These proposals are at different stages of development. Europe is farthest along the road, with a directive that was largely implemented in member countries by the beginning of 1998. In the United States, legislation on the matter is currently in Congress. The WIPO proposal is likely to be discussed for some time before any further action. Although there are key differences between the three proposals, all have the objective of creating a new kind of intellectual property right specifically tailored for developers and publishers of databases. The requirement for protection is not a concept of original authorship, but rather a notion of substantial investment in the creation of a database. No creativity is required. Furthermore, the definition of *database* in the new laws is extremely wide: "a collection of independent works, data or other materials arranged in a systematic or methodical way and capable of being individually accessed by electronic or other means" (World Intellectual Property, 1996).

The most significant issue for the public domain lies in the nature of the extensive new rights these proposals give database owners over the extraction of data and its reuse. In addition, the United States and WIPO proposals contain sanctions against anyone attempting to circumvent technological protections for data (e.g., encryption). These laws raise a host of policy issues that will require careful examination at national and international levels. The proposals are notably remote from the conventions of copyright law. In copyright, notions of fair use or fair dealing have been used to strike a balance between the legitimate rights of creators and the public benefit in the circulation of information—hence the idea of fair use for educational and scientific purposes. But the new database rules have the potential to restrict the scope of fair dealing of this kind. Educators, librarians, and scientists in the United States have raised concerns that the proposed changes would significantly inhibit researchers seeking to reuse and combine data for publication or for research, as well as educators wishing to use portions of data sets for instructional purposes.

These new proposals have appeared at a time of increasing fiscal pressure on educational and research institutions in many countries. Governments around the world increasingly look to these bodies to adopt a more commercial approach. The new information technologies provide them with an infrastructure for commercialized data services. Laws along the lines of the current proposals would provide a stronger regulatory infrastructure, but the consequences of this approach, particularly for the public sector and developing countries, are a long way from being fully understood.

## CONCLUSION

Questions of proprietary rights and content management are technical issues that have long been at the heart of national media and cultural policies. The story of what has been called the digital agenda for policy underlines the complexity of this technologically driven transition. This is not simply the result of the supposed profundity of the digital revolution. It is also because of the delicacy or, indeed, obscurity of the policy compromises embodied in the persistent historical accretion of law and regulation in these fields. The Net does not mean that public citizens will all become private users, that states will become variant forms of user groups, or that liberal cultural governance will evaporate in the heat of cross-border data traffic. Nevertheless, the refraction of cultural and media policy into information rules is a critical juncture for these delicate settlements between public and private interests. Within an expanding mesh of stateless legal systems, including contracts, human rights, and technical standards

(Teubner, 1997), liberal machines are intended both to sustain and reform certain forms of government. Current policy debate continues to search for the limits of that project.

## REFERENCES

ACLU vs Reno. (1996). U.S. District Court for the Eastern District of Pennsylvania, June.
Castells, M. (1997). *The information age: Economy, society and culture* (Vol. 3). Oxford, UK: Blackwell.
Commonwealth of Australia. (1998). *A strategic framework for the information economy*. Canberra: Author.
Human Rights Watch. (1998). *Freedom of expression on the Internet* [Online]. Available: http://www.hrw.org/hrw/worldreport99/special/internet.html
Kahin, B., & Nesson, C. (Eds.). (1997). *Borders in cyberspace*. Cambridge, MA: MIT Press.
Mason, A. (1998). Public interest objectives and the law of copyright. *Journal of Law and Information Science, 2.*
Melody, W. H. (1996). Toward a framework for designing information policies. *Telecommunications Policy, 20*(4), 243-259.
Ministry for Research and Information Technology (Denmark) (1994). *Info-Society 2000*, Copenhagen.
Pool, I. de S. (1983). *Technologies of freedom*. Harvard: Belknap Press.
Rabb, C. D. (1997). Privacy, democracy, information. In B. D. Loader (Ed.), *The governance of cyberspace* (pp. 155-174). London: Routledge.
Ris, A. M. (1997). The information welfare society: An assessment of Danish government initiatives preparing for the Information Age. In B. Kahin & E. Wilson (Eds.), *National information infrastructure initiatives: Vision and policy design* (pp. 424-456). Cambridge, MA: MIT Press.
Teubner, G. (Ed.). (1997). *Global law without a state*. Aldershot, UK: Dartmouth.
United Nations. (1998a, May). Secretary-General says communications technology has great democratizing power waiting to be harnessed to global struggle for peace and development (Press Release SG/SM/6502 SAG/4). New York: Author.
United Nations. (1998b, December). Expert seminar supports expanded use of information and communications technologies in advocacy for reproductive health and rights (Press Release POP/693). New York: Author.
U.S. Government. (1994). *National Information Infrastructure: Agenda for action*, Washington, DC.
U.S. Government. (1995). *Global Information Infrastructure: Agenda for co-operation*, Washington, DC.
World Intellectual Property Organization. (1996). Document CRNR/DC/6, Basic proposal for the protection of databases, Article 2, Geneva.